Wilde the Irishman

Wilde the Irishman

EDITED BY
JERUSHA McCORMACK

Yale University Press
New Haven and London

The essay 'Oscar Wilde: The Artist as Irishman' is reprinted by permission of the publisher from *Inventing Ireland* by Declan Kiberd, Cambridge: Mass.: Harvard University Press, copyright © 1995 by Declan Kiberd.

For permission to reprint extracts from copyright material the author and publishers gratefully acknowledge the following: Julian Symons 'The Detling Secret' Penguin, 1984; Seamus Heaney 'Punishment', Faber & Faber.

Typeset in Walbaum
Printed and bound in Great Britain by Bookcraft, Midsomer Norton, Somerset

Library of Congress Catalog Card Number 97–80783
ISBN 0–300–07296–1
A catalogue record for this book is available from the British Library.

10 9 8 7 6 5 4 3 2 1

for DARA MCCORMACK
1942–1996

What thou lovest well remains

Contents

Part Two: CONTINUITIES

Contributors

ANGELA BOURKE Short-story writer and Director of the M.Phil. in Irish Studies at University College Dublin, Angela Bourke is known as a cultural commentator who makes frequent appearances on radio and television. She is the author of *Caoineadh ná dTrí Muire* (1983) and of numerous articles on the Irish oral tradition and has twice acted as judge for *The Irish Times* Literature Awards. Her short-story collection, *By Salt Water*, was published in 1996.

OWEN DUDLEY EDWARDS was born in Dublin in 1938, educated at Belvedere College, University College Dublin, and Johns Hopkins University. He has taught at various universities, and is now at the University of Edinburgh (where he was appointed in 1968) and where he holds the position of Reader in History. He is the editor of *The Fireworks of Oscar Wilde* (1989) and worked, at an earlier date, as an assistant to Sir Rupert Hart-Davis in editing *The Letters of Oscar Wilde* (1962) and *More Letters of Oscar Wilde* (1985). He is writing an account of the life of Oscar Wilde for the new *Dictionary of National Biography*.

JOHN WILSON FOSTER was born and educated in Belfast, receiving his BA and MA from Queen's University, Belfast, and his Ph.D. from the University of Oregon. Now Professor of English at the University of British Columbia, Canada, his books include *Fictions of the Irish Literary Revival* (1987), *Colonial Consequences: Essays in Irish Literature and Culture* (1991) and *The Achievement of Seamus Heaney* (1995).

SEAMUS HEANEY's first book of poems, *Death of a Naturalist*, appeared in 1966 and since then he has published many volumes of poetry, criticism, and translations, the most recent of which was *The Spirit Level* in 1996. He has taught in colleges and universities in Ireland and the USA, and from 1984 until 1997 was Boylston Professor of Rhetoric and Oratory at Harvard University. In 1995 Seamus Heaney was awarded the Nobel Prize for Literature.

DECLAN KIBERD has lectured on Irish literature and cultural politics in over twenty countries and writes regularly in Irish newspapers. Among his books are *Synge and the Irish Language* (1993), *Men and Feminism in Modern Literature* (1985), *Inventing Ireland* (1995) and *Idir Dhá Chultúr* (1993). He edited *An Crann Faoi Bhláth: The Flowering Tree* (1991) (a collection of modern Gaelic poetry with verse translations) and the Penguin Classics edition of *The Students' Annotated Ulysses* (1992). A former director of the Yeats Summer School, he is now Professor of Anglo-Irish Literature and Drama at University College Dublin.

THOMAS KILROY has written seven stage plays, a novel, *The Big Chapel* (which won the *Guardian* Award for Fiction), as well as adaptations of Chekhov, Ibsen and Pirandello. He is currently writing a screenplay of *The Madame MacAdam Travelling Theatre* for Channel 4 and his version of *The Seagull* has been planned for a BBC 2 TV Performance Series. *The Secret Fall of Constance Wilde* was first performed by the Abbey Theatre in October 1997 as part of the Dublin Theatre Festival.

JERUSHA MCCORMACK has written the biography of the man reputed to be the 'real' Dorian Gray in *John Gray: Poet, Dandy, and Priest* (1991), as well as editing his *Selected Prose* (1992). A lecturer in English and American literature at University College Dublin, she acted as a judge for *The Irish Times* Literature Awards during the period 1996/97.

W. J. MCCORMACK's field of expertise is Anglo-Irish literature and, in particular, the Irish Gothic novel and the work of Maria Edgeworth. After many years at Trinity College, Dublin, he now lectures in the English Department of Goldsmiths College, London. In his other incarnation, as Hugh Maxton, he is best known as a poet (*The Engraved Passion: New and Selected Poems 1970–91*) and as a translator of Hungarian poetry.

FRANK MCGUINNESS's plays include *Observe the Sons of Ulster Marching Towards the Somme* (1986), for which he won the London *Evening Standard* Award for Most Promising Playwright. His other plays include *Innocence* (1987), *Carthaginians* (1988), *The Breadman* (1991) and *The Bird Sanctuary* (1994); a recent play, *Someone Who'll Watch Over Me* (1992), was nominated for an Olivier Award in London in 1993 and won a Tony in New York. He has translated works by Lorca, Chekhov and Ibsen. At present, he lectures in the English Department of University College Dublin.

DEREK MAHON is widely regarded as one of the most important Irish poets of his generation. Born in Belfast and educated at Trinity College Dublin, his publications include *Night-Crossing* (1968), a Poetry Book Society Choice, *Lives* (1972), and *The Snow Party* (1975), for which he received the Denis Devlin Award. These poems, some revised, were subsequently published in *Poems 1962–1978* by Oxford University Press; his *Selected Poems* appeared in 1991. Recently, he has published *The Bacchae* (1992), *The Hudson Letter* (1995), *The Yellow Book* (1997), a version of *Phaedra* (1996) and *Journalism* (1996).

PAULA MURPHY lectures in the History of Art in University College Dublin and has published extensively on Irish art of the nineteenth and twentieth centuries, particularly public sculpture. She is currently on the board of the Irish Museum of Modern Art and of the Sculptors' Society of Ireland.

BERNARD O'DONOGHUE was born in County Cork in 1945 and still spends part of the year there. He moved to England in 1962, and studied English at Lincoln College, Oxford. He taught Medieval English, Linguistics and Anglo-Irish Literature at Magdalen College from 1971 to 1995 when he moved to Wadham College, where he is a Fellow in English. He has published a number of critical studies, including *Seamus Heaney and the Language of Poetry* (1994) and three collections of poetry: *Poaching Rights* (1987), *The Weakness* (1991), and *Gunpowder* (1995), which won the Whitbread Poetry Prize. He is currently preparing an anthology of *Medieval Secular Lyrics*.

FINTAN O'TOOLE is the author of *The Politics of Magic* (1987), a study of the plays of Tom Murphy; *No More Heroes* (1990); essays on Shakespeare's tragedies; and *A Mass for Jesse James* (1990), a journey through Ireland in the 1980s. A journalist with *The Irish Times* and currently working as theatre critic for the New York *Daily News*, his biography of Richard Brinsley Sheridan, *A Traitor's Kiss*, appeared in October 1997.

GABRIEL ROSENSTOCK is the author/translator of over sixty books, including ten volumes of poetry. He has translated into Irish the selected poems of Francisco X. Alarcón, Seamus Heaney, J. W. Hackett, Georg Trakl, Willem M. Roggeman, Peter Huchel, Günter Grass, Georg Heym and others. He has translated into English the selected stories of Pádraic Breathnach and Dara Ó Conaola.

ALAN STANFORD has nearly thirty years' experience as a leading actor in the Irish Theatre, working with most of the major companies. Best known for his work at the Gate Theatre, Dublin over the past sixteen years, his performances with the Gate of Herod in Oscar Wilde's *Salomé*, Pozzo in *Waiting for Godot* and Hamm in *Endgame* won international acclaim. He has directed a wide variety of plays, done much film and television work and, as a teacher, is well known in Ireland as one of the founders of both the Dublin Theatre School and the Drama course in Trinity College Dublin.

DEIRDRE TOOMEY is a co-editor of *The Collected Letters of W. B. Yeats*, Volume II, *1896–1900* (1997) and is editor of *Yeats and Women* (revised edition, 1997). She is working on an authorized edition of *Yeats's Occult Diaries (1898–1901)*.

VICTORIA WHITE is Arts Editor of *The Irish Times*. She has published a book, *Raving Autumn and Other Stories* (1990), and, while on the editorial board of *Theatre Ireland*, produced its 1993 issue on 'Women and the Theatre'.

Preface

As I recall, this book first took shape over lunch with a colleague at which I expressed my frustration at having to explain to Irish students that Oscar Wilde was, yes, indeed, Irish. And then having to do battle with whatever that meant: 'Irish' being a moot designation, even now. It seemed as good a place as any to start a project which had long been in my mind.

But the project refused to write itself. One end of the equation was fine: Wilde will always provoke. But Ireland? After twenty-five years in this, my adopted country, it eluded me in so many directions − historical, cultural, even linguistic − that I decided that this was a project I would have to undertake with others: not academic colleagues only, but those creative spirits who are, at this present time, redefining what it means to be Irish.

So my first order of thanks must be to those who also wrote this book. That conspirator over lunch, Declan Kiberd, will be the earliest named: for his enthusiasm, wit, and (when things got rough) his hard head. He offered me his essay on Wilde before it appeared in his magisterial *Inventing Ireland*. He also helped me compile the list of fellow conspirators, the creative critics and critical artists whose names appear in this book. It is to their credit (not to say, their glory) that, when approached, there was not in even one instance a question about a fee or a publisher (at that point, there was none) − or even the names of other contributors. The writers here were given no brief; or, if they asked, told simply: 'Off the wall. Write what you think needs to be written. Or send me what you have already done.' It was an Irish approach to an Irish project: arseways forward. Carried on talk and trust. It is a tribute to them all that it worked, and worked well.

What came in from the contributors arrived in amazing disarray: from smeared ballpoint through steam typewriter and on to crazily formatted disk. Writing styles, referencing systems − or lack of them − were equally various and unpredictable. The wonderful Beverly Sperry of the Night Owl Early Bird Bureau and her team restored sanity to the manuscript − and to me − by typing it all into one authoritative version. At a critical point, Jonathan Williams, my literary agent, took the whole manuscript away and did an initial ruthless copy edit. His work was later refined by a second and even more scrupulous Yale editor, Peter

James. Finally, Ray O'Neill helped double-check and coordinate Wilde quotations from varied editions. All three improved a sloppy manuscript beyond measure.

My own life was even more chaotic; much is owed to those who helped me through a difficult year. My valued colleagues at University College Dublin I thank here, as I have tried to thank them each in person. Professor Jim Mays and the Dean of the Faculty of Arts, Professor Fergus D'Arcy, and my colleague Dr Ron Callan have been, in particular, kind and protective. There are others that I cannot thank in any official way: those friends of the heart and soul who have been with me through it all − and my family, here and in America.

The book is dedicated to my beloved Dara, who brought me to this country. He loved Ireland passionately and at times with the despair of one who tries to serve a nation divided and at odds with itself. He infected me with his exasperated love. He taught me how it could mutate into a particularly Irish wit, a fierce joy in the world's absurdity. For all that joy, I thank him, and for our sons, David and Thomas, who keep that joy alive. May the reader still find its echo in the pages of this book.

Introduction: The Irish Wilde

JERUSHA McCORMACK

Who is Oscar Wilde? He had trouble answering the question himself. From his home in Dublin, a youthful Wilde sent Lord Houghton a copy of a sonnet on Keats's grave, calling him the 'sweetest singer of our English land'. Ten years later, from his residence in London, Wilde declined to write for an anti-Home Rule paper, claiming himself to be 'a most recalcitrant patriot'. Like many another, Wilde had in the interval discovered his true home from abroad: it was during his tour of America in 1881 that he first found himself giving qualified endorsement to Irish nationalism, saying: 'I do not wish to see the empire dismembered, but only to see the Irish people free, and Ireland still as a willing and integral part of the British empire.'

Given a choice between being English or Irish, then, Wilde chose both: 'Good man yourself there, Oscar,/Every way you had it.' To fellow Irishman and prisoner of the British, Brendan Behan, Wilde's gift was not to choose; although 'holy Death' was to be the price of his 'path of sin', it was also to liberate Wilde for ever from the false dichotomies of choice itself. Was Wilde Irish or British? The true answer is, he was both: born into a class known as the Anglo-Irish, at once the pillar of a rotting imperial regime in Dublin and more Irish than the Irish themselves. Born into an oxymoron, and doomed to live out his life as paradox, Wilde became adept at living on both sides of the hyphen: a self-proclaimed republican (also socialist and sometime anarchist) who infiltrated the highest ranks of London society; fond of a duke and besotted with a lord; at the same time, a Byronic explorer of the London underworld of rentboys and petty criminals.

Wilde's desire to have it every way makes it impossible, in common terms, to define him. If he was both Irish and British, both mock-aristocrat and avowed republican, he was also – depending on the year – heterosexual, bisexual and gay (probably in that chronological order). He was at once the champion of the 'new woman', and, as editor of the *Woman's World*, a force for her intellectual liberation, yet, within a few short years, he was penning *Salomé*, a play of violent, not to say hysterical, misogyny. An intellectual who wrote a novel which is still an urban myth, a self-styled 'lord of language' who wrote some of the most gorgeous nonsense ever spoken: how shall we define him? What may we say that *is* true of Oscar Wilde? Only that, of any truth advanced about Wilde, the contrary will also be equally true.

To phrase it otherwise: Oscar Wilde is not politically correct. We must not say so. In an age of labels and factions, not least those sponsored by committed critics, complexity of such high order gives offence. Perhaps — the thought occurs — it was to simplify exactly such complexity that the British put him away in the first place: that it was an act of concentrated social revenge is no longer in any doubt. For years, it was followed by a decent, not to say terrified, silence. But in the last decade, following the lead of his biographer Richard Ellmann in opening up unexplored facets of his life, new efforts have been made to place Wilde: as 'homintern martyr', in Auden's phrase, and as Irishman, born and bred.

Either of these appropriations of Wilde could be read as exercises in crude thinking: Wilde as martyr to the gay cause; Wilde as a member of that exorcized class, the Anglo-Irish, which might at last provide a bridge between British and nationalist Irish in the cause of a New Ireland. In fact, both Alan Sinfield's *The Wilde Century* and Davis Coakley's *Oscar Wilde: The Importance of Being Irish* (or, more recently, Richard Pine's *The Thief of Reason: Oscar Wilde and Modern Ireland*) only demonstrate the complexity of their categories. What does it mean to be gay — or Irish? Is it something one is born to? Or is it a kind of infection, a state one is culturally inducted into? What does the gay — or the Irishman — of a century ago have to do with the gay/Irishman of today? How can one define a person by a label that is itself so contingent and context-bound, a label, in both cases, that is defined by a hegemony of the dominant community and is therefore in itself not to be delineated in any stable and secure fashion?

To say that Wilde is Irish, therefore, is to define him in terms of a question: what does it mean to be Irish? How many things does it include? And what must it, implicitly or explicitly, exclude? At various stages of his career, Wilde invoked different definitions of Irishness; to some extent, it would be fair to argue (in terms already advanced by both Declan Kiberd and Richard Pine) that Wilde was inventing Ireland as he proceeded to invent himself, and, in inventing himself, helped to invent what is now modern Ireland.

But there is a constant beneath the variables: Wilde's identification with Ireland had perhaps less to do ultimately with historical fact or party-political affiliation than a consistent cultural identification with what he called 'Celtic'. The Celt, as defined by Ernest Renan and Matthew Arnold, was not merely Irish, but also Breton, Scottish and Welsh; he was of the oppressed peoples which embodied all that was alien and rejected by the English; in turn the Celt rejected what Wilde called the 'inherited stupidity' of the master-race: its common sense, its philistinism, its puritanism. Indolent, unmanageable, imaginative, dreamy, 'in vehement reaction against the despotism of fact', the Celt was heir to an ancient and rich race-experience. But to understand oneself in such terms, as Wilde evidently did, was also to reject terms of moral choice. Making one's life becomes a matter of fate: that of representing the master-race to itself, by embodying that secret self it has rejected or denied, to perform, with whatever degree of irony one could summon, the script already dictated by one's audience.

In embracing this fate, Wilde redefined what it means to be Irish. What Wilde's life demonstrates is that to be Irish is to have multiple, and divided, loyalties: to be both colonizer and colonized, native and official, within the Pale and beyond it: to inhabit a space where contraries meet and are transvalued into something else, a something which by definition escapes definition: to be in a provisional and mutating stage, not a recognized state but a state of mind. 'I am a problem for which there is no solution', Wilde once said, silently conceding by that phrase that he was part of the larger Irish question. Precisely because Ireland is still a question, it is appropriate that Wilde should now be made part of it, and its destabilizing energies in turn destabilize and transmute our interpretations of him.

This is an exercise, therefore, not only in crossing borders, but in blurring and even eliminating them, by showing how the complexity of being Irish elicits other complexities. Those who write here aim, by changing the paradigm within which Oscar Wilde is interpreted, to change the perspective by which we read him. Traditionally, Wilde has been regarded as a 'British' writer — a category in which even Irish critics colluded in placing him. What difference does it make to read him as Irish?

Every difference; a radical difference, judging from the essays of this book. First of all, as Owen Dudley Edwards demonstrates, the legacy of Wilde's childhood complicated his sense of Irishness from his earliest years. From his parents, who in their various modes recorded its effects, Wilde would have been initiated into the memory of the Great Famine and its exposure of the double-think of the empire at home. That same kind of double-think also saturated his education at Portora Royal School, Enniskillen, where he was taught a strangely exclusive version of English history — one that made virtually no reference to the history or condition of Ireland itself. Yet Wilde's father was passionately interested in the native oral culture, the focus of Deirdre Toomey's essay. Wilde's debt to this culture, she argues, must make us question whether we can any longer think of him as a writer at all, rather than as a talker, a performer of his own tales and a transcriber of an ancient oral tradition. What does this do to the notion of authorship? How may Wilde be accused of plagiarism if the teller of tales makes, *in effect*, no claim to such originality?

Wilde invented his stories from the lore his parents collected in the West of Ireland, from an ancient, but increasingly marginalized and despised native tradition. Was it the exotic (that is, backward) appeal of this version of Ireland that led one of Wilde's English friends, the enigmatic E. F. Benson, to travel to County Tipperary to report on the Irish scandal of the day, the burning of a woman by her husband for being 'away with the fairies'? Was it an accident of history that Benson's essay appeared in the same month that Wilde began to serve his two-year gaol sentence: or was it, as Angela Bourke suspects, a coded message about being a 'fairy' in London, and the price of suspect activity in either country? Or — as Bernard O'Donoghue asks — is there something natively Irish about the idea of sacrifice, especially when linked to violence?

Turning to relations between England and Ireland, Declan Kiberd examines the way in which the ambiguities of colonial subjectivity reflect issues of sexual ambiguity. As he trenchantly argues, the colony is a repository for the 'other', a mirror-image which reverses the colonizer's vision of himself. Fintan O'Toole in turn recounts how Wilde discovered in the American West a paradigm of the renegade turned hero; was it only the magic of publicity — or the new potency of a once colonized people (now in the process of becoming colonizers themselves) — which made the son of Irish parents, the outlaw Jesse James, into a star? Wilde's identification with the enemy within — the anarchists and nationalists of his day — as those 'souls in revolt', the demonic dandy who plots to overthrow not only the empire but the self-justifying logic by which it is sustained, is the subject of my own essay, 'The Wilde Irishman'. In another commentary on Wilde's political context, W. J. McCormack explores Wilde's silent fixation on Parnell, and in doing so opens up the question of Wilde's eloquent reticence — one that in fact extends (except for notable instances, such as the essay on Froude) to Ireland as well. It was for his later contemporary James Joyce to articulate that silence as a weapon of the Irishman in exile. Yet others who shared his exile in London, Yeats and Shaw, recognized in Wilde his instinctive Irishness, the complicated game of seduction and subversion played out in his art.

Closing this section, John Wilson Foster meticulously unearths another layer of Wilde's Irish legacy: the scientific interests that were a direct if unacknowledged inheritance from his father and the intellectual tradition of his class and time. Wilde's espousal of the then current notions of race-membership and race-consciousness — upon which Yeats's Celtic Revival ultimately rested — are here seen as crucial to Wilde's strong sense of cultural identity.

These appropriations are explicit, and their fruits are here abundant and obvious. For the second half of the book, Irish writers, both creative and critical, had the task of forging continuities between the Oscar Wilde of a century ago and the Oscar Wilde of today. These essays lead off with an account by Paula Murphy of the competition for the first public statue of Oscar Wilde in his native country. In her record of the various submissions, upon which both the judging panel and the sculptors comment, as well as Wilde's own reflections on the role of sculpture in his own aesthetic, one comes to understand something of how reputations are made and unmade in the public consciousness. As itself a record of how Ireland has come to acknowledge its own native son, this account is invaluable testimony. Those who follow bear witness to the impress of Wilde in their own way and their own voice; they were given no brief and follow none, except to appropriate him as they see fit, according to the opportunities afforded them. All take risks in their own way, and several are bound to be controversial; so much the better. They celebrate, on their own terms and in their own idiom, the homecoming of one of the prodigal sons of Irish letters.

'Swift haunts me: he is always just around the next corner', Yeats once wrote, retracing in old age the steps of the Dean of St Patrick's. Where his own ghost now treads, Yeats is shadowed by the more urgent apparition of Joyce, soliciting the tourist from street and pub. But — one hundred years after his trial in London — not one of my Irish students knew that Oscar Wilde was born in Dublin; that he attended Trinity College and spent holidays in the West, in Mayo and Galway. Perhaps to them he was the ghost of the old class, whom the new republic had exorcized: the ghost of colonialism, of the bad old days, of the Castle and the jackboot, the Famine and the Ascendancy; a dark and murky past that would betray republican simplicities.

Yet it is daily becoming clearer that simplicities no longer respond in any way to the complicated fate of being — or becoming — Irish. Perhaps they never did. Through the mediators of the new political climate, those who have restlessly revised our versions of Irish history and those who are, through opening commerce with the extremes of both loyalist and nationalist opinion, expanding the debate on who belongs to this island, the adumbrations of Wilde's ghost may be registered. For the first time since his death, Wilde is being recognized as Irish. No one who has read Davis Coakley's book will again be able to read Wilde's story 'The Selfish Giant' without imagining the young Oscar playing inside the private garden that was Merrion Square, while the dirty urchins of the slums pressed their faces against the railings. Wilde's effigy now haunts the same garden. Perhaps this will be the year when we shall at last glimpse his ghost disappearing around the corner.

One cannot appropriate a ghost. This book does not seek to do so. What it seeks to do is to reinstate his spirit back in its own haunting grounds: to relocate its origins and its effects in its native Ireland and in that spiritual territory that Wilde himself understood as home to the collective unconscious of his race.

DUBLIN, 1997

Part One
APPROPRIATIONS

Oscar Wilde:
The Artist as Irishman

DECLAN KIBERD

'Was there ever an Irish man of genius who did not get himself turned into an Englishman as fast as he could?'[1] asked Henry Craik in an immortal line; and no better illustration could be found than the career of Oscar Wilde, which began with his arrival as a student in Oxford in the autumn of 1874. Having put the Irish Sea between himself and his parents, the young genius proceeded to reconstruct his image through the art of the pose. According to Yeats, Wilde in England 'perpetually performed a play which was in all things the opposite of all that he had known in childhood and youth. [He] never put off completely his wonder at opening his eyes every morning on his own beautiful house and in remembering that he had dined yesterday with a Duchess . . . .'[2]

The home which Wilde had left in Dublin was, on the other hand, 'the sort that had fed the imagination of Charles Lever, dirty, untidy and daring,'[3] and it was presided over by two eccentric parents who seemed to have stepped out of a bad stage-Irish melodrama. Sir William Wilde, although a most eminent surgeon and scholar, was reputed to be the dirtiest man in Dublin. 'Why are Sir William's nails so black?' asked the mordant students who assisted at his operations, and the answer was 'Because he has scratched himself.'[4] The Lord Lieutenant's wife one evening refused the soup at the Wilde home, because she had spotted her host dipping his thumb into the tureen. That same hand, it was alleged, on one notorious occasion administered a whiff of chloroform to a female patient as a prelude to an amorous overture.[5] Lady Wilde turned a blind eye to the peccadilloes of her husband, just as he indulged the strident patriotism of his wife, who wrote under the pen-name 'Speranza' for nationalist journals. His monumental studies of the antiquities and archaeology of Ireland were matched by her collections of folklore and outpourings of nationalist verse. To her second son, Lady Wilde bequeathed a love of the pose and a theatrical personality.

From the outset, her attitude to Oscar was ambivalent. She had longed for a girl and so, when the boy-child arrived like an uninvited guest, she was somewhat miffed. Thereafter, this ardent feminist and radical alternately pampered and neglected him. His love for her was melodramatic but genuine, as was his repeated espousal in later writings of her doctrines – especially her belief in a woman's

9

right to work and to engage in political activity. Persistent rumours about his parents' sexual adventurism may, however, have given rise to doubts about his own legitimacy, which would ultimately be put in the mouth of Jack Worthing in *The Importance of Being Earnest*: 'I said I had lost my parents. It would be nearer the truth to say that my parents seemed to have lost me . . . I don't actually know who I am by birth. I was . . . well, I was found.'[6] The mild fear of technical illegitimacy concealed in Wilde a far deeper concern to establish his true personal identity. His famous parents were probably too busy to offer the one commodity that is signally lacking in all his plays, that continuous tenderness and intimacy which might have given him a sense of himself.

The future master of paradox was already flickering between national extremes, emulating his mother's Irish patriotism in one poem, only to salute Keats as 'poet–painter of our English land'[7] in the next. Already, he was evolving the doctrine of the androgyny of the integrated personality, which would find immortal expression in the wisecrack that 'All women become like their mothers. That is their tragedy. No man does. That's his.'[8] The loutish sexism of the first half of the proposition is fully retrieved by the sharp intelligence of the conclusion.

The sexual uncertainty induced by a neglectful but dominant mother was heightened by the disappointment of Wilde's first love for Florence Balcombe, the beautiful daughter of a retired army officer. Having met her in the summer of 1876, he wrote to a friend: 'She is just seventeen with the most perfectly beautiful face I ever saw and not a sixpence of money.'[9] That he was serious about her is confirmed by the characteristically flippant reference to cash: but she spurned the young dandy for the more Gothic thrills of life with a minor civil servant named Bram Stoker, thereby causing Wilde to fire off a letter in which he vowed to 'leave Ireland' and live in England 'probably for good'.[10] Here was yet another nightmare from the Irish past to be suppressed by a famous career in England. Wilde easily cut the cord which bound him to the land of his parents, for Sir William died while he was at Oxford. The loss of one parent was a misfortune, but the loss of two might indicate carelessness, so Wilde installed his mother in proximity to himself in London after his graduation, but at a chaste distance from his own quarters. He announced to startled guests at their weekly soirées that mother and son had formed a society for the suppression of virtue. It was only later that they saw what he meant.

In the meantime, he busied himself with the task of arranging a pose based on the art of elegant inversion. All the norms of his childhood were to be reversed. His father had been laughed at by society, so he would mock society first. His father had been unkempt, so he would be fastidious. From his mother he had inherited a large and ungainly body, which Lady Colin Campbell compared to 'a great white caterpillar'[11] and which recalled all too poignantly the gorilla-like frame of the stage-Irishman in Sir John Tenniel's cartoons. To disarm such critics, Wilde concealed his massive form with costly clothes and studied the art of elegant deportment. His mother had sought to reconquer Ireland, so he would surpass her by invading and conquering England. She had wished to repossess Irish folklore and the native language, but he would go one better and achieve a total mastery of English.

'I am Irish by race,' he told Edmond de Goncourt, 'but the English have condemned me to speak the language of Shakespeare.'[12] It was not the most onerous of sentences and he admitted as much to an audience in San Francisco: 'The Saxon took our lands from us and made them destitute . . . but we took their language and added new beauties to it.'[13] Decades later, the same diagnosis would be offered by James Joyce:

> In spite of everything Ireland remains the brain of the United Kingdom. The English, judiciously practical and ponderous, furnish the over-stuffed stomach of humanity with a perfect gadget — the water closet. The Irish, condemned to express themselves in a language not their own, have stamped on it the mark of their own genius and compete for glory with the civilized nations. The result is then called English literature.[14]

Wilde's entire literary career constituted an ironic comment on the tendency of Victorian Englishmen to attribute to the Irish those emotions which they had repressed within themselves. His essays on Ireland question the assumption that, just because the English are one thing, the Irish must be its opposite. The man who believed that a truth in art is that whose opposite is also true was quick to point out that every good man has an element of the woman in him, just as every sensitive Irishman must have a secret Englishman within himself — and vice versa. With his sharp intelligence, Wilde saw that the image of the stage Irishman tells far more about English fears than Irish realities, just as the 'Irish joke' revealed less about Irishmen's innate foolishness than about Englishmen's persistent and poignant desire to say something funny. Wilde opted to say that something funny for them in a lifelong performance of 'Englishness' which was really a parody of the very notion. The ease with which Wilde effected the transition from stage-Ireland to stage-England was his ultimate comment on the shallowness of such categories. Earnest intellectuals back in Dublin missed this element of parody and saw in Wilde's career an act of national apostasy: but he did not lack defenders. Yeats saw Wilde's snobbery not as such, but as the clever strategy of an Irishman marooned in London, whose only weapon against Anglo-Saxon prejudice was to become more English than the English themselves, thereby challenging many time-honoured myths about the Irish.[15]

The costs of such a gamble, however, might be too high, entailing a comprehensive suppression of personality. In rejecting the stage-Irish mask, Wilde took a step towards selfhood, but in exchanging it for the pose of urbane Englishman, he seemed merely to have exchanged one mask for another, and to have given rise to the suspicion that what these masks hid was no face at all — that the exponent of 'personality' was fatally lacking in 'character'. To his mortification and intermittent delight, Wilde found that his English mask was not by any means a perfect fit. The more he suppressed his inherited personality, the more it seemed to assert itself. 'The two great turning-points of my life', he wrote in *De Profundis*, 'were when my father sent me to Oxford, and when society sent me to prison.'[16] It was a revealing equation, for in both institutions he learned what it was to be an outsider, an uninvited guest, an Irishman in England.

To his friends in Oxford, he was not so much an Anglo-Irishman as a flashy and fastidious Paddy with 'a suspicion of brogue' and 'an unfamiliar turn to his phrasing'. At the university's gate-lodges, he took to signing himself 'Oscar Fingal O'Flahertie Wills Wilde', filling two lines of the roll-book with the indisputable proof of his Irish identity. His flirtation with Roman Catholicism at Magdalen College was rather more serious and much more costly than that of his English peers: for an Englishman, the Catholic Church evoked incense and Mariolatry, but for an Irishman it was the historic faith of an oppressed people.[17] As a consequence of his devotion to the Scarlet Lady, Wilde was punished by exclusion from his half-brother's will at a time when he was sorely in need of funds. Yet he refused to deny his interest in Catholicism, which may have been enhanced by the dim recollection of having been brought as a child, at the whim of his mother, for a second baptism in the Catholic Church at Glencree, County Wicklow. It is possible that the 'desire for immediate baptism' expressed by the two leading men of his greatest play may arise from that experience: certainly, the playwright made sure to have a Dublin Passionist Father at his bedside just before he died.

At all events, Oxford strengthened in Wilde the conviction that an Irishman discovers himself only when he goes abroad, just as it reinforced his belief that 'man is least himself when he talks in his own person', but 'Give him a mask, and he will tell you the truth.'[18] Years later, when Parnell was at the height of his power in 1889, Wilde wrote in celebration of his own Celtic intellect which 'at home . . . had but learned the pathetic weakness of nationality; [but] in a strange land it realized what indomitable forces nationality possesses'.[19] Wilde saw his own career as running parallel to that of Parnell, another urbane Irishman who surprised the English by his self-control and cold exterior. Always a separatist, Wilde poured scorn on the latest English debate on 'how best to misgovern Ireland' and wrote a mocking review of one of James Anthony Froude's books on the subject.

In his view, Froude on Ireland was a perfect example of all that was amiss with Britain's attitudes: 'If in the last century she tried to govern Ireland with an insolence that was intensified by race hatred and religious prejudice, she has sought to rule her in this century with a stupidity that is aggravated by good intentions.' The man who complained that the modern attempt to solve the problem of slavery took the form of devising amusements to distract the slaves, saw the political version of such distraction in the endless rehearsals of the Irish Question at Westminster. He closed a review of Froude's *The Two Chiefs of Dunboy* with a straight-faced inversion of the author's purpose: 'as a record of the incapacity of a Teutonic to rule a Celtic people against their own wishes his book is not without value'. (West Indians coined the term 'Froudacity' to describe Froude's lofty condescension: in his *The English in the West Indies* [1888] Froude had found it impossible to think that the former slaves of the area could ever hope to run their own government.) Wilde brilliantly glossed the latest Froudacity: 'there are some who will welcome with delight the idea of solving the Irish question by doing away with the Irish people'. His solution was more complex and daring: to become a very Irish kind of Englishman, just as in Ireland his had been a rather English kind of Irish family. The truth, in life as well as in art, was that whose opposite could also be true: every great power evolved its own opposite in order to achieve itself, as Giordano Bruno had written, but from such opposition might spring reunion.

Wilde's art, as well as his public persona, was founded on a critique of the manic Victorian urge to antithesis, an antithesis not only between all things English and Irish, but also between male and female, master and servant, good and evil, and so on. He inveighed against the specialization deemed essential in men fit to run an empire, and showed that no matter how manfully they tried to project qualities of softness, poetry and femininity on to their subject peoples, these repressed instincts would return to take a merry revenge. Arnold's theory had been that the Celts were doomed by a multiple selfhood, which allowed them to see so many options in a situation that they were immobilized, unlike the English specialist, who might have simplified himself but who did not succumb to pitfalls which he had not the imagination to discern. Wilde knew that in such Celtic psychology was the shape of things to come.

Wilde was the first major artist to discredit the romantic ideal of sincerity and to replace it with the darker imperative of authenticity: he saw that in being true to a single self, a sincere man may be false to half a dozen other selves.[20] Those Victorians who saluted a man as having 'character' were, in Wilde's judgement, simply indicating the predictability of his devotion to a single self-image. The Puritan distrust of play-acting and the rise of romantic poetry had simply augmented this commitment to the ideal of a unitary self. This, along with the scope for psychological exploration provided by the novel, may have been a further reason for the failure of nineteenth-century artists before Wilde to shape a genuinely theatrical play, Shelley's *The Cenci* being far better as poetry than as drama. Wilde argued that these prevailing cultural tendencies also led to some very poor poems written in the first person singular: all bad poetry, he bleakly quipped, sprang from genuine feeling. In the same way, he mocked the drab black suit worn by the Victorian male – Marx called it a social hieroglyphic – as a sign of the stable, imperial self. He, on the contrary, was interested in the subversive potential of a theatricality which caused people to forget their assigned place and to assert the plasticity of social conditions. Wilde wrote from the perspective of one who realizes that the only real fool is the conventionally 'sincere' man who fails to see that he, too, is wearing a mask, the mask of sincerity. If all art must contain the essential criticism of its prevailing codes, for Wilde an authentic life must recognize all that is most opposed to it.

In consequence, in *The Importance of Being Earnest*, each person turns out to be his own secret opposite: Algy becomes Bunbury, Jack Ernest, as in Wilde's career the Irelander turned Englander. Whatever seems like an opposite in the play materializes as a double. For example, many critics have found in it a traditional contrast between the brilliant cynicism of the town-dwellers and the tedious rectitude of the rural people; but that is not how things work out. Characters like Canon Chasuble and Miss Prism are revealed to have contained the seeds of corruption and knowingness all along, while Cecily has her most interesting (that is, evil) inspirations in a garden (rather reminiscent of her biblical predecessor). So every dichotomy dichotomizes. Wilde's is an art of inversion and this applies to gender stereotypes above all: so the women in the play read heavy works of German philosophy and attend university courses, while the men lounge elegantly on sofas and eat dainty cucumber sandwiches.

Far from the men engaging in the traditional discussion of the finer points of the female form, it is the women who discuss the physical appeal of the men: when Algernon proposes to Cecily, it is *she* who runs her fingers through *his* hair and asks sternly: 'I hope your hair curls naturally. Does it?'[21] (The answer is 'Yes, darling, with a little help from others.') When Algy rushes out, Cecily's instant response is: 'What an impetuous boy he is! I like his hair so much!' The last word on these inversions of gender roles is spoken by Gwendolen, when she praises her own father for conceding that a man's place is in the home and that public affairs may be safely entrusted to women:

> Outside the family circle, papa, I am glad to say, is entirely unknown. I think that is quite as it should be. The home seems to me to be the proper sphere for the man. And, certainly once a man begins to neglect his domestic duties he becomes painfully effeminate, does he not? And I don't like that. It makes men so very attractive.[22]

It would be possible to see this cult of inversion as Wilde's private little joke about his own homosexuality, but it is much more than that: at the root of these devices is his profound scorn for the extreme Victorian division between male and female. A historian of clothing remarked in 1969 that, if a Martian had visited Victorian England and seen the clothes worn there, that Martian might have been forgiven for thinking that men and women belonged to different species.[23] In the history of men's fashions over the previous four centuries, it was only in the Victorian age that men presented themselves with no trace of the 'feminine'. The Elizabethan gallant had been admired for his shapely legs, starched ruff and earrings; the Restoration rake for his ribbons, muff and scent; the Romantics for their nipped-in waists, exotic perfumes and hourglass shapes. Such details indicate that the androgyny of the male and female had never been fully suppressed.

Wilde always liked to create manly women and womanly men, as a challenge to the stratified thinking of his day. He had seen in his mother a woman who could edit journals and organize political campaigns in an age when women had no right to vote; and it was from her that he inherited his lifelong commitment to feminism. 'Why should there be one law for men, and another for women?'[24] asks Jack of Miss Prism near the end of *Earnest*: if the double standard is right for men, then it is right also for women; and if it is wrong for women, then it is wrong also for men. Wilde demonstrates that the gender-antitheses of the age were almost meaningless: in the play, it is the women who are businesslike in making shrewd calculations about the attractions of a proposed marriage, while it is the men who are sentimental, breathless and impractical.

By rejecting such antithetical thinking, Wilde was also repudiating the philosophy of determinism, that bleak late-nineteenth-century belief that lives are preordained by the circumstances of birth, background and upbringing, a conviction shared by a surprising range of the age's thinkers.[25] The extreme sects of Protestantism had long believed in the notion of the elect and the damned, but radical critics such as Marx and Freud evolved secular versions of the theory, viewing the person as primarily the effect of childhood training and social conditioning. For these figures, environmental factors often overwhelmed the initiatives of the individual, a view summed up in the Marxian claim that consciousness did not determine social being but that social being determined consciousness. To Wilde, who believed in the radical autonomy of the self, this was hateful stuff. He saw the self as an artwork, to be made and remade: for him, it was society that was the dreary imposition. 'The real life is the life we do not lead'[26] — that is, the one lived in pure imagination and in acts of playful dissent which deliver us from the earnestness of duty and destiny.

The Importance of Being Earnest challenges ideas of manifest destiny by the strategy of depicting characters reduced to automatons by their blind faith in the preordained. Gwendolen idiotically accepts Jack in the mistaken belief that he is Ernest: 'The moment Algernon first mentioned to me that he had a friend called Ernest, I knew I was destined to love you.'[27] The whole plot machinery creaks with an intentional over-obviousness. Jack, for instance, says that the two girls will call one another 'sister' only after they have called each other many worse things as well, and this is exactly what happens. The women, perhaps because they seem to have been more exposed to Victorian education than the men, show a touching faith in determinism. Ever since Cecily heard of her wicked uncle, she talked of nothing else. Her faith, however, takes on a radical form, as she finds in it the courage to reject the tedious, all-female regime of Miss Prism and to bring her *animus* to full consciousness in the ideal Ernest, with whom she conducts a wholly imaginary affair before Algy's actual arrival. In doing this, she was already rejecting the notion of an antithesis between herself and others, because she had already recognized the existence of that antithesis in herself. Just before meeting her wicked uncle, she denies the idea of a black-and-white world: 'I have never met any really wicked person before. I feel rather frightened. I am afraid he will look just like everyone else.'[28] Wilde insists that men and women know themselves in all their aspects and that they cease to repress in themselves whatever they find unflattering or painful. In abandoning this practice, people would also end the determinist tyranny which led them to impute all despised qualities to subject peoples. Anglo-Saxonist theory, as we have seen, insisted that the Irish were gushing and dirty by inexorable inheritance, and as unable to change any of that as they were unable to alter the colour of their eyes.[29] But Wilde showed otherwise.

The Wildean moment is that at which all polar oppositions are transcended. 'One of the facts of physiology', he told the actress Marie Prescott, 'is the desire of any very intensified emotion to be relieved by some emotion that is its opposite.'[30] The trivial comedy turns out, upon inspection, to have a serious point; the audience itself is acting each night and must be congratulated or castigated for its performance; and the world will be an imitation of the play's utopia, rather than the play imitating an existing reality. That utopia is a place built out of those moments when all hierarchies are reversed as a prelude to revolution. So the butler begins the play with subversive witticisms which excel those of his master, and the master thereafter goes in search of his half-suppressed double.

The psychologist Otto Rank has argued that the double, being a handy device for the offloading of all that embarrasses, may epitomize one's noble soul or one's base guilts, or indeed both at the same time.[31] That is to say that the double is a close relation of the Englishman's Celtic Other. Many characters in literature have sought to murder their double in order to do away with guilt (as England had tried to annihilate Irish culture), but have then found that it is not so easily repressed, since it may also contain man's utopian self (those redemptive qualities found by Arnold in Ireland). Bunbury is Algy's double, embodying in a single fiction all that is most creative and most corrupt in his creator. Bunbury is the shadow which symbolizes Algy's need for immortality, for an influential soul that survives death; and, at the same time, Bunbury is that ignoble being to whom the irresponsible Algy transfers all responsibility for his more questionable deeds. The service which the Irish performed for the English, Bunbury discharges for his creator: he epitomizes his master's need for a human likeness on the planet and, simultaneously, his desire to retain his own difference. Hence the play is one long debate about whether or not to do away with Bunbury. Lady Bracknell's complaints sound suspiciously like English claims that, in trying to solve the Irish Question, the Irish kept on changing it: 'I think it is high time that Mr Bunbury made up his mind whether he was going to live or to die. This shilly-shallying with the question is absurd. Nor do I in any way approve of the modern sympathy with invalids. I consider it morbid.'[32]

Erich Stern has written that 'in order to escape the fear of death, the person resorts to suicide which, however, he carries out on his double because he loves and esteems his ego so much'.[33] Many analysts would contend that the double is the creation of a pathologically self-absorbed type, usually male, often chauvinistic, sometimes imperialist: only by this device of splitting can such a one live with himself. Rank actually argued that the double arose from a morbid self-love which prevented the development of a balanced personality.[34] If this is so, however, then killing or annihilating the double is no final solution, for his life and welfare are as closely linked to that of his author as are the Irish to the English, women to men, and so on. No sooner is the double denied than it becomes man's fate. Like the 'Celtic feminine' in a culture of imperial machismo, it comes back to haunt its begetters, enacting what Wilde called the tyranny of the weak over the strong, the only kind of tyranny which lasts. So, in the play, whenever he is most stridently denied, the double always turns out to be closest at hand. When Jack exclaims, 'My brother is in the dining-room? I don't know what it all means. I think it is perfectly absurd,' Algy asks, perhaps on behalf of all uninvited Irish guests: 'Why on earth don't you go up and change? . . . It is perfectly childish to be in deep mourning for a man who is actually staying for a whole week with you in your house as a guest. I call it grotesque.'[35] The denied double thus ends up setting the agenda of its creator, who, being unaware of it, becomes its unconscious slave. The women in the play set the agenda for men, Bunbury for Algy, butlers for masters, and so on, even as the Irish Parnellites were setting the agenda for England, repeatedly paralysing politics at Westminster.

Writers throughout history have found their version of the double in art, that diabolical enterprise which paradoxically guarantees immortality; and this is the one employment of the double which may not be a form of neurosis, since it is presented 'in an acceptable form, justifying the survival of the irrational in our over-rational civilization'.[36] But other uses are pathological and doomed, since the double is devised to cope with the fear of death but reappears as its very portent. That fear gives rise to an exaggerated attitude to one's own ego, leading to an inability to love and a wild longing to be loved. These, sure enough, are attributes of Algy and Jack before the women break up their self-enclosed rituals (and, it might be added, attributes of British policy in Ireland before independence).

There could hardly be a more convincing psychological explanation of the strange oscillation between conciliation and coercion in imperial policy towards Ireland than Rank's report on the tactics employed in the making of the double. The notion of the 'innocent' and 'spontaneous' Irish may have been an emotional convenience to those Victorians who were increasingly unable to find satisfaction for feelings of guilt in universally accepted religious forms. The myth of an unspoilt peasantry, in Cumberland or Connemara, was, after all, a convenient means of emotional absolution from guilt in a society for which natural instinct was often tantamount to a vice. The sequence of coercion following upon conciliation could be explained in terms of outrage with the symbol when it failed to live up to these high expectations.

If this is so, then *The Importance of Being Earnest* becomes (among other things, of course) a parable of Anglo-Irish relations and a pointer to their resolution. This should not seem surprising. Wilde, in London, offering witty critiques of imperial culture, was one of the first in a long line of native intellectuals who were equipped by an analytic education to pen the most thorough repudiation of their masters. The violent denunciation of Europe produced by Frantz Fanon would be written to a Hegelian method in the elegant style of a Sartre. In a somewhat similar fashion, the English did not just create their own colonialism in Ireland; they also informed most hostile interpretations of it.

The Irish, by way of resistance, could go in either of two ways; and Wilde, being Wilde, went in both. On one side, he duplicated many of the attributes of the colonizer, becoming a sort of urbane, epigrammatic Englishman (just as militant nationalists, going even further, emulated the muscular imperial ethic with their own Gaelic games, Cuchulanoid models and local versions of the public schools). On another, more subversive level, he pointed to a subterranean, radical tradition of English culture, which might form a useful alliance with Irish nationalism and thus remain true to its own deepest imperatives. Sensing that England might be the last, most completely occupied of the British colonies, Wilde offered, in saving Ireland, to save the masters from themselves. For the Irish, of course, knew more than their island neighbours: their problem was that of a quick-witted people being governed by a dull one. As Hegel had observed, the losers of history, in learning what it is to lose, learn also what it must be like to win. They have no choice but to know their masters even better than the masters know themselves. To them, the masters (though tyrants) remain always human, but to the masters the subjects are not human, not persons, not really there at all. Hope therefore comes from the initiatives launched by the slaves.[37]

The psychologist Ashis Nandy observed these tendencies at work in occupied India, whose citizens often sought to become more like the British, either in friendship or in enmity. A martial ethos was cultivated, ostensibly to threaten the occupiers with violent insurrection; but this was really a subtler form of collaboration with the British culture. The new muscular Indians came, nevertheless, to view the feminized Indian male as one whose identity was nullified by these self-cancelling polarities, a victim of a pathology even more dangerous than that of femininity itself.[38] Hesitant European well-wishers like E. M. Forster would provide in a character like Dr Aziz a portrayal of the Indian's lack of manly fibre, as if secretly willing the nationalists to open revolt. A liberationist reading followed, rejecting the either/or polarities of male and female, England and India, and embracing instead an alternative both/and mode of thought, which opposed male or female to the ideal of androgyny, English or Indian nationalism to the ideal of liberation.[39]

This was at once the occupiers' darkest fear and deepest need: that 'instead of trying to redeem their masculinity by becoming counter-players of the rulers according to established rules, the colonized will discover an alternative frame of reference within which the oppressed do not seem weak, degraded . . .'.[40] This led Indian subjects to see their rulers as morally inferior and, with their new-found confidence, to feed that information back to the British in devious ways. This was also Wilde's mission in London, a place (he said) of intellectual fog, where only thought was not catching. 'Considered as an instrument of thought, the English mind is coarse and undeveloped', he wrote. 'The only thing that can cure it is the growth of the critical instinct.'[41] That instinct was not always welcomed. Two weeks before Wilde's first trial, a versifier for *Punch* magazine called for the extradition of such colonial androgynes:

If such be 'Artists' then may Philistines
  Arise, plain sturdy Britons as of yore,
And sweep them off and purge away the signs,
  That England e'er such noxious offspring bore.[42]

Indians like Nandy came to see Wilde as embarked on the attempt to save England from the deforming effects of industrial pollution. 'I would give Manchester back to the shepherds and Leeds to the stock farmers',[43] Wilde proclaimed as a young student of Ruskin; but years later he sensed that a psychological repair-job was called for as well. The colonial adventure had not only led to suffering and injustice overseas, but had corrupted domestic British society to the core. The projection of despised 'feminine' qualities on to Celts or Indians had led, inexorably, to a diminution of womanhood at home. Wilde's first act on taking up the editorship of the *Lady's World* in 1887 was to rename it *Woman's World*; and in his plays he argued for those feminine qualities deemed irrelevant to a thrusting industrial society.

The hierarchical view of humankind, on which imperialism justified itself, led to a purely instrumental view of the English working class, but that class would never rise in revolt, since the empire also *reduced* class tensions by opening up careers overseas to talented members of the lower orders. Nandy held that Wilde's effeminacy thus threatened a fundamental postulate of the colonial mentality in Britain itself.[44] Certainly, Wilde seemed at all times anxious to feed back his most subversive ideas to the ruling class, as when he published his essay 'The Soul of Man under Socialism' in the upmarket *Fortnightly Review* (1891). In such challenges may be found the essence of that carnivalesque moment towards which each of his plays moves: when the wit and laughter of the low rejuvenate the jaded culture of the high, and when polyphonic voices override the monotones of perfunctory authority. 'Rather more than a socialist,' Wilde described himself with real accuracy as 'something of an anarchist.'[45]

What is canvassed throughout *The Importance of Being Earnest* is nothing less than the revolutionary ideal of the self-created man or woman. Even the odious Lady Bracknell finds herself inadvertently proposing a Nietzschean idea: that if nature has not equipped you with a good father, you had better go and manufacture one: 'I would strongly advise you, Mr Worthing, to try and acquire some relations as soon as possible.'[46] Jack, therefore, has to create himself *ex nihilo*, inventing the tradition of himself; allegedly born and first bred in a railway station, he appears to have defied all notions of paternity (or what Lady Bracknell calls 'a recognized position in good society'). In Edward Said's terms, he exemplifies *affiliation* (the radical creation of one's own world and contexts and versions of tradition) rather than conservative *filiation*. Lady Bracknell has no doubts about where all this is leading: to the break-up of family life into its individual units and to 'the worst excesses of the French Revolution'.[47] Revolution is a spectre which she raises when the education of the lower classes is mentioned. If successful, it may lead to a home-grown uprising and acts of violence in Grosvenor Square.

The politics and psychology of the play are quintessentially republican: Bunbury must be interred not in England but in Paris, home of European radicals and Fenian exiles. All this is scarcely surprising from the pen of one whose mother had determined to 'rear him a Hero perhaps and President of the future Irish Republic';[48] from one whose first play *Vera, or The Nihilists* was deemed too republican for the London stage and was performed instead in the United States; from one who told an American audience after the Phoenix Park killings in 1882 that England was 'reaping the fruit of seven centuries of injustice'[49] and who said that England would be fully saved only when it too became a republic. Wilde's republicanism was a declared feature of his agenda in London from the outset. In 1881, he sent a political pamphlet by his mother to the editor of the *Nineteenth Century*, adding, 'I don't think age has dimmed the fire and enthusiasm of that pen which set the young Irelanders in a blaze.'[50] Contrary to many aesthetes who yearned for Renaissance-style patrons, Wilde asserted that the republican form of government was the one most favourable to art.[51]

The debate about republicanism had been very much in the air during Wilde's teenage years. In 1871 a radical politician named Charles Dilke had called at a meeting of working men for the abolition of monarchy. For this he was ostracized and his subsequent gatherings broken up. *The Times* editorialized: 'these are evidently improper points, to be handled, and that with little candour or delicacy, before an assembly of working men'.[52] Prime Minister Gladstone assured the Queen on 21 December 1871 that 'it could never be satisfactory that there should exist even a fraction of the nation republican in its views';[53] and together they ran a nationwide campaign for royalism. So successful was this that the subject was not widely debated again until 1922–23, the years immediately following Irish independence, when the matter was raised at Labour Party meetings in the north-east of England.[54] This gives some sense of Wilde's daring as a thinker, as well as illustrating that the so-called Irish Question was truly parabolic, a device by which British radicals could explore contentious topics at a somewhat safe remove. For example, some years after Wilde's fall from grace the question of homosexuality was raised, once again in a charged Irish context, by the allegations made at the trial of Sir Roger Casement in 1916. The Irish Question was merely the sounding-board for unacknowledged English questions.

Certain questions recur in each of Wilde's plays, and so also do certain observations. *Lady Windermere's Fan*, for instance, suggests that England has no room for the 'heart', which it invariably breaks. The most vital character on stage, Mrs Erlynne, chooses to emigrate, taking with her Lord Augustus Lorton; and he feels set free of his country rather than deprived of it. Imperialism has, apparently, sapped English society of two elements, the creative and the criminal, leaving only dull suburban types. What life there is in it comes from the outside, from the visiting Mr Hopper of Australia, who takes the one unattached young woman in the play back with him. Wilde's implication is prophetic of the end of empire. For while Britain wins further victories overseas through such innovators, it will be in a state of terminal decay at home. A society which has no place for its dissidents, its creators or its youth is a society in trouble. Wilde knew this only too well, since he came from such a place: Ireland. And he said that the remedy was for England to adopt some Irish qualities while shedding Irish territories.

If the English used Ireland as a laboratory in which to test their society, Wilde was happy to use England as a testing-ground for Irish ideas and debates: for, in his mind, the two could not be separated. Though it was never viewed as such in Ireland, he saw his own art as part of the Irish Renaissance, jokingly telling Shaw that their mission was to dispel English fog so that it could make way for the 'Celtic School'.[55] What he meant by the latter phrase he explained in 'The Critic as Artist': 'it is the Celt who leads in art, there is no reason why in future years this strange Renaissance should not be almost as mighty in its way as that new birth of Art that woke many centuries ago in the cities of Italy'.[56]

But this did not mean that Wilde could write directly of the Ireland of his youth. That would have entailed him in the bad faith of reproducing an environment which he knew he should be contesting; and that is something which no radical author could countenance (unless, like Shaw, he wrote of the contrast between how the land was and how it should be). Ireland in the nineteenth century was a confused and devastated place, suspended between two languages; and Wilde was committed to sketching the lineaments of no-place, otherwise known as utopia, something which Ireland or indeed England might yet become. Where Arnold had hoped to see the object in itself as it really was, Wilde wished to see it as it really was not. At a time when the Irish were often accused by the English of mischievously changing the question, Wilde was thinking further ahead than either side in the debate. So far from responding to the questions posed by the epoch, art (for him) offered answers even before the questions had been asked.

There is a further reason why, in order to deal with Ireland, a play such as *The Importance of Being Earnest* had to be set in England. Wilde had discovered that an Irishman came to consciousness of himself as such only when he left his country. Wearing the mask of the English Oxonian, Wilde was paradoxically freed to become more 'Irish' than he could ever have been back in Ireland. 'It is only by contact with the art of foreign nations that the art of a country gains that individual and separate life that we call nationality....'[57] Identity was dialogic; the other was also the truest friend, since it was from that other that a sense of self was derived. A person went out to the other and returned with a self, getting to know others simply to find out what they thought of him- or herself. This seeing of the entire world through the other's eyes was an essential process in the formation of a balanced individual; and so Wilde loved England as genuinely as Goethe loved the French. He quoted Goethe on the point: 'How could I, to whom culture and barbarism are alone of importance, hate a nation which is among the most cultivated of the earth, and to which I owe so great a part of my own cultivation?'[58]

That was a universal theme: the persons who gave its name to France were indeed Germanic Franks, for a culture could be surveyed and known as such only from the outside or, at least, from the margins. Identity was predicated on difference, but the colonizers of the 1880s and 1890s were conveniently forgetting that fact in their anxiety to make over the world in their own image; and they would have to be reminded. A somewhat similar jolt must also be given to those chauvinists who were too eager to deny any value to the occupier culture; and Wilde, by announcing the Irish Renaissance with works which appeared to be set in England, administered that rebuke. One says 'appeared to be set in England', of course, for a reason which must be finally explained.

English literature had a liberating effect on Wilde: it equipped him with a mask behind which he was able to compose the lineaments of his Irish face. This was to be a strategy followed by many decolonizing writers; and, as so often, it was the Argentinian Jorge Luis Borges who gave the fullest account of the method. He described the insistence that Argentine artists deal with national traits and local colour as 'arbitrary' and as a 'European cult' which nationalists ought to reject as foreign. There were no camels in the Koran, he said, because only a falsifier, a tourist or a nationalist would have seen them; but Mohammed, happily unconcerned, knew that he could be an Arab without camels. Borges, indeed, confessed that for years he had tried and failed to capture Buenos Aires in his stories, but that it was only when he called Paseo Colón the rue de Toulon and only when he dubbed the Adrogue country house Fiste-le-Roy that his readers found the true Argentinian flavour. 'Precisely because I did not set out to find that flavour, because I had abandoned myself to a dream, I was able to accomplish, after so many years, what I had previously sought in vain.'[59] Wilde advanced the same argument when he said that the more imitative art is, the less it expresses its time and place: what compels belief in a portrait is not its fidelity to the subject so much as its embodiment of the spirit of the artist. Borges, for his part, found that being Argentinian was either a fate or a mere affectation. If the former, it was futile to try consciously for an Argentinian subject or tone; and if the latter, that was one mask better left unworn, for it could be donned only in the degrading pretence that the mask actually was the face.

In Ireland, writers soon found that it was — as George Russell said — foolish to try consciously for a Celtic feeling.[60] Wilde never made that elementary mistake. His few recorded comments on the 'realistic' Anglo-Irish novelists of the nineteenth century are caustic. Croker and Lover did not really see Ireland so much as 'a humorist's Arcadia'. They 'came from a class that did not — mainly for political reasons — take the populace seriously . . . of its passion, its gloom, its tragedy, they knew nothing.'[61] Wilde charged them with making the error of magnifying the one sort they did encounter — affable carmen and feckless servants — into a type of the nation. They produced a literature of the 'I know my natives' kind, a set of texts purporting to record native psychology as quaint and reassuring to rulers who might otherwise have feared that, if the natives eluded knowledge and control, then anything was possible. Wilde wanted no truck with such representational fallacies. Implicit in his comments on these novelists was the recognition that one of the objects of colonial policy was to maintain conditions in which the production of serious works of literature describing a society in all its complexity was well-nigh impossible. In an address to an American audience, he linked artistic and national freedom, telling his listeners somewhat luridly that 'with the coming of the English, art in Ireland came to an end . . . for art could not live and flourish under a tyrant'.[62] This was, in any strict sense, untrue: what became problematic was not art, as such, but rather that form of art called literary realism.

Wilde refused to write realist accounts of that degraded Ireland which he only partly knew, and he took instead utopia for theme, knowing that this would provide not only an image of revolutionary possibility for Ireland but also a rebuke to contemporary Britain. 'England will never be civilized till she has added Utopia to her dominions', he concluded in 'The Critic as Artist', adding the vital afterthought that 'there is more than one of her colonies that she might with advantage surrender for so fair a land.'[63]

The Story-Teller at Fault:
Oscar Wilde and Irish Orality

DEIRDRE TOOMEY

When Yeats recalls Oscar Wilde in 'Four Years',[1] it is not as a writer (Wilde's books merely date the experiences recalled) nor as 'the lion of the season', but as a talker – 'an excellent talker'.[2] Speech, conversation, the oral takes precedence over writing. Yeats asserts this aggressively: 'only when [Wilde] spoke, or when his writing was the mirror of his speech, or in some simple, faery-tale, had he words exact enough to hold a subtle ear . . . his plays and dialogues have what merit they possess from being now an imitation, now a record, of his talk'.[3] And later, in 'The Tragic Generation', he recalls the oral version of Wilde's story 'The Doer of Good', which Wilde called 'the best short story in the world':

> Christ came from a white plain to a purple city, and as He passed through the first street He heard voices overhead, and saw a young man lying drunk upon a window-sill. 'Why do you waste your soul in drunkenness?' He said. 'Lord, I was a leper and You healed me, what else can I do?' A little further through the town He saw a young man following a harlot, and said, 'Why do you dissolve your soul in debauchery?' and the young man answered, 'Lord, I was blind and You healed me, what else can I do?' At last, in the middle of the city He saw an old man crouching, weeping upon the ground, and when He asked why he wept, the old man answered, 'Lord I was dead, and you raised me into life, what else can I do but weep?'

Yeats concludes with heroic disparagement: 'Wilde published that story a little later, but spoiled it with the verbal decoration of his epoch, and I have to repeat it to myself as I first heard it, before I can see its terrible beauty.'[4] A year later, in 1923, when Yeats wrote an introduction to *The Happy Prince and Other Tales*, he expanded this stance: 'indeed, when I remember him with pleasure it is always the talker I remember. . . . Behind his words was the whole power of his intellect, but that intellect had given itself to pure contemplation. . . . The further Wilde goes in his writings from the *method of speech* [my italics], from improvisation, from sympathy with some especial audience, the less original he is, the less accomplished.' Again Yeats recalled and praised 'The Doer of Good':

It has definiteness, the simplicity of great sculpture, it adds something new to the imagination of the world, it suddenly confronts the mind — as does all great art — with the fundamental and the insoluble. It puts into almost as few as possible words, a melancholy that comes upon a man at the moment of triumph. . . .[5]

Yeats, when reading a story such as 'The Fisherman and his Soul', tried to recreate it in its primary oral version:

> I try to imagine it as it must have been when he spoke it, half consciously watching that he might not bore by a repeated effect or unnecessary description, some child or some little company of young painters or writers. Only when I so imagine it do I discover that the incident of the young fisherman's dissatisfaction with his mermaid mistress, upon hearing of a girl dancing with bare feet was witty, charming and characteristic. . . . In the written story that incident is so lost in decorations that we let it pass unnoticed at a first reading, yet it is the crisis of the tale. To enjoy it I must hear his voice once more, and listen once more to that incomparable talker.[6]

Yeats's privileging of the oral over the written does not indicate hostility or envy; Yeats admired Wilde as a man and was almost incapable of literary envy. Yeats's aesthetic judgement is also a mark of an Irish cultural valuing of the oral over the written. Wilde himself had praised the young Yeats for his story-telling: 'he made me tell him long Irish stories and compared my art of story-telling to Homer's'.[7] Both writers came from the most oral culture in Western Europe, a culture which retained primary orality as well as oral/writing *diglossia* well into the twentieth century. Yeats himself manifested a productive tension between extreme endorsement of oral culture (his concern with folklore, his gathering of oral texts, his experiments with chaunting) and extreme concern with the text elaborately realized in an object, the book. In contrast, the tension between writing and talking for Wilde was a hostile symbiosis. He told a journalist that there should be a more satisfactory way of 'conveying "poetry to the mind"' than by printing it, and he frankly told Gide that writing bored him.[8]

Many of Wilde's listeners did not have an Irish context into which to place his orality; but they still valued his oral tales over their written versions. André Gide ('*Dorian Gray*, at the very beginning, was a splendid story, how superior to *Peau de Chagrin* . . . Alas! written down, what a masterpiece *manqué*'[9]), Charles Ricketts, Gabrielle Enthoven, Aimée Lowther, Ernest La Jeunesse, Henri de Régnier, Jean Lorrain and many others have recorded Wilde's tales and over eighty were collected by Guillot de Saix.[10] Vincent O'Sullivan, who recorded several tales, glossed Wilde's inability to write after 1897 thus:

> the impulse to write was *never* very strong in Wilde. The impulse to compose — yes. But that he satisfied by talking . . . it was not very hard to break utterly such impulse to write as he had. He had not much left when he came out of prison. It soon died down in the socket.

Vincent O'Sullivan also comments on the importance of 'immediate applause' for Wilde. Certainly Wilde's late rejection of writing is tied to the difficulty of being published – although Leonard Smithers would have published anything Wilde wrote. Wilde told Laurence Housman, 'I told you that I was going to write something: I tell everyone that . . . in my heart – that chamber of leaden echoes – I know that I never shall. It is enough to know that the stories have been invented, that they actually exist, that I have been able, in my own mind, to give them the form that they demand.' By contrast, if Yeats had been proscribed by all the publishers in the world, he would still have spent half the day writing, despite his authentic, demonstrable love of oral culture. Yeats isolates this difference in identifying Wilde as a 'man of action' whose 'half-civilised' Irish blood could not tolerate the 'sedentary toil' of writing.[11]

Wilde lacked any strong sense of ownership in his oral tales – an identifying characteristic of oral cultures, in which the text belongs to the whole community. Thus in Ireland in the 1840s, when Peter O'Leary heard the great Munster folk tale *Séadna*, the tale was the property of the whole community, although told by Peig Labhrais and memorized by the young O'Leary, who published it from memory fifty years later.[12] When the adolescent W. B. Maxwell, Mary Braddon's son, confessed to Wilde that he had published a tale of Wilde's which he had heard at his mother's house, Wilde responded amiably, 'stealing my story was the act of a gentleman, but not telling me you had stolen it was to ignore the claims of friendship'. Wilde merely asked him not to appropriate another tale – the tale 'I told you about a man and a picture' – that is the oral version of *Dorian Gray*.[13] Wilde was equally mild in his response to Aimée Lowther's announcement that she was about to publish his fine oral tale 'The Poet'.[14] Once Wilde was dead any pretence of restraint ceased. Guillot de Saix has noted much French appropriation of Wilde's tales. Frank Harris published a plodding version of 'The Miracle of the Stigmata',[15] a tale which was also obviously of use to George Moore in *The Brook Kerith*; Arthur Symons's tale 'Esther Kahn' is a plagiarism with naturalistic colouring of Wilde's oral tale 'The Actress'.[16] A more unexpected plagiarist is found in Evelyn Waugh, who had evidently heard Wilde's oral tale 'Aunt Jane's Ball' at second hand, possibly in Ireland. Waugh published an embarrassingly inferior version, 'Bella Fleace Gave a Party', as late as 1933.[17]

Oral texts are, by their very nature, contextualized and responsive to a particular audience. Oral poets 'rhapsodize' differently to a different audience; the audience's reaction is part of the tale – the so-called 'sounding-board' effect.[18] The beholder's or listener's share in an oral culture is of comprehensive constructive significance; it directs the tale. What is not accepted is not the text. The context in which the tale is told will also alter the text; thus when – say – on Christmas Eve 1899, in the Kalisaya Bar, Paris, surrounded by the usual suspects (Jean de Mitty, Ernest La Jeunesse, Robert Sherard), Wilde told 'The Miracle of the Stigmata', it would have been in a version which responded to this time and context.[19] Yeats points to the way in which Wilde would adjust the telling of a story in progress to the impatience of children or the unsophisticated.

Vincent O'Sullivan, discussing what he terms 'the machinery of [Wilde's] talk', emphasizes Wilde's 'extraordinary tact in choosing subjects which would suit his listeners and in judging his effects . . . he did not try to enforce his moods; he gave the impression of adapting himself to the moods of others'.[20] La Jeunesse, who spent much time in the Kalisaya Bar with Wilde, gives a gripping account of the process of oral story-telling:

> slowly, word for word, he would invent in his feverish stumbling agony of art, curious fleeting parables. . . . He wasted himself entirely in words . . . the chaos of hope of words and laughter, the mad sequence of half completed sentences with which this poet plunged, proving to himself his still unextinguished fancy. . . . He attempted his stories all over again. It is like nothing save the bitter, blinding brilliance of a superhuman firework.[21]

The struggle which La Jeunesse represents here is not so much that of composition as of 'stitching and unstitching', of adjustment of a tale to a particular audience, a particular context.

In oral cultures, words are not *things*, dead, 'out there' on a flat surface, as they are to literates living in a chirographic–typographic culture. In Walter Ong's account, to pre-literates living in verbomotor cultures, words are *events*:

> The fact that oral peoples commonly and in all likelihood universally consider words to have magical potency is clearly tied in, at least unconsciously, with their sense of the words as necessarily spoken, sounded and hence power-driven . . . in a primary oral culture, where the word has its existence only in sound . . . the phenomenology of sound enters deeply into human beings' feeling for existence, as processed by the spoken word. For the way in which the word is experienced is always momentous in psychic life.[22]

Ong's account of the magical, penetrative and internalized experience of the spoken word is perfectly realized in Chapter Two of *The Picture of Dorian Gray* — a work which began as an oral tale — as Dorian meditates:

> Words! Mere words! How terrible they were! How clear, and vivid, and cruel! One could not escape from them. And yet what a subtle magic there was in them! They seemed to be able to give a plastic form to formless things. . . . Mere words! Was there anything so real as words?[23]

It is worth noting that Dorian's will is penetrated and corrupted by the magical *spoken* word: the fatal book — so overemphasized in analysis of this novel — is a subsidiary matter in the catastrophe.

Gesture and the somatic element are vital in oral cultures and related to the physicality of the story-telling mode. Ong points to the totality of the oral experience:

the oral word . . . never exists in a simply verbal context as a written word does. Spoken words are always part of a total existential situation, which always engages the body. Bodily activity beyond mere vocalisation is not adventitious or contrived in oral communication, but is natural and even inevitable.[24]

Eric Havelock, in analysing Greek oral poetry, has suggested an erotic element in this somatic component, shared by artist and audience.[25] And Havelock's position on oral composition is anticipated by Wilde in 'The Critic as Artist': 'the great poet is always a seer, seeing less with the eyes of the body than he does with the eyes of the soul . . . a true singer also, building his song out of music, repeating each line over and over again to himself . . . chaunting in darkness'.[26] Charles Ricketts remembered Wilde's tendency to pause upon certain key words and to gesture as if to arrest their sound, his subtle but expressive use of gesture and mimesis:

a chance word, even an interruption, might conjure up a prose poem. . . . The poet, we divine in his early verse, remained ever present and spontaneous in his speech. There was, besides, the cadenced and varied intonation, pausing on a word, a sentence, as a violinist accents and phrases his music. Wilde possessed and used all vocabularies, slang alone excepted – even that of the Victorian philistines and moralists, ever his accusers. One heard also the beloved voices of men he had admired in his youth . . . Ruskin . . . Tennyson . . . Rossetti . . . Swinburne . . . . I would not describe this gift as mimicry, it was hardly more than a variation in intonation or a movement of the eyes.[27]

Other characteristics of orality – the agonistic structure found in 'The Decay of Lying' and 'The Critic as Artist', the lack of a hierarchy between text and interpretation (a profound element in Wilde's aesthetic) – can be identified in his written oeuvre. Wilde's love of the aphorism (and his elevation of aphorism above narrative in *The Picture of Dorian Gray*) is also typical of the oral mode.[28] 'The Decay of Lying' endorses that very aspect of oral culture which, according to Havelock, Plato attacked in *The Republic*.[29]

Another sphere in which oral culture differs absolutely from literate culture is in its attitude to cliché, stereotype and plagiarism. These cardinal sins of literacy are cardinal virtues of orality. Originality in an oral culture consists not in inventing an absolutely new story but in stitching together the familiar in a manner suitable to a particular audience, or by introducing new elements into an old story. The persistent charge of plagiarism against Wilde seems oxymoronic in an oral culture. Wilde's tendency to start from the very familiar or traditional in his oral tales – something already given and known, the Bible, fairy tales – is again fully characteristic of orality. A remarkable defence of Wilde's type of artist is given by Ernest La Jeunesse:

When a thaumaturg (sic) – and I choose the words purposely, one that Wilde respected highly – undertakes to fool the public, he has the right to choose his material where he finds it; one does not expect of him moral and social lessons, but inventions, tricks, *words*, a touch of heaven and a touch of hell, and what not else; he must be Proteus and Prometheus, must be able to transform all things and himself . . . he must be confessor, prophet and magician; he must dissect the world with the exactness of a doctrinarian and recreate it all anew the moment after, by the light of his poetic fancy; he must produce formulas and paradoxes, and even barbaric puns with nothing save their antiquity to save them.

For this price — a well paid one — he can find distraction after the manner of the gods or the fallen angels and seek for himself excitements and deceptions, since he has advanced, and eventually crossed, the borders of ordinary human emotions and sensations.[30]

Wilde's major cycle of biblical tales exemplifies this characteristic of the oral in its dependence on traditional material known to all his listeners. Some tales are endearingly slight, such as the versions of 'The Woman Taken in Adultery' which represent her indignant husband's position — he casts the first stone.[31] Others are expressive of Wilde's profoundest conceptions and beliefs — specifically his identification of Christ with the figure of the Artist. Christ is the type of the perfectly realized personality 'entirely and absolutely himself', the 'very basis of his nature was the same as that of the nature of the artist. . . . Christ's place indeed is with the poets.'[32] Jean Lorrain recalled an oral tale which extends the Raising of Lazarus, noting that the first half of the tale was no more than an elegant redaction of John 11. After Lazarus has been raised from the dead, the 'variante du poète' begins:

And Lazarus walked. And all cried, a miracle.
But Lazarus, raised from the dead, remained sad.
Instead of falling at the feet of Jesus, he remained apart, with a reproachful
    countenance.
And Jesus, approaching, asked him gently:
— You who have come back from the dead, won't you say anything to me,
    Lazarus?
And Lazarus said to him:
— Why did you lie to me, why do you lie still by speaking of heaven, of the
    glory of God? There is nothing, Rabbi, nothing beyond death, and he who
    is dead is really dead — I know this — I who have come back from there.
And Jesus, putting a finger to his mouth, with an imploring look towards
    Lazarus, replied:
— I know it. Do not tell them.[33]

Another biblical story told to Yeats is recalled by him in epitome:

One day [Wilde] began, 'I have been inventing a Christian heresy,' and he told a detailed story, in the style of some early Father, of how Christ recovered after the Crucifixion, and, escaping from the tomb, lived on for many years, the one man on earth who knew the falsehood of Christianity. Once Saint Paul visited his town and he alone in the carpenters' quarter did not go to hear him preach. Henceforth the other carpenters noticed, that, for some unknown reason, he kept his hands covered.[34]

A full version of the tale, entitled 'The Miracle of the Stigmata', was collected by Guillot de Saix, who gives the context of its telling, of its specified setting (AD 35 in the Jewish quarter in Rome) and presents a variant ending to Yeats's version. After Christ's death, his fellow carpenters discover the nail marks in his hands and feet and declare this to be a great miracle. To Coulson Kernahan, his editor at Ward, Lock & Co., Wilde talked very seriously about his obsession with the figure of Christ (Kernahan was deeply religious):

Shall I tell you what is my greatest ambition — even more than an ambition — the dream of my life? Not to be remembered hereafter as an artist, poet, thinker or playwright, but as the man who reclothed the sublimest conception the world has ever known . . . with new and burning words, with new and illuminating symbols, with new and divine vision, free from the accretions of cant which the centuries have gathered around it. I should therefore be giving the world back again the greatest gift ever given to mankind since Christ Himself gave it. . . .

Wilde is arguing — as he so often did — for a new Evangel, a heterodox fifth Gospel. He told Kernahan part of a story of the return of Christ, 'The Useless Resurrection', but was interrupted at the crisis and never returned to finish this, the most ambitious and most ideologically and aesthetically charged of his tales of Christ.[35] It was later collected and printed in full by Guillot de Saix, as follows:

One day, an Arab labourer, working for an archaeological entrepreneur, who was simply searching for old coins, struck his pick by chance into the stone of a tomb on the side of the hill of Calvary. With the help of his comrades he lifted this heavy flagstone, and discovered, at the bottom of the narrow sepulchre carved out of the rock, a body, still wrapped in its intact winding cloth.

The archaeological entrepreneur had this macabre discovery transported to a museum where savants in spectacles examined it carefully, unwrapped the bandages from the dead person and discovered with stupefaction a mummified corpse, still displaying clearly the wounds in the wrists, the feet and the side rimmed with dried blood, blackened and crackling. It was truly, without doubt, the body of he whom had been crucified under Pontius Pilate.

Thus generations had been deluded just like the holy women and the first disciples, deluded just as much as those who believed that they had found with certainty the site of the tomb belonging to Joseph of Arimathea and built on this place a sanctuary where the knees of the faithful had come to wear away the stones.

The newspapers seized on the event, the Pope was chased out of the Vatican, which became a kind of temple of scientific truth, where was exposed to the public, under glass, the corpse which had killed the secular lie. And as a result Christianity, based on the dogma of the Resurrection, suffered a temporary eclipse.

But the next Easter Sunday, a sad Sunday, without bells, at the first pale ray of sunlight which came to touch it late in the morning, the inert corpse came alive, broke the glass of its transparent coffin, and, in front of prostrated visitors and guards, crossed the Vatican vault in a glorious soaring flight and disappeared from their sight. A new religion had to be born and to spread, with other apostles and also other martyrs. Here and there Christ appeared to other pilgrims to justify himself to men and to found a cult of beauty on new foundations. He preached that, if one followed his doctrine, there would be neither rich nor poor, nor class struggle, nor war, but only, in the grand unity of divided races, men who loved one another in the presence of the ephemeral and constant miracle of life. He affirmed that he had come back to abolish the suffering of those who are legion and whose dwelling is in the tombs, all the oppressed, the factory children, thieves, vagabonds on the highway, prisoners, the proscribed, in brief all those who are dumb under the sword of the oppressor and whose silence is understood by God alone.[36] He said to each one, 'Be thyself. Thy perfection is in thyself.'[37] But without doubt he had come too late in a world that was too old.

This supreme revelation from a mouth of light was rationally and scientifically explained by the savants. Jesus forever renounced appearing before men and all reverted again into the old apathy of days without belief or joy.[38]

In all these tales, Christ is the type of the Artist, a thaumaturge and a perfectly realized personality but doomed to rejection and to a failure which is central, not extraneous to his power. In 'The Useless Resurrection' the themes of both 'The Critic as Artist' and 'The Soul of Man under Socialism' are dramatized. It is a tale in which Wilde's Joachimism can be detected; the Christ who returns is a Third Age Christ, Christ as the Holy Spirit, a Divine Being who preaches with a mouth of light not flesh. His gospel, 'Be thyself', the gospel of 'The Soul of Man under Socialism', is a Third Status gospel, a gospel of the Age of the Spirit.[39] It fails, and 'The Useless Resurrection' has the same trajectory as Yeats's occult tales, 'Rosa Alchemica', 'The Tables of the Law' and 'The Adoration of the Magi', ending in greyness, apathy, despair.[40]

One of Wilde's most popular oral tales, 'The Poet', survives in many accounts – told sometimes as a trifle to amuse a journalist, at other times as a serious, highly worked exposition of the nature of imagination and its relation to experience. Gide gives a crude résumé of this tale in his memoirs of Wilde, omitting a crucial episode.[41] Equally reduced résumés are given by Coulson

Kernahan, Henri de Régnier and Jean Joseph Renaud. Full versions are given by Gabrielle Enthoven, Aimée Lowther and Charles Ricketts. Ricketts, who had first heard this tale about 1889, published it in 1932, in a version which is probably very close to the most refined oral text. Ricketts acknowledges having heard it many times:

Now a certain man was greatly beloved by the people of his village, for, when they gathered round him at dusk and questioned him, he would relate many strange things he had seen. He would say, 'I beheld three mermaids by the sea who combed their green hair with a golden comb.' And, when they besought him to tell more, he answered — 'By a hollow rock I spied a centaur; and, when his eyes met mine, he turned slowly to depart, gazing on me sadly over his shoulder.' And when they asked eagerly, 'Tell us, what else have you seen?' he told them, 'In a little copse a young faun played upon a flute to the dwellers in the woods who danced to his piping.' One day when he had left the village, as was his wont, three mermaids rose from the waves who combed their green hair with a comb of gold, and, when they had departed, a centaur peeped at him behind a hollow rock, and later, as he passed a little copse, he beheld a faun who played upon a pipe to the dwellers in the wood.

That night, when the people of the village gathered at dusk, saying, 'Tell us, what have you seen to-day?' he answered them sadly: 'To-day I have seen nothing.'[42]

This tale, and in particular the motif of the centaur slowly turning his head, obsessed Ricketts, who was puzzled by Gide's omission of this detail. 'Strangely enough Gide omits the episode of the centaur, yet this detail has remained vivid in my memory, for Wilde, by an almost imperceptible turn of the head, when speaking, conjured up the movement of the receding creature.'[43] And in 1923, when Wilde came through on the astral plane to the famous Dublin medium Hester Dowden (he discussed *inter alia* his dislike of *Ulysses*, which he had been absorbing in the ether),[44] Ricketts wrote to the medium, asking her to cross-examine Wilde's ghost about the correct version of 'The Poet' and the detail of the centaur's head.[45] This fine motif of the centaur's twisted head, expressed by the story-teller's gesture, is probably an unconscious absorption of Wilde's own experience at the Olympia excavations in April 1877 — Wilde was always to claim that he had been present when the great statue of Apollo was discovered. The west pediment of the Temple of Zeus at Olympia is a magnificent centauromachy and a memory of the twisted head of the centaur Eurytion is preserved in this tale — and in the story-teller's gesture while telling it.[46]

Yeats alone of Wilde's friends had the Irish nationalist context in which to place a valuing of the oral over the written, and to understand the larger cultural and political implications of such a stance. In *Autobiographies* Yeats recalls J. F.

Taylor's speech at Trinity College Dublin defending, the Irish language — which Yeats called the greatest extempore speech ever made. Taylor had responded to arguments which insisted on the marginality and poverty of Irish language and culture with a speech which ended with a vision of Moses defying Pharaoh: 'I see a man at the edge of the crowd; he is standing listening there, but he will not obey . . . had he obeyed he would never have come down the mountain carrying in his hands the Tables of the Law in the language of the outlaw.'[47] To be committed to folk culture and 'the language of the outlaw' was, in Ireland, to be radically nationalist. As late as 1899, it was being argued by Professor Robert Atkinson that modern Irish was not an authentic language and that Irish folk tales were disgusting and worthless. Atkinson was Todd Professor of Celtic Languages in the Royal Irish Academy, Professor of Sanskrit and of Romance Languages at Trinity College Dublin, and he had edited facsimiles of Old Irish texts such as *The Book of Leinster*. Atkinson was a lexicographer, but had abandoned the *Dictionary of Irish* which the Royal Irish Academy had commissioned from him. In February 1899 he gave expert evidence to the Intermediate Education (Ireland) Commission, chaired by Baron Parkes. The teaching of Irish in Irish schools was undervalued, and in the Intermediate Examination it counted for only five-twelfths of the value of Greek. Douglas Hyde was in favour of, and John Pentland Mahaffy against, a revaluation of the subject. Atkinson accepted that Old and Middle Irish were fine classical languages but argued that modern Irish, even as spoken by Douglas Hyde, was merely a 'patois', an 'imbroglio, mélange, an omnium gatherum'.[48] Atkinson's objections to modern Irish were read (by Yeats, Hyde and others) as being essentially political: 'the true explanation is that Dr. Atkinson, like most people on both sides in politics of the generation which had to endure the bitterness of the agrarian revolution, is still in a fume of political excitement, and cannot consider any Irish matter without this excitement'.[49]

However, it is also clear from Atkinson's evidence that much of his hostility to modern Irish was that during the nineteenth century it had become primarily an *oral* language, with its principal texts being oral folk tales or poetry. Atkinson's vehement attack on folk literature — not obviously relevant to the Commission's terms of reference — exhibits his visceral hostility to oral culture. Irish folklore was condemned as being 'low', 'near the sod'. All folklore was at bottom 'abominable . . . so low! I do not want to know about the vulgar exploits of a dirty wretch who never washed his feet . . . that he never washed his feet and had an interview with the Pope, and married the Princess So-and-so' was his response to 'Guleesh na Guss Dhu' from Douglas Hyde's *Beside the Fire*.[50] Atkinson's neurotic fear of the 'low', the 'primitive' and pre-literate seems to indicate a construction of oral and folk texts as dangerous and expressive of uncontrollable unconscious forces. Somewhat out of control himself, Atkinson went on to inform the bemused Commissioners that even Old Irish literature (his own field) was contaminated by its 'disgusting' subject matter. He insisted that a recent edition of Old Irish texts, easily identifiable as Standish Hayes

O'Grady's *Silva Gadelica*, was a work which 'no human being could read through . . . without feeling that he had been absolutely degraded by contact with it − filth that I will not demean myself even to mention. Instances, no doubt, are not numerous in it, but . . . if you will call at any time upon me in my rooms, I will show you them. . . .'[51]

Atkinson's hostility to oral literature also had a manifest political dimension. And when folk-tale collectors such as Sir William Wilde or Douglas Hyde took down the tales of pre-literate peasants in the West, they were engaging in something more than an anthropological or literary exercise; they were making a statement of cultural and political nationalism. Oscar Wilde can be associated with those Protestant nationalists (Sir William Wilde, Lady Wilde, Douglas Hyde, Lady Gregory, Yeats, Synge) who, by linking themselves to a despised, indigenous, pre-literate culture, with folk-tales and folk parables, reidentified with Ireland,[52] with 'the unwritten tradition which binds the unlettered . . . to the beginning of time and to the foundation of the world'.[53] Douglas Hyde had defended Irish oral culture as being 'as truly literature as the deathless lays of that "blind old man of Scio's rocky isle," which were for ages chanted traditionally. . . . I would willingly go on to give some description of that store of poems, epigrams and stories, which, instead of being enshrined between the leaves of a dead book, are inscribed upon the living page of the hearts of the Irish people.'[54] And Wilde ended his life, like Raftery − the last wandering Irish poet − 'playing music to empty pockets'.[55]

Wilde himself drew on tales collected in the West of Ireland by his father and published by his mother − Lady Wilde's 'The Priest's Soul' became an after-dinner tale for him in Paris.[56] Some of the images of Irish folk tales affected Wilde's sensibility. Wilde's description of his experiences with rough trade as being like 'feasting with panthers' seems to have more than an accidental link with Lady Wilde's 'A Wolf Story', an uncanny homoerotic version of the Grateful Beast motif. A young farmer seeking strayed animals is benighted in a hut with a ferocious old couple. Two wolves walk in and transform themselves into dark, handsome but sinister young men with glittering eyes; one shows much affection for the farmer and protects him, thanking him for having once removed a thorn from his side.[57]

Yeats thought that 'all art should be a Centaur finding in the popular lore its back and its strong legs',[58] and Wilde's 'The Poet' − the classicized tale which obsessed Ricketts enough to badger Wilde's ghost as to its essential elements − is rooted in Irish folk culture. It is an inversion of the formula of a celebrated Irish folk tale, 'The Story-Teller at Fault', first published by Griffin in *Tales of the Jury Room*, and collected in many oral versions: the folk-motif is apparently unique to Ireland.[59] A King's story-teller finds himself at a loss for a new tale. His wife points to an old grey ragged beggar man who has suddenly appeared on their land; the story-teller gambles with the beggar and loses horse, hounds, land and wife and eventually gambles himself away; the beggar then transforms the story-teller into a hare and the story-teller's own horses chase him, while his wife watches.

Transformed back, the story-teller, by an extraordinary narrative manoeuvre, becomes the assumed observer of the beggar's magical antics at the court of a neighbouring lord. Here the beggar plays a variety of tricks, including that of producing a silken rope from a bag, throwing a hare and a red-eared hound up it and sending a young woman and a young man after the animals. The beggar then returns to the court of the story-teller's lord and reassembles story-teller and wife on their own land — pulling them out of narrative space to do so — and reveals himself to be Aengus Og, the Irish god of love and revelry. The story-teller then has only to tell the King of his own magical adventures that day and he has a never-ending, never-failing tale.

As so often in his oral tables, Wilde respects the morphology of the original tale, but inverts the 'moral'; the 'fault' concludes his tale, rather than being its occasion. So 'The Poet', this richly classicized tale with its *l'art pour l'art* aesthetic and its centaur from the Olympia pediment, is an Irish folk tale inverted, a product of the dying oral culture to which Wilde was tied by what Yeats called 'his half-civilised blood', the culture of those who listened to spoken tales, undivided by book culture — 'friend by friend, lover by lover'.[60]

Hunting Out the Fairies:
E. F. Benson, Oscar Wilde and the
Burning of Bridget Cleary[1]

ANGELA BOURKE

> Man is least himself when he talks in his own person.
> Give him a mask, and he will tell you the truth. (Oscar Wilde)

Oscar Wilde's life and work are characterized by doubleness. A devoted husband and father at home, and a frequenter of rentboys in hotels, he mixed with the English upper class while repeatedly asserting his Irishness. A consummate performer of the flippant paradox, he was passionately sincere, and the characters he created are similarly doubled and divided. Yet, as Richard Ellmann has noted, 'the denouement of his dramas and narratives is that masks have to go. We must acknowledge what we are.'[2] Ultimately, this acknowledgement led to Wilde's downfall, but many of his contemporaries were less brave than him. One of them was the young novelist, aesthete and socialite E. F. Benson, whom Wilde had met just a year earlier. He remained a closet homosexual all his life and maintained silence on the Wilde case for most of it.[3]

Yet, for all his caution, Benson did publish one article which reads like a masked or coded commentary on Wilde's fate.[4] It appeared in June 1895, just as Wilde was beginning a two-year sentence of imprisonment with hard labour in Pentonville for acts of gross indecency. Its subject was the case known as the 'Tipperary witch-burning', the trial of nine people for the murder of twenty-six-year-old Bridget Cleary in rural Ireland. This was a sensational story, which had attracted widespread newspaper coverage at the same time as the Wilde case, but it was not the sort of subject in which Benson usually expressed interest.

Bridget Cleary burned to death in her own kitchen in Ballyvadlea, near Clonmel, County Tipperary, on the night of 15 March 1895, in the presence of several of her relatives and neighbours. She had been ill, and rumours were in circulation that her sickness had a supernatural cause. Her body was buried in a rough grave, where it was discovered a week later by members of the Royal Irish Constabulary; a magistrate's inquiry followed which remanded ten prisoners for trial the following July. Reports of these events appeared daily in the Dublin and London newspapers at the end of March and beginning of April 1895.[5] This was the week when the Marquess of Queensberry stood trial at the

Old Bailey for criminally libelling Oscar Wilde, and Wilde himself was arrested and charged.

Several articles offered analyses of the Cleary case, but Benson's was unusual.[6] It appeared while the prisoners were still on remand and the case was *sub judice*, and argued that the defendants merited clemency. This intervention in the court's business did not go unnoticed; in December of the same year an article in the journal *Folk-Lore* rapped Benson firmly over the knuckles.[7] Even without mentioning Oscar Wilde, therefore, he was taking a risk. He added to it by invoking a story which obliquely paralleled the Wilde case, with its public humiliation of an Irish male defendant and its theme of folklore and magic.

Only a few years earlier, in December 1889, the cause of Home Rule for Ireland had been irreparably damaged when its champion, Charles Stewart Parnell, was named as co-respondent by Captain O'Shea in his divorce case. Oscar Wilde's disgrace bore out the conservative contention that the Irish were unfit for self-government, as even their upper classes were portrayed as immoral and ungentlemanly. Now the opponents of Home Rule seized on the story of Bridget Cleary's death as propaganda.[8] This time the irregularity attributed to the Irish was not sexual. Called a 'witch-burning' by journalists, it involved an apparent attempt to banish a fairy changeling, believed to have been left by the fairies when they abducted a young married woman.[9] Persons present during the events that led to it told the crown court in Clonmel that they had been 'hunting out the fairies'. This 'primitive and savage superstition', as Benson and others called it, seemed to support the conservative argument that the Irish had not achieved the state of evolution which would fit them for self-government. Fairies and changelings belonged to folklore, a category of human thought which fascinated the Victorians as long as it stayed firmly within the framework of literary fiction, but which must be exterminated as dangerous when it leaked into real life.

Oscar Wilde's downfall was another sort of witch-hunt, conducted when parts of his life, masked as fiction in *The Picture of Dorian Gray*, became common knowledge. It can also fairly be described as a case of 'hunting out the fairies'. 'Fairy' may have been in use to denote a male homosexual as early as the sixteenth century, but is attested in print from 1896, when its primary meaning, an imaginary or supernatural being of human form, also had considerable currency in antiquarian and folklore writings.[10] Many gay men left England permanently after the Wilde trials, for Capri and other more tolerant places, while the Prime Minister, Lord Rosebery, took to his bed. Rosebery's relations with Lord Alfred Douglas's brother had been held responsible for that brother's recent suicide; their father, the Marquess of Queensberry, had once referred to him as a 'snob queer'. Daily bulletins in the newspapers reported that Rosebery was suffering from severe insomnia and was 'quite unable to attend to any but the most urgent business'. Many of Wilde's acquaintance expected, and even urged, him to leave England instead of standing trial.[11]

A recent study of Wilde as gay man has asserted that, with his fall, 'sane thinkers, rather than being liberated to speak their minds, were driven further underground, where they and their successors remained for several decades'.[12] This imagery, common though it is, is startlingly reminiscent of Irish fairy tradition: the invisible, non-human race, which embodies all that seems both enviable and reprehensible to established society, lives chiefly under the ground, inside hills.[13] As a derogatory term for a gay man, 'fairy' still carries with it the sense of deviance and danger which we find consistently in Irish oral traditions about the 'good people' or 'wee gentry'.[14]

Although the stories of Oscar Wilde and Bridget Cleary rest on different senses of the word 'fairy', they share a body of imagery that reveals much about how societies deal with their marginal members: rendering them invisible; driving them underground; consigning them to wild or barren areas of the shared landscape; punishing them viciously when they refuse to disappear. Like Wilde's writings, Irish fairy legends are works of art – not factual reports – which offer explorations of ambivalence and multiple personalities. The changelings they describe are alternative selves, which may be either assigned by others or assumed by the subject. Like Wilde's writings, these legends are richly entertaining and imaginative, and apparently frivolous. Only on closer examination do they reveal the serious themes which underlie them. Bridget Cleary was first labelled a changeling, then brutally tortured, and finally killed. Her killing and Wilde's downfall were, as it happened, reported in the same issues of *The Times*; for us, they are linked both by Wilde's Irishness and by the figure of E. F. Benson.

In Benson's essay, it is as though the space consciously left blank for Oscar Wilde has been occupied by Bridget Cleary, so that the account of her death masks an unspoken preoccupation with Wilde. Wittingly or unwittingly, in drawing attention away from Wilde and towards the Cleary case, Benson has given us a refracted picture of Oscar as Irishman, as story-teller and as misunderstood victim.

Edward Frederick Benson was the fifth child and third son of the Archbishop of Canterbury, in the spring of 1895 living with his parents at Lambeth Palace. He was not yet twenty-eight, but his first novel, the frivolous *Dodo*, published in 1893, had gone into twelve editions in its first year, making him both rich and famous. In 1894 he had met Lord Alfred Douglas in Cairo, during one of Douglas's estrangements from Wilde, and was one of a party which, in Ellmann's words, 'vied with one another in quoting bits of [*The Picture of Dorian Gray*] as they floated up the Nile to Luxor'. He was engaged at the time in an archaeological investigation in Athens, where Douglas visited him and stayed in his rooms for a week.[15]

According to Benson's biographer, Brian Masters, 'Bosie' Douglas was a friend of his, but 'not one who ever visited the Benson family'.[16] Back in London, Douglas introduced him to Wilde in June 1894, when Wilde presented him with a copy of *The Sphinx*, just published in a limited edition of 250 copies. The Marquess of Queensberry's campaign of harassment against his son and Wilde was in full swing by this time, so the gift of a book of homoerotic verse set in Egypt, inscribed 'To E. F. Benson, with the compliments of the author, Oscar Wilde', made Benson complicit in a dangerous business.[17]

Sociable and popular, 'Fred' Benson was nevertheless an intensely private person. More than thirty years later, he wrote about the Wilde case, hiding it behind another Victorian scandal about cheating at cards in the Prince of Wales's circle; but at the time, he remained silent.[18] Masters makes clear that the Archbishop's family, including Benson's mother Minnie, were well aware of male homosexuality, but he writes, 'there is no evidence whatever that the scandal which consumed Oscar Wilde and Fred's friend Lord Alfred Douglas in 1895 reverberated within the walls of Lambeth Palace, although it would be impossible to believe that they never discussed it'.[19] When Benson did come to write about the Wilde case, in his celebrated portrait of Victorian and Edwardian life, *As We Were*, he showed considerable ambivalence, making many alterations and additions to his manuscript.[20] Wilde had surrendered to intemperate and bestial perversions, according to the sixty-two-year-old Benson, yet 'no decent man can feel anything but sheer pity and sympathy for one so gifted and so brittle and withal so lovable'.[21]

Masters comments that 'there is a paradox, an ambivalence, at the heart of [Benson's] attitudes towards sensuality, which he considers at one and the same time a liberating influence – an avenue towards self-expression – and a dangerous toxin leading to perdition'.[22] A similar ambivalence finds expression in Irish fairy legend, where being 'away with the fairies' has connotations of imaginative and sexual liberation, at the same time marking a separation from society: alienation, ostracism or even death.

Most of the human protagonists of fairy legends told in Ireland are either marginal to adult society or in transition within it: elderly bachelors and widows, young unmarried men and women, brides, pregnant women, nursing mothers and children. Many legends give alternative explanations for stories of unhappiness and misadventure; others may provide veiled accounts of sexual exploits, both heterosexual and homosexual. Among the most poignant are those that tell of doomed encounters between human men and fairy women, or of young people and children led ambiguously astray. Those taken were often the most beautiful.

W. B. Yeats was the writer who most comprehensively articulated this ambivalent view of Irish fairy tradition in the 1890s. Presenting character after character as tempted by the dangerous seductions of faery in poems and plays, as well as prose works, Yeats retold the oral legends of rural Ireland for a discriminating metropolitan audience fascinated by the occult.[23] Unlike the 'old bitter world where they marry in churches', the fairy otherworld he encountered in the stories of the West of Ireland offered eternal youth and freedom from social constraint; but the price was high – if not for the protagonist, then for the wider society. We are inevitably reminded of Wilde's *Dorian Gray*, in which a beautiful young man is led astray, becomes a 'fairy' and in his turn leads other young people to perdition.

For many educated people, Yeats provided an introduction to the newly fashionable matter of Irish folklore, but Oscar Wilde had grown up among such tales. In his *Irish Fairy Tales* (1892), Yeats freely acknowledged his debt to Lady Wilde's *Ancient Legends, Mystic Charms and Superstitions of Ireland*, published in London four years earlier.[24] Oscar Wilde was, of course, adult when his mother's work appeared, but during his childhood, and indeed before his parents' marriage, his father, a noted antiquarian, had been a keen collector and student of Irish oral traditions in various parts of Ireland. Sir William Wilde's *Irish Popular Superstitions* (1852) includes many legends of human encounters with and abductions by the fairies, and (as Yeats was aware) it was his collection of notes, preserved since his death in 1876, which had provided the material for his widow's book. Reviewing its sequel, *Ancient Cures, Charms and Usages of Ireland* (1890), Yeats wrote that Sir William 'collected a vast bulk of tales and spells and proverbs, then threw all his gatherings into a big box, and thence it is that Lady Wilde has gathered the materials of her new book'.[25] Elsewhere Yeats recounted how the distinguished eye and ear surgeon combined his interest in folklore with his profession: 'old men and women, too, when going away cured from his hospital, would ask leave to send eggs or fowl, or some such country gift, and he would bargain for a fairy tale instead'.[26]

When Yeats's *Fairy and Folk Tales of the Irish Peasantry* appeared in 1889, Oscar Wilde returned the compliment to his mother by reviewing it in the *Woman's World*. A devoted and admiring son, he concludes a long excerpt from Yeats's Introduction with the poet's tribute to the *Ancient Legends*:

> But the best book since Croker is Lady Wilde's 'Ancient Legends'. The humour has all given way to pathos and tenderness. We have here the innermost heart of the Celt in the moments he has grown to love through years of persecution, when, cushioning himself about with dreams, and hearing fairy songs in the twilight, he ponders on the soul and on the dead. Here is the Celt, only it is the Celt dreaming.[27]

Wilde's closing remarks show his own familiarity with the material and his appreciation of these stories as works of art:

> Mr Yeats has certainly done his work very well. He has shown great critical capacity in his selection of the stories, and his little introductions are charmingly written. It is delightful to come across a collection of purely imaginative work, and Mr Yeats has a very quick instinct in finding out the best and most beautiful things in Irish folk-lore. . . .
>
> All lovers of fairy tales and folk-lore should get this little book. 'The Horned Woman', 'The Priest's Soul', and 'Teig O'Kane', are really marvellous in their way: and, indeed, there is hardly a single story that is not worth reading and thinking over.[28]

Wilde's own stories, *The Happy Prince and Other Tales*, had been published to considerable acclaim in 1888, and 'The Happy Prince' at least had started life as an oral narrative, told to entertain his friends. At Moytura, the villa Sir William Wilde built overlooking Lough Corrib in County Mayo when his second son was ten years old, Oscar had accompanied his father on archaeological expeditions. His interest in archaeology, which he described as 'intense', was one he later shared with E. F. Benson, but it was also the means of exposing him to the story-telling, singing and belief traditions of the West of Ireland, as even in the remotest districts his father maintained excellent relations with local people, many of whom had been his patients.[29]

When the story of Bridget Cleary's disappearance and the arrest of her husband, father and several neighbours appeared in *The Times* on 27 March 1895, Oscar Wilde had other things on his mind. Still, however horrified he might have been by this account, its terms would certainly have been familiar to him:

Dublin, March 26

A special court was held at Clonmel yesterday by Colonel Evanson and Mr Cambridge Grubb to hear the case against ten persons, charged with having murdered, by burning to death, a woman named Cleary, who was supposed by the prisoners to be possessed of an evil spirit. The prisoners included the husband and the father of the deceased, and a local herb doctor. It appeared from the evidence of a woman named Burke, who had been nursing Mrs Cleary, that the latter was suffering from nervous excitement and from a mild attack of bronchitis, and her husband thought she was a witch. He gave her herbs which he obtained from the herb doctor, the other prisoners holding her while she was forced to take them. The man then called on her to say, in the name of God, that she was not his wife. She was held over the fire to make her say this. These proceedings were repeated on the following night, when the husband knocked her down, stripped off all her clothes, poured paraffin oil over her, and set fire to her with a burning stick from the hearth. While she was burning to death there were present six of the male prisoners and two women, all relatives of the deceased. Some of them remonstrated with the husband, but did nothing more. He told them that it was not his wife he was burning but a witch, and that she would disappear up the chimney. He rolled a sheet round the charred body and, with the aid of one of the prisoners, buried it in a dyke near his house. Here the remains were discovered a week afterwards by Sergeant Rodgers of the Royal Irish Constabulary. The prisoners were remanded. They were hissed and groaned at as they passed through the streets in custody.

Murders were not usually committed in the name of fairy belief, but stories of fairy interference in human life were common in Irish oral tradition. They appear often in the ethnographic writings of Sir William Wilde and in Lady Wilde's *Ancient Legends*, as do 'herb doctors', or 'fairy doctors'. These traditional healers, also called 'fairy women' as in the passage quoted below, were commonly called on to deal with mysterious and intractable maladies like tuberculosis, stroke, sudden infant death and post-natal depression, said to be caused by fairy intervention in human life. I have discussed elsewhere the use of such fairy discourse as euphemism and metaphor, and several scholars have written about it as a medium of social control.[30] Chief among the ways fairies are said to interfere with humans is by stealing healthy, happy children or women and replacing them with sickly, wizened and bad-tempered changelings. Lady Wilde reports that:

> This superstition makes the peasant-women often very cruel towards weakly children; and the trial by fire is sometimes resorted to in order to test the nature of the child who is suspected of being a changeling. For this purpose a fairy woman is usually sent for, who makes a drink for the little patient of certain herbs of whose power she alone has the secret knowledge. . . . Should there be no improvement in the child after the treatment with herbs, then the witch-women sometimes resort to terrible measures to test the fairy nature of the sufferer.[31]

Several times in the same book, Lady Wilde describes the trial by fire. One story tells of a child stolen by the fairies and discovered by a man on his way home. He gives the child into his own mother's care, and next morning hears that the first-born son of the local lord has died. At the wake, the man laughs when he sees the dead child in the cradle, 'shrunk and wizened like a little old man', and orders the parents to 'put down a good fire . . . .'

> Then he went over to the cradle and said to the hideous little creature, in a loud voice before all the people —
> 'If you don't rise up this minute and leave the place, I will burn you on the fire, for I know right well who you are, and where you came from.'
> At once the child sat up and began to grin at him; and made a rush to the door to get away; but the man caught hold of it and threw it on the fire. And the moment it felt the heat it turned into a black kitten, and flew up the chimney and was seen no more.
> Then the man sent word to his mother to bring the other child. . . .[32]

The black kitten is an unusual touch: more commonly, in changeling narratives of the sort Oscar Wilde must have heard often during his childhood, the wizened, elderly changeling runs out the door when threatened with fire, and the plump healthy baby is magically returned to the cradle. When adults are taken, the changeling often appears to die, but if the coffin is opened some time later, only a broom is found inside.

Davis Coakley finds Wilde's debt to Irish folk narrative most apparent in *The Picture of Dorian Gray*, noting that 'folklore and myth form the basis and structure of the novel, setting it apart from other works of the same genre in the English language'.[33] Coakley focuses on style and imagery, but with its suggestion of alternative identities inhabiting the same person, changeling tradition offers a rural, oral and traditional antecedent to *The Picture of Dorian Gray*: as in Yeats's 'The Stolen Child', the 'real' person spirited away by fairies remains youthful and carefree, while the simulacrum ages and withers away. The notion of fairy abduction also allows a person to be absent, mentally or physically or both, without explanation or responsibility, much as a double identity does for Jack/Ernest in Wilde's *The Importance of Being Earnest.*

What would Oscar Wilde have made of the story of Bridget Cleary? 'The Celt dreaming' was how he characterized fairy fiction, giving the native Irish story-teller and audience credit for creativity and agency, but this was a case of the Celt acting. Benson's essay presents Bridget's husband, father, cousins and neighbours as lacking autonomy, blindly following the dictates of a primitive and exotic belief-system. Wilde's interpretation would surely have been more subtle. No despiser of the working class, he was more astute than most of his contemporaries in dissecting the bizarre customs and belief-systems of the privileged people among whom he lived. He supported the cause of Home Rule for Ireland, so would hardly have subscribed to the social-Darwinist doctrine which found the Irish lower on the tree of life than other northern Europeans. Above all he understood how porous is the membrane that separates fiction from real life.

Wilde's Irish background would have given him an understanding of the transactions between the lives lived by rural people and the oral fictions they told. Traditional fairy belief is encoded in a meshed repertoire of legend told all over Ireland (and in Scotland and Canada's Atlantic provinces), to entertain, amuse, educate and frighten. In these narratives are found many examples of adult changelings, usually women, often 'swept', or 'changed', at times of transition, as brides or during childbirth. Times of literal change in women's lives are thus marked metaphorically as occasions of fairy intervention.

Newspaper accounts of the Cleary case were themselves an unsettling mixture of fact and legend. On 29 March 1895, *The Times* reported that Bridget Cleary had been buried in Cloneen cemetery, near her home, but that her funeral was conducted entirely by the police, all her relatives and neighbours having boycotted it. The report continued: 'the people believe − or, perhaps, with a view to the defence of the prisoners, affect to believe − that the real Bridget Cleary will come back, riding on a white horse sent by the fairies, and that if they can succeed in cutting the reins of the horse they will secure her . . .'. Reports published on 2 and 3 April added the detail that she was believed to be in Kylenagranagh 'fort'. In the district of Cloneen and Ballyvadlea, where the Clearys lived, the 'fort' of Kylenagranagh was identified as a fairy habitation. Such 'forts' are found all over Ireland, but their prominence in the landscape and in oral tradition no more indicates universal credulity than does the figure of Santa Claus in cities in the weeks before Christmas. They provide sites for fiction, and, to borrow Adrienne Rich's phrase, for lies, secrets and silence. Available as a complex and flexible abstract model of the society that traffics in it, fairy legend holds open a space in community discourse within which to contemplate anomaly and change. Here is where the two meanings of the word 'fairy' begin to overlap.

This idiom of fairy legend, anchored in and illustrated by the known and conspicuous 'fairy fort', could be used metaphorically to express tensions and difficulties of social and interpersonal relations. So a child who whinged or misbehaved, as well as one who was sickly, might be labelled a changeling and threatened with a hot shovel. A woman unhappy in her marriage or dissatisfied with her situation might be similarly labelled, or might label herself, as being 'in the fairies'.[34] 'She's away with the fairies' may be no more than a colloquial way of saying that a woman does not pay attention, or that she thinks herself better than her neighbours; 'I must have been away with the fairies' may mean 'I don't know what came over me', or 'I don't know what you're talking about' — in other words 'I refuse to explain or take responsibility for my behaviour.' A man who behaved eccentrically, or whom parents did not trust to be alone with their children, might also be described as 'in the fairies'.

A changeling, or person 'in the fairies', is someone who has changed, or a person who fails or is unwilling to fulfil society's expectations. Bridget Cleary was twenty-six years old and had been married for six years, but had no children. This made her anomalous in a society which accorded much higher status to married than to single women, but expected a woman to become pregnant within a year of marriage. Newspaper reports of the investigation of her death show her as a strong-minded and independent woman, in better financial circumstances than many of her neighbours. This may have been enough to lead to an accusation of fairy substitution when she fell ill, or it may have been suspected that she was suffering from tuberculosis, as later accounts from the locality assert.[35] Calling gay men 'fairies' is a way of conveying the same sense of repudiation and stigma.

Some of the abduction narratives collected by Sir William Wilde and later students of folklore read as metaphors for illness, disability and accident, but others clearly frame a negotiation with the reality of domestic violence.[36] Both types are narratives which make the unbearable at least speakable. Fairy legends in the oral tradition tell of the desperate measures adopted by mothers to 'recover' their children, and by men to 'recover' their wives: attacking changelings with fire irons and farm implements. Significantly, stories are lacking in which adult male changelings are banished by violence.[37]

A diagnosis of fairy abduction, like an accusation of witchcraft or an arrest warrant, is a way of singling out one person for negative attention by a group, and sometimes for brutal and abusive treatment. While witchcraft is presented as analogous to crime, implying volition on the part of the witch, changeling status is compared to illness. Witnesses in the Bridget Cleary case spoke of the herbs and fire administered to her as part of a 'cure', while the local man who had prescribed the herbs was called a 'herb doctor' and a 'fairy doctor'. But diagnosis can function as accusation and both can be strategies for rejection. Recently we have seen tuberculosis give way to AIDS as a focus of such social contamination. By the end of the nineteenth century, medicine and the law had been strengthened and refined as discourses of social control, displacing oral traditions of witchcraft and fairy abduction in all but those areas classified as 'remote and isolated', then as now, a euphemism for 'savage and barbarous'.[38] In 1895, the statement that the woman known to her family and neighbours as Bridget Cleary had been replaced by a fairy changeling might have been acceptable as part of a coded oral narrative of social deviance or disruption, but to the modern mind of newspaper and courtroom it was both repugnant and ridiculous.

Analyses of what went on in Bridget Cleary's house during her last days have tended to leave out of consideration the intensity of emotional upheaval which must have prevailed there, and which contemporary accounts assure us did prevail. They have focused instead on the exotic logic of the belief-traditions described in court and corroborated by folklorists. But these traditions belong to verbal art, not to legal discourse, and they are not so much a charter for action as a way of rationalizing events which have got out of control.

The Times, quoted above, attributes a sort of crazed ritualistic deliberation to Bridget's husband, Michael Cleary, when he 'stripped off all her clothes, poured paraffin oil over her, and set fire to her with a burning stick from the hearth'. Irish newspapers, by contrast, show Michael's disastrous action as a sudden outburst of individual violence which followed several sleepless nights and a trial by fire carried out by several men together. Their reports, much longer than those in English papers, make clear that this ritual attempt at cure, cruel though it was, had taken place earlier and was believed to have been successful. Michael Cleary, at the end, acted alone.

Hubert Butler's well-known essay on the fate of Bridget Cleary made much of a remark by Michael, referred to once in court, that Bridget 'was always talking about Kylenagranagh', and that 'She used to be meeting an egg man on the low road . . .' beside the fairy fort.[39] Butler inferred that jealousy of his wife's relationship with the egg man was what drove Michael Cleary to violence. Clearly something in Bridget's behaviour had given her husband cause for concern, but her interest in the fairy fort alone would have been enough to trouble him. Representing a whole area within which she was beyond his control, it was probably at least as important as the egg man in driving him to violent action.

Benson, for his part, argues that Michael Cleary and his neighbours acted 'strictly in accordance with a primitive and savage superstition', and proceeds to draw comparisons, after the manner of contemporary folklorists, between the belief-tradition of rural Ireland and the 'primitive and elementary' forms of religious belief found in societies from Western Australia to Vancouver to Patagonia.[40] His essay quotes from anthropological studies which were part of the discourse of colonization, and heavily indebted to Darwinian ideas about the relative humanity of the world's peoples.[41]

Something of the same ambivalence Benson displayed about Wilde in his later book, *As We Were*, is already evident in his article on the Cleary case. He condemns the actions of Michael Cleary and his neighbours as primitive and savage, but appeals for leniency on their behalf on the grounds that they have acted 'honestly . . . and for the best'. The reader is reminded of the 'sheer pity and sympathy' he expressed finally for Oscar Wilde. 'We cannot imagine', he writes, 'that they, by pure chance, invented a course of reasoning to excuse their act which entirely tallies with a widely spread and primitive superstition, nor is there the smallest evidence to show that any of those motives which, for the most part, lead to murder were influencing, or had influenced, any of the actors. The story is too strange not to be true.'[42]

The story is certainly too strange to have been invented out of thin air at the time of Bridget Cleary's death, but its correspondence to familiar fictions is no guarantee of its truth. A readiness to believe that working-class or rural or colonized people 'believe' things which seem nonsensical to the metropolitan mind suits a certain colonial attitude. It also apparently suited Benson, who in this essay extended his interest in the exotic and archaic to embrace Ireland.

As his biographer remarks in another context, Benson was an exceedingly private person, who had an 'inherited need to divert prying eyes';[43] his essay on the Cleary case appears to be an expression of just that need. The diversionary tactics he employed would have had the effect in London that the telling of fairy legends can have in rural Ireland. At a time of potential confrontation, they deflected attention away from the immediate community, with all its tensions, towards the faraway, the wild and the incomprehensible – in this case, Ireland. Oscar, of course, was both Wilde and Irish, and, in one kind of language, he was a fairy. Larger than life, he was difficult to overlook. Largely invisible, his image floats between the lines of Benson's essay.

Impressions of an Irish Sphinx

OWEN DUDLEY EDWARDS

> In a dim corner of my room for longer than my fancy thinks
> A beautiful and silent Sphinx has watched me through the shifting gloom.
>
> Inviolate and immobile she does not rise she does not stir
> For silver moons are naught to her and naught to her the suns that reel.
>
> Red follows grey across the air, the waves of moonlight ebb and flow
> But with the Dawn she does not go and in the night-time she is there.
>
> Dawn follows Dawn and Nights grow old and all the while this curious cat
> Lies crouching on the Chinese mat with eyes of satin rimmed with gold.
>
> Upon the mat she lies and leers and on the tawny throat of her
> Flutters the soft and silky fur or ripples to her pointed ears.
>
> Come forth, my lovely seneschal! so somnolent, so statuesque!
> Come forth you exquisite grotesque! half woman and half animal!
>
> Come forth my lovely languorous Sphinx! And put your head upon my knee!
> And let me stroke your throat and see your body spotted like the Lynx!
>
> And let me touch those curving claws of yellow ivory and grasp
> The tail that like a monstrous Asp coils round your heavy velvet paws!¹

I

'He shuns the mysterious,' concludes Vincent O'Sullivan's *Aspects of Wilde*, 'and in himself he was not mysterious, nor had he the aura of mystery and its attractions. It is not in the desert that his Sphinx proposes her riddles, but in a room – a room in an hotel.'² Wilde would have liked that ending, I suppose; like his poem, it sounds well: graceful, ironic, questioning. There are still questions from that hotel-room Sphinx — how far did his sense of humour impair his sexual stimulus, for one thing, when feasting with panthers of the banality of Charlie Parker and Fred Atkins? But whether Wilde was as unmysterious as Unitarianism, himself a Sphinx without a Secret, or whether his mystery begins not in 21 Westland Row but in the cloakroom of the railway-station opposite (the Bray rather than the Brighton line), mystery surrounds him. Let us agree with O'Sullivan, however momentarily, and acknowledge that Wilde gave himself no aura of mystery such as that with which his political leader, Charles Stewart Parnell, surrounded *him*self.

Wilde did not contrive his life, and indeed built it far less designedly than most of us: he could not have contrived it, for one thing, because he discovered repeatedly that he was not what he had thought he was. He did not build much mystery into his life: he should have built a great deal more than he did, to protect himself and his family. But what happened to him made mysteries, and his Sphinx is everywhere, beginning in Westland Row. He asked it many questions as he went along. *The Sphinx*, taking nearly twenty years to write, recorded Wilde's life-long struggle with the charm of Catholicism. He knew how Irish he was, and when, and where, and why: we know far less than him, on that and so much else. Indeed our desert is so barren of information on his Irish life that the Sphinx needs new style and new symbol in our questions.

We must interrogate works about life, and life about works, with homage to Wilde's insistence on Nature imitating Art in 'The Decay of Lying': it is an old theme that Lord Alfred Douglas was Nature's revenge on the creator of Dorian Gray. Much more tantalizing is what Richard Ellmann diagnosed as Wilde's consistent use of betrayal of the lover by the beloved, of friend by friend, long before *The Picture of Dorian Gray*. The list is considerable: the Nightingale betrayed by the shallowness of the Student, Hans by the greed and hypocrisy of Hugh 'the Devoted Friend', the Dwarf by the selfishness and condescension of the Infanta; his family, benefactors and *origins* by the Star-Child; in later works, Basil Hallward's betrayal and, ultimately, murder by Dorian Gray; Gerald Arbuthnot's betrayal of his mother (until inadvertently steered back to her by the follies of his father) in *A Woman of No Importance*, Sir Robert Chiltern's betrayal of Lord Goring after Goring's rescue of him in *An Ideal Husband*, Jack's betrayal of Algy in the unrevised four-act *The Importance of Being Earnest*. Whence did this hunger and virtual demand for betrayal derive? Graham Greene concluded his essay 'The Lost Childhood' with a quotation — unusually for him — from an Irish source, AE's 'Germinal':

In ancient shadows and twilights
    Where childhood had strayed,
The world's great sorrows were born
    And its heroes were made.
In the lost boyhood of Judas
    Christ was betrayed.

This is directly helpful on Greene; but with Wilde any such search is infinitely more difficult. Ellmann notes betrayals going back to his Oxford days. Was there some such betrayal in his youth? Was he himself Christ or Judas if there was? The theme is present in his earliest, repudiated dramatic works: *Vera*, composed in 1879–80, and the *Duchess of Padua* in 1883, although in both these cases the betrayal is temporary and for more justifiable motives than the self-absorption of the later traitors. And it leads much more directly to those lines from '*The Ballad of Reading Gaol*' –

> Yet each man kills the thing he loves

(Vera intended to stab her love.)

> The kindest use a knife, because
> The dead so soon grow cold.

(Theme is one thing, technique another: the boy of twenty-five who wrote *Vera* could not have written that last line.) But the harder, Judas theme thrusts itself into those verses too:

> Some do it with a bitter look,
>   Some with a flattering word.
> The coward does it with a kiss. . . .[3]

Who? Or maybe what? Any quest, for treacherous loved ones rather than lovers, should include the unknown Irish years. Did some treachery happen in Ireland?

There is one strong clue that it did, and that is the absence of personal reminiscences. Richard Ellmann pointed out that Wilde's Portora years are reduced from seven to one, and are even eliminated completely, in different accounts Wilde supplied to interviewers about his early years – recalling Mrs Cheveley's remark: 'I have forgotten my schooldays. I have a vague impression that they were detestable.' As to his later Irish Protestant education, his friendship with the Rev. John Pentland Mahaffy seems to have been the most enduring legacy from his three years at Trinity College Dublin, apart from his fairly close acquaintance with Edward Henry Carson. Wilde would be betrayed by both men – but not until 1895.

Betrayal need not always be by persons; perhaps it was an inevitable outcome of the very conditions of Wilde's childhood in Ireland.

II

Wilde was fascinated by masks and masques pictures and portraits. 'The Birthday of the Infanta' comes *from* a painting (Velàzquez's *Las Meninas*); 'The Portrait of

Mr W. H.' turns *on* a painting (actually two paintings, the second of which catastrophically proves the first a forgery); and *The Picture of Dorian Gray* transfers mutation in physiognomy from an original *to* a painting. Our first sight of Oscar Wilde is in a photograph of a large child, holding on to a chair-back, dressed in female attire or just possibly somebody's notion of archaic Gaelic court dress. The work is often captioned as Oscar aged two, but, as Ellmann sensibly states, the child is 'about four'. There is nothing particularly feminine about it. It is plump, and could be tall for its age. It also seems poised, in the manner of a child on parade in a tableau, or even amateur theatricals. The sash running from beneath the right shoulder to above the left hip adds a faintly military touch. It is a child which just might typify the infant Oscar of Fianna celebrity after whom he was named. In any event, the dress is Romantic. The child probably is not, but is evidently self-assured, if unenthusiastic. It sees no reason to defer to whoever faces it, or otherwise seek reassurance. It reflects confidence, and fears no challenge. It is unaware of any superior. It is an Irish Protestant.

Was there, in the 1850s, any people on the surface of the globe possessed of self-esteem comparable to that of the Irish Protestant? An Irish Protestant, of course, means a Protestant Episcopalian, communicant of the Established Church of Ireland, heir of the eighteenth-century Protestant Ascendancy which built its own Houses of Parliament to throw the Westminster edifice into the shade and then in 1800 allowed itself to be bribed into the Union of both legislatures on the despised Thames. It claimed Jonathan Swift, George Berkeley, Edmund Burke (actually of Roman Catholic stock and sympathies), Oliver Goldsmith, Richard Brinsley Sheridan, Henry Flood, Henry Grattan, Theobald Wolfe Tone, Robert Emmet; it claimed some of the noblest architecture raised by human hands; it claimed every farthing it could grasp in tithes exacted from Papist, Presbyterian, Methodist, Quaker and Jew in addition to its own. It knew itself the superior of what it called Non-Conformists, although their pride was as angular in its own way, all the more in that they had sold no birthright for the glittering pottage of Erastian rewards. As for the despised Roman Catholics, fast narrowing the political and economic − but not the social − gaps, the Irish Protestant knew his magnificence by his cultural distance from the rabble of beggars constituting the great bulk of Irish Catholicism: or, if the Great Famine had removed the mendicant masses, why, what remained was an animated lump of aspirations above their proper station, manipulated by their greedy clergy, instead of by their greedy landlords. In fact the landlords still held most political control, but spectacular clerical wins from time to time enabled the Protestants to lament the ouster of true Irish patriotism from public counsels. On their side, the Catholics bided their time, and under their own more deferential manner hid the blazing pride of a faith surviving its own outlawry in the land where its votaries remained a majority, however hapless. And of course good Catholics knew Protestants to be damned, the better ones perhaps being saved after a long stretch in Purgatory in which, as the cream of the joke, Protestants did not believe.

The Irish Protestant was answerable to nobody. He might, for various reasons, defer to the Westminster government, or even to the rising economic or political power of the Papists, and be heartily despised in consequence by his fellows, but even there the Protestant truckler for Catholic votes or readers, the Protestant snouter for London jobs and favours, despised his critics no less than he despised the flunkeys of Whitehall and the shavelings of Rome, much though he might hope to get from either. He might idle the day away gambling, or reading, or experimenting, or hunting, or fishing, or rack-renting; he might kill himself tending scores of fever-ridden famine victims on his estate or he might kill scores of the same victims by evicting them from his estate; he might luxuriate in the development of scholarship on Irish antiquities and pride himself on their proof of civilization a millennium before the Saxon came to Rye and out on Severn strode, oblivious of his own possibly exclusively Saxon ancestry; he could define his Irishness as unsurpassed, regardless of whether he chose to identify it with Wellington, Wolfe Tone or Brian Boru; he might found some new religious cult incomprehensible to all including himself, or he might go to the far more extreme limit of excess and become a Papist, yet he remained the Irish Protestant.

(Anyone acquainted with Irish Protestant converts to Roman Catholicism should have little difficulty in accepting the last point.)

III

Declan Kiberd, on the whole the most constructive commentator on literature to proclaim Wilde's Irishness, falls short of his normal high standards when in his *Inventing Ireland* he seeks to tie Wilde in with a theory that the great men of the Irish Renaissance had fathers who were failures.[4] In general the argument is impossible: (a) because the Oedipus complex is far rarer than Freud imagined (Oedipus himself being one of its numerous exceptions); (b) because Irish Protestants by definition could not be failures; (c) because Sir William Wilde combined the zenith of achievement of his time in demography, aural surgery, optical surgery, topography, ethnology, ethnography, medico-biography, public health and Irish character. The assumption by some students of Wilde (most unwisely following in the biographical footsteps of Frank Harris) that the Wildes were ruined in Dublin society by the suit of an eccentric female patient, Mary Travers, in 1864 is to impose mid-Victorian standards on a society which acknowledged no superior to its own: Irish Catholics and Presbyterians in their search for social acceptance were far more respectful to the English norm. Isaac Butt QC appeared for Miss Travers, ruthlessly cross-examined Lady Wilde in the witness-box, ruthlessly denounced Sir William Wilde, who did not appear in the witness-box, and was happily known throughout Dublin for a private life much wilder than Wilde's. Neither the public nor the private life of Butt stood in the way of William Wilde's joining Butt's Home Government Association six years later. No doubt the memory of the Travers case weighed on the sensitive Oscar. But he showed it in behaviour asserting invulnerability to public opinion when threatened by legal proceedings in his own turn. If Irish Protestants had sustained their title to rule regardless of majority rights and wrongs, why should they care for anything as artificial as Victorian public opinion? So Oscar Wilde would ultimately go to his fate as though an adverse outcome in *Regina (Wilde)* v. *Queensberry* was nobody else's business, much as Parnell four years earlier had seen nobody else's business in the outcome of *O'Shea* v. *O'Shea and Parnell.*

Wilde was to grow up very interested in Greek legend, but (unlike Yeats) not particularly in Oedipus. If we want to generalize from Greek legend, can we invent a Hippolytus complex? The father and mother are both heroic, but the father is heterosexually promiscuous both before and after marriage, with widely bruited results. The son responds by distaste at the prospect of his own repetition of his father's gallantries, especially when to do so would seem to dishonour his mother. It is a sufficiently frequent pattern in homosexual men, but also in evangelicals, enthusiasts, votaries of some kind. It induces a degree of special devotion to virgins (such as Artemis, or Athena, or Mary the mother of Jesus, or Elizabeth I of England, or Florence Nightingale). The sexual preference, if any, is not the most important part of the story, although it may become the most notorious. Nor is the Hippolytus figure hostile to his father: he may be very proud of him, as was Hippolytus of Theseus, and as was Oscar of Sir William. But on certain things father and son find communication difficult, sometimes fatally so.

Psychiatrists, historians and plain journalists thirst for evidence of conflict, but the most important parental influences on children may be where there is no conflict, where independently Mother and Father find themselves in agreement (as did Theseus and Hippolyta on hunting and heroics), and where the child either follows suit or has a giant-size rebellion. As Richard Pine points out in his seminal, if not comprehensive, *The Thief of Reason: Oscar Wilde and Modern Ireland,*[5] the Irish Great Famine, still raging less than five years before Wilde's birth, offers a coincidence of parental obsessions. Taking Wilde's eponymous story, he feels that 'The redemptive quality of the young King's true poverty and humility might speak for all those whose degradation under the Famine had been noted by his father's coldly analytic pen and the strident sympathy of his mother's verse.'

William Wilde's phenomenal work compiling the medical statistics of the Famine and Jane Francesca ('Speranza') Elgee's 'The Famine Year' are formidable inheritances by any standard. The homage of modern economic historians is given to no Famine contemporary analyst more generously than to William Wilde. Speranza was apparently writing in mid-Famine, to judge by her poem's title. Today, we rightly recognize Prime Minister Sir Robert Peel as doing more than might be expected from any other contemporary premier or putative Irish self-ruling government, in distributing relief and funding schemes of public works, but the worship of *laissez-faire* under the ensuing Whigs implanted the traditional horror-story of corn-laden ships leaving the Famine-stricken island in inexorable pursuit of the wealth of nations. Shaw, born two years after Wilde, recorded its enduring hold on Irish-America when in *Man and Superman* he had old Malone tell the supercilious Violet of 'the starvation. When a country is full of food and exporting it, there can be no famine.' Speranza began 'The Famine Year':

Weary men, what reap ye? – Golden corn for the stranger.
What sow ye? – Human corses that wait for the avenger.
Fainting forms, hunger stricken, what see you in the offing?
Stately ships to bear our food away, amid the stranger's scoffing.
There's a proud array of soldiers – what do they round your door?
They guard our masters' granaries from the thin hands of the poor.
Pale mothers, wherefore weeping? – Would to God that we were dead –
Our children swoon before us, and we cannot give them bread.

Speranza was assailing suffering in her own country, and charging her own caste
and their English cousins with its responsibility.

We are fainting in our misery, but God will hear our groan;
Yet, if fellow-men desert us, will He hearken from His Throne?
Accursed are we in our own land, yet toil we still and toil;
But the stranger reaps our harvest – the alien owns our soil.
O Christ! how have we sinned, that on our native plains
We perish houseless, naked, starved, with branded brow, like Cain's?
Dying, dying wearily, with a torture sure and slow –
Dying, as a dog would die, by the wayside as we go.[6]

Her information is good enough, medically and socially, to show it is reliable,
including starving children left with dead mothers. She knows of the vagrant
and nomadic fathers, however kind a construction she puts on their desertion of
wives and children. She has the imagination to see the Famine from a dying
infant's standpoint, above all the terror of what to them was inexplicable
hunger and a dying they could not define. Lines such as these indicate Wilde
had a mother whose imagination would reach out to his, rather than turning
from, or thwarting, it. It gave Wilde a vocabulary of horror and suffering he
was to use with effect in *The Ballad of Reading Gaol* half a century after the
Famine.

But in the interval it was no slumbering imagery. It certainly prompted this
moment in 'The Young King':

From the darkness of a cavern Death and Avarice watched them, and Death
said, 'I am weary; give me a third of them and let me go.'

But Avarice shook her head. 'They are my servants,' she answered.

And Death said to her, 'What hast thou in thy hand?'

'I have three grains of corn,' she answered, 'what is that to thee?'

'Give me one of them,' cried Death, 'to plant in my garden; only one of them,
and I will go away.'

'I will not give thee anything,' said Avarice, and she hid her hand in the fold
of her raiment.

And Death laughed, and took a cup, and dipped it into a pool of water, and out of the cup rose Ague. She passed through the great multitude, and a third of them lay dead. A cold mist followed her, and the water-snakes ran by her side.

And when Avarice saw that a third of the multitude was dead she beat her breast and wept. She beat her barren bosom, and cried aloud. 'Thou hast slain a third of my servants,' she cried, 'get thee gone. There is war in the mountains of Tartary, and the kings of each side are calling to thee. The Afghans have slain the black ox, and are marching to battle. They have beaten upon their shields with their spears, and have put on their helmets of iron. What is my valley to thee, that thou shouldst tarry in it? Get thee gone, and come here no more.'

'Nay,' answered Death, 'but till thou hast given me a grain of corn I will not go.'

But Avarice shut her hand, and clenched her teeth. 'I will not give thee anything,' she muttered.

And Death laughed, and took up a black stone, and threw it into the forest, and out of a thicket of wild hemlock came Fever in a robe of flame. She passed through the multitude, and touched them, and each man that she touched died. The grass withered beneath her feet as she walked.

And Avarice shuddered, and put ashes on her head. 'Thou art cruel,' she cried; 'thou art cruel. There is famine in the walled cities of India, and the cisterns of Samarcand have run dry. There is famine in the walled cities of Egypt, and the locusts have come up from the desert. The Nile has not overflowed its banks, and the priests have nursed Isis and Osiris. Get thee gone to those who need thee, and leave me my servants.'

'Nay,' answered Death, 'but till thou hast given me a grain of corn I will not go.'

'I will not give thee anything,' said Avarice.

And Death laughed again, and he whistled through his fingers, and a woman came flying through the air. Plague was written upon her forehead, and a crowd of lean vultures wheeled round her. She covered the valley with her wings, and no man was left alive.

And Avarice fled shrieking through the forest, and Death leaped upon his red horse and galloped away, and his galloping was faster than the wind.[7]

Put in the context of his father's expertise and his mother's enthusiasm, the passage takes on new meaning. William Wilde knew how much disease followed in the wake of famine, the starvation itself probably accounting for less than half the deaths (although weakening countless thousands beyond any resistance to ague, fever or plague). The bewilderment of the educated classes, in Dublin and England, that this disaster should have struck so near at hand, instead of being something reported from Asia or Africa, finds clear echoes here.

Above all, Avarice has evidently convinced herself she is a paternalistic landlord and, hardly conscious of hypocritical intention, cries for the preservation of her servants. But, by definition, what she regards as natural is but grist to her Avarice. Wilde is hard enough in his exposure of the human plea that the suffering should fall elsewhere than on one's own people — Orwell uses it as Winston Smith's final capitulation in *1984* — and Avarice ends pitiably enough, but useless, bankrupt, incompetent. He was later to explore the Socialist's insistence on Capitalism as its own executioner, in 'The Soul of Man under Socialism.' It is also probably the finest measurement of the relations of Death and Avarice in the Irish context: Ireland's rulers did not want to kill the people, but (to their own grief and mortification) aided the Death they sought to avert. And Wilde's achievement is the greater in his professional linguistic use of the Authorized Version of the Bible, a reminder of the skill he would show in *Salomé* some five years later; he was, after all, the nephew of three Protestant Episcopalian priests and related to several others. The evangelical strain present in the ancestry of Shaw, Yeats, Synge, O'Casey and other giants of the Irish theatre — even Sheridan and Goldsmith — works its way out in Wilde, as in so many others, to evangelize from platform and proscenium in place of pulpit.

> One by one they're falling round us, their pale faces to the sky;
> We've no strength left to dig them graves — there let them lie.
> The wild bird, if he's stricken, is mournèd by the others,
> But we — we die in Christian land — we die amid our brothers,
> In the land which God has given, like a wild beast in his cave,
> Without a tear, a prayer, a shroud, a coffin, or a grave.
> Ha! but think ye the contortions on each livid face ye see,
> Will not be read on judgement-day by eyes of Deity?
>
> We are wretches, famished, scorned, human tools to build your pride,
> But God will yet take vengeance for the souls for whom Christ died.
> Now is your hour of pleasure — bask ye in the world's caress;
> But our whitening bones against ye will rise as witnesses,
> From the cabins and the ditches, in their charred, uncoffin'd masses,
> For the Angel of the Trumpet will know them as he passes.
> A ghastly, spectral army, before the great God we'll stand,
> And arraign ye as our murderers, the spoilers of our land.[8]

Speranza's 'Famine Year' was written, we must remember, some fifteen years before Julia Ward Howe's 'Battle-Hymn of the Republic': the quandary of a forgiving Christ and an unforgivable wrong is resolved in the same way, by confidence in the vengeance of the Old Testament God. Confronted with the absolute in moral horror, she instinctively responds as an archdeacon's granddaughter with two clerical uncles.

Thus the Great Famine and its revelation of human responsibility for human suffering were probably the greatest individual legacies in creative response which Wilde inherited from his parents. It was part of that legacy that he was left with a permanent denial of his own caste's title to rule in Ireland, and that of the English aristocratic ruling class, whose superiors they took themselves to be — with title to rule now questioned not simply for Ireland, but also for Britain: Wilde belonged by birth to a bourgeoisie economically in power but socially afraid to assert itself.

IV

Wilde as talker is agreed to be one of his most extraordinary if least recorded art-forms. No doubt we get something of it from Vivian in 'The Decay of Lying'; various monologues from the dandy philosophers of the plays, even the longer epigrams of Prince Paul Maraloffski in *Vera*, give a touch of it; but theatre required more break-up of conversation than any intelligent person in real life would want. Julian Symons (brother and biographer of A. J. A. Symons) gives us a flavour of Wilde at full tilt in his detective-novel *The Detling Secret*:

'. . . I have followed your brilliant career with deep admiration, and know you have that gift of imagination which is valued above all others by the Irish temperament. Show my countrymen that you understand their longing for freedom and their genius for suffering, and they will greet you as a brother.'

With that he passed on, to tell a promising actress that he had in mind a play which would include a wonderful part for her, and at last to encounter the youthful Eglantine, who stood mute in a corner now that his reading had finished. The shape of those sonnets was perfect, Mr Wilde said, making shapes himself in the air with his large hands, they were perfect as the flower that now bore a poet's name. A brief quotation about sweet musk-rose and eglantine, and another about eglantine in the warm hedge, and Oscar Wilde was gone, perhaps to another party, leaving an impression of conceited dandyism among those who had not spoken to him, and of warmth and generosity in those who had. He had done more than anybody else could have done to make the party a success.[9]

The last point is critical: Wilde was a very amusing talker, but a very kindly one.

The problem of the talker in Dublin is best summed up by Micheál macLíammóir in his magnificent one-person recital *The Importance of Being Oscar* (crowning a lifetime's evangelization of Wilde in the dangerous surroundings of that prophet's own country):

He wanted something, of course, that his own country could never have given him. He wanted world-wide fame, and he decided to begin by being widely talked about everywhere.

Dublin, doubtless, would have talked about him too: had indeed done so already. He had seen to that. But in Dublin talk was merely for talk's sake: there would have been no real result of the talk at all: no world-wide fame, no rich reward, no jewelled elegance; and the dinner tables he so rightly felt himself destined to dominate would have been in Dublin far less opulent than those in London, and far more conversationally competitive. An English lady once gently rebuking the poet for his faith in a fortune teller had said: 'Fortune-telling? Oh, but do you not think that is rather tempting Providence, Mr Wilde?' And he had answered: 'Dear lady, surely Providence can resist temptation by this time.'

Now, who in Ireland would have listened to a crack like that without trying either to cap or to capsize it?[10]

We think of Wilde as an essentially urban figure, and when we remember his Dublin origins we recall Merrion Square: nothing rural about Merrion Square. Speranza's salon in Chelsea recalls an equally fixed domicile in fashionable Dublin. But Wilde's experience of talking as a boy would be far from limited to Dublin drawing-rooms and dinner-tables, even if they did include the Protestant poet Samuel Ferguson and the Catholic (convert) poet Aubrey de Vere. His parents were among the leading folklorists of their time, and the subject of folk-narrative would necessarily be a frequently overheard theme of discussion between them. William Wilde recorded a vast number of stories, possibly songs, certainly examples of custom and belief; his wife, in turn, showed a profound grasp of folk material and would have based her extensive studies in part at least on her late husband's researches, papers and communications to herself and the boys. They all travelled in the West of Ireland, questioning informants. Lady Wilde worked up her material initially into *Ancient Legends, Mystic Charms and Superstitions of Ireland* (1887, 1888) — a second work, *Ancient Cures, Charms and Usages of Ireland*, following in 1890 — and her belated preparation of her material significantly coincided in time with her son Oscar's conception of his first prose book, *The Happy Prince and Other Tales* (published May 1888).

The *Happy Prince* stories work very well for telling to children — Wilde was a father when he wrote them, and if his sons (born in 1885 and 1886) were very young listeners, they would have been very much the audience in his creating mind. So we are thinking of a transition from rural story-telling to Victorian nursery-fare. Lady Wilde knew all about such a process: the great William Carleton, conserver of the folklore and folk history of southern Ulster — especially Catholic southern Ulster — had been one of her closest friends, and was commemorated by her in a poem. Carleton's work ranged from reporting avowed fireside narrative, through short stories embodying folk culture, to the formal novel. The privileged status of the old bards was in some degree inherited in Irish Catholic peasant society by the *seanchaí*, story-teller or folk-raconteur. The most illustrious example of all such categories was of course the legendary Oisín, son of Fionn Mac Cumhaill, or Finn MacCool or Fingal, whose stories (produced to a surprisingly credulous Christian audience after 300 years' preservation of the narrator in *Tír na n-Og*) turned chiefly on his father or his heroic son Oscar. The Wildes proclaimed their own bardic or at least folk-narrator-conserver status by giving their second son the names 'Oscar' and 'Fingal'. Your name conditions your perceptions of your identity in its relation to your world. All that was asked of Oscar Wilde by his name was that he be a hero, but a hero existing by parental story-getting and story-telling. The eldest son was given firm forebear names: William Charles Kingsbury Wilde. The second — Oscar Fingal O'Flahertie Wilde — was a hostage to Irish cultural identity.

Oscar Wilde's awareness of Irish folk-belief, whatever his experience in assisting his parents to report it, was likely to surface only with an Irish inter-locutor, and one of Catholic origins; but to one such, Vincent O'Sullivan, he was explicit enough:

> He told me that as a child he heard the Banshee, and woke up crying: 'Why are they beating that dog? Tell them to stop beating the dog.'
> The next day one of the family died.
> His mother died while he was in prison. He told me quite seriously that on the night of her death she appeared to him in his cell. She was dressed for out-of-doors, and he asked her to take off her hat and cloak and sit down. But she shook her head sadly and vanished. When they came to tell him of her death he said quietly: 'I know it already.'[11]

Obviously the idea of a revenant was something he associated with his mother's custody of such legends. But while Lady Wilde's *Ancient Legends* discusses both Banshees and dogs (with instructive comparative data from other cultures considered both as possible origins and as interesting correlations), she does not bring both together. And the thin wail of a suffering dog can sound like the Banshee. O'Sullivan does not suggest that Wilde made much of a story of the Banshee, not nearly as much as he did of his mother's epiphany, neither of them as elaborate as he would have made a 'good story' for an enraptured audience. What O'Sullivan documents is the extent to which parental folklore remained strongly present in Oscar Wilde's mind to his final years.

Richard Pine and others have picked up several themes linking Gaelic folklore and Wildean fiction. The preservation of youth in *The Picture of Dorian Gray* as echo of *Tír na n-Og* is the most obvious: the link to Oisín tightens its personal immediacy. Lady Wilde in 1864 congratulated Ferguson ecstatically on his poetic use of the Oisín legend. Wilde himself reviewed Yeats's *The Wanderings of Oisín* a few months before writing *Dorian Gray*:

> when he is at his best he is very good. If he has not the grand simplicity of epic treatment, he has at least something of the largeness of vision that belongs to the epical temper. He does not rob of their stature the great heroes of Celtic mythology. He is very naïve, and very primitive, and speaks of his giants with the awe of a child.[12]

This was in its way a truly charming compliment (all the more in a notice hailing 'a volume . . . so far above the average that one can hardly resist the fascinating temptation of recklessly prophesying a fine future for its author'): it covertly identified Yeats with the child Christ or at least His child playmates in 'The Selfish Giant', published the previous year (and presumably Yeats, and Lady Wilde, would have been expected to see the linkage). The lesson is important for *Dorian Gray*: it too describes figures retaining their heroic stature, for all of the damnation Dorian shares with the Yeats Oisín. The two poets also come together as inheritors of the folk-story recorded by Lady Wilde as 'The Priest's Soul'. Yeats's 'The Hour-Glass' is virtually a dramatization of it (with the innocent child, immune from the apostate priest's corrupting materialism, becoming in Yeats's hands a 'Fool'). Wilde, in turn, appropriated the idea of soul as existing independently of body into 'The Fisherman and his Soul' as well as into *Dorian Gray*. Both Wilde stories also employ the 'changeling' theme firmly identified by Lady Wilde. Debts to Irish folklore extend even to details of Wilde's stories. In *Wilde's Use of Irish Celtic Elements in The Picture of Dorian Gray*, David Upchurch believes 'the delicate perfume of the pink-flowering thorn' (ending the novel's first paragraph) to derive from the magic fairy-sheltering hawthorn with which Lady Wilde opens her discussion of 'Sacred Trees'.[13] Certainly it gives as good an explanation as any for the forces who grant Dorian Gray's wish for eternal youth in exchange for the ageing of the picture.

Wilde's parents, especially his father, would have collected much material in Irish Gaelic, which Oscar Wilde's son Vyvyan remembered his father using to sing nursery lullabies. As Pine surmises, it must have been the product of family holidays in Connaught where William Wilde bought his estate at Moytura, defined the topography of Lough Corrib, and presumably took his sons on folklore expeditions. This in turn brings us back to the earliest fairy stories: how do they translate into Gaelic? It seems our only way of finding a direct connection. One association there certainly is: Patrick Pearse directly drew on 'The Selfish Giant' for his short story 'Íosagán' and, less obviously, on 'The Happy Prince' for its companion 'Eoghainín na n-Éan'. It was in itself a symbolic act: Wilde was still very much a non-person in 1907. Admittedly, Pearse had the advantage that nobody could admit to familiarity with the work of a non-person. But we do not need to take matters too far. Pearse had limited creativity; but as a teacher he saw the facility of Irish transposition of theme, material and even words. He set the stories in the Connaught where the Wildes had worked and played. 'The Selfish Giant' in particular suggests not just a peasant context, where Pearse put it, but the Giant as owner of the Big House with the little children as peasants and, presumably, Catholics.

Following Pearse's perception, can we go further? 'The Happy Prince' is a story of urban bourgeois greed and proletarian poverty: Pearse had hard work to do to build its rural counterpart, and made the Prince a tubercular child. 'The Nightingale and the Rose' is set in a town with a regal court as well as a university, and as such might derive from Dublin with its Viceregal Lodge more naturally than from Oxford, but (other than in Thomas Moore's *Lallah Rookh*) its plot lies outside Irish tradition (contrast with the work of Liam O'Flaherty, as affecting as

Wilde about the self-sacrifice of animals, but as naturalism not symbolism). 'The Remarkable Rocket', a fable in pyrotechnics, has no place in rural Ireland (where even the Protestants hardly required Guy Fawkes Night, given the abundance of their own festivals). But 'The Devoted Friend' is very rural indeed, with its introductory Water-Rat, Duck and narrator Green Linnet, followed by as nasty an example of gombeen-man ethics as any countryman could recount. 'Green Linnet' is found as a folk-motif in nineteenth-century agrarian and patriotic song, being successive codes for Napoleon, Daniel O'Connell and Michael Davitt. The Miller's self-serving philosophy has its links to the rationale for crop-export during the Famine, although he is firmly in the New Ireland as a rising capitalist rather than a decaying landlord. It should translate well into Irish Gaelic.

Of direct translations, 'The Happy Prince' and 'The Selfish Giant' have been rendered into acceptable, but unfortunately abridged, Irish versions. To say this is not to say that all Wilde would translate well into Irish. He translates very badly into English, in the case of *Salomé*, apart from the Iokanaan borrowings from Ezekiel. But in this, as in other cases, Wilde's awareness of Irish lying behind his English stood him in good stead for bilingual expression, whether dealing with French or with Greek. It also explains why he should have had such verbal felicity from the first. He never really regarded English as a language entirely enclosing him.

V

Of the family in Wilde's Irish life, the one who seems to have made the greatest impact on his fictional creativity is the one of whom we know least: his sister Isola.

Isola was born in 2 April 1857. She died on 2 February 1867. Oscar was still overshadowed by her death even after his imprisonment, his family still possesses the envelope in which he retained a lock of her hair until he died. It is decorated with various legends such as schoolboys like to draw, but not on schoolboy themes. There are four crosses forming points of a trapezoid, strong, black crosses, radiating light. Four scrolls occupy roughly the corners of the envelope, reading top left 'Thy Will be done', bottom left 'God is love', bottom right 'She rests in peace', top right 'Resurgam'. On the base of the envelope is a radiant crown. Above it are the words, again given radii, 'She is not dead, but sleepeth', with the citation 'Mark.v.xxxix'. The passage in question is in fact Jesus' raising of the daughter of Jairus to life (with 'the damsel' where Oscar wrote 'she', and the words being those of Jesus). Four wreaths surround the words, the upper two being separated by 'Obiit Feb xxiii' and below it '1867'. Above that are the words, boxed, 'My Isola's Hair'. Above them are two more wreaths, but this time linked, the left-hand one surrounding an 'O', the right-hand one, slightly falling out of line, surrounding an 'I'. The top-left cross is between an 'O' and an 'I', the top right-hand cross between an 'I' and an 'O'.

He was twenty-one, and in Avignon after his first year at Oxford, when he wrote 'Requiescat':

Tread lightly, she is near
   Under the snow,
Speak gently, she can hear
   The daisies grow.

All her bright golden hair
   Tarnished with rust,
She that was young and fair
   Fallen to dust.
Lily-like, white as snow,
   She hardly knew
She was a woman, so
   Sweetly she grew.

Coffin-board, heavy stone
   Lie on her breast,
I vex my heart alone,
   She is at rest.

Peace, Peace, she cannot hear
   Lyre or sonnet,
All my life's buried here,
   Heap earth upon it.[14]

Yeats asked for the right to reproduce it in an anthology in 1894. Wilde, while granting permission, hinted he would prefer another choice. He did not think it 'very typical of my work. Still, I am glad you like it.'[15] He had included it in his *Poems* (1881) — Yeats, often a perverse anthologist, was eminently sound here, it is surely the best thing in it — but by 1894 Wilde wanted no more mauling of his grief.

By then, in any case, Wilde had worked new ideas into his loss. He was still haunted by the idea of Isola's survival: whether as Jairus's daughter or as the listener beneath the snow, or even as the connected wreaths labelled 'O' and 'I' which he drew as a schoolboy on the envelope containing Isola's hair; they resemble bushes linked up, much as in folk poetry lovers' graves grew rose and briar ultimately intertwining. His story 'The Canterville Ghost' is about a little girl, and an undying ghost, two different characters who ultimately unite to dissolve the enchantment by which the Ghost is cursed. Virginia Otis is nominally fifteen in the story, partly to give her a charming young duke whom she can marry in a few years, but in the crisis of the story she is described as 'a little child' both in the old prophecy and by the Ghost (and her Duke, going back to Eton in 'floods of tears' when he is not allowed to propose to her, seems rather closer to the twelve years that were Oscar's when Isola died — a probable memory of his own return to Portora after Isola's funeral). Above all, the word 'Resurgam', 'I will rise again' (Matthew 27: 63, Latin vulgate), is suggestive, apart from the indication that Oscar was even then finding religious support in Roman Catholic usages. (He won the Greek New Testament prize at his school.) *Resurgam* is the title given to the first collection of Wilde's private letters (six only, to the composer Dalhousie Young), published in 1917 by Clement Shorter, husband of the Irish revolutionary poet Dora Sigerson Shorter. There it is applied to the resurrection of Wilde's name, but the boy Wilde himself was haunted by it, and responded by having his invented Ghost haunt and be put to rest by a living girl. Of course the very American Virginia Otis is not Isola, but something of her affection and sympathy may be. The Christian name is obviously American, yet it also reflects Isola, who 'hardly knew she was a woman'.

Virginia's departure on her mission to save the Ghost − all we ever learn about how she saved him − surely derives from the memory of Isola's being 'taken' by, or 'lost' to, death. (no doubt it had its influence on Yeats's 'The Stolen Child' − a poem in any case indebted to Wilde's mother):

> Suddenly she stood up, very pale, and with a strange light in her eyes. 'I am not afraid,' she said firmly, 'and I will ask the Angel to have mercy on you.'
>
> He rose from his seat with a faint cry of joy, and taking her hand bent over it with old-fashioned grace and kissed it. His fingers were as cold as ice, and his lips burned like fire, but Virginia did not falter, as he led her across the dusky room. On the faded green tapestry were broidered little huntsmen. They blew their horns and with their tiny hands waved to her to go back. 'Go back! little Virginia,' they cried, 'go back!' but the Ghost clutched her hand more tightly, and she shut her eyes against them. Horrible animals with lizard tails, and goggle eyes, blinked at her from the carven chimney-piece, and murmured 'Beware! little Virginia, beware! we may never see you again,' but the Ghost glided on more swiftly, and Virginia did not listen. When they reached the end of the room he stopped, and muttered some words she could not understand. She opened her eyes, and saw the wall slowly fading away like a mist, and a great black cavern in front of her. A bitter cold wind swept round them, and she felt something pulling at her dress. 'Quick, quick,' cried the Ghost, 'or it will be too late,' and, in a moment, the wainscoting had closed behind them, and the Tapestry Chamber was empty.[16]

The folk-motif is obvious: people endangered by fairy importunity are warned by signs and beings, and their salvation often turns on heeding the warnings. For all Wilde's debt to Maturin's *Melmoth the Wanderer*, his mother's translations and reports, Sheridan Le Fanu's stories and so forth, the passage and indeed story is misunderstood if its originality is not acknowledged. Dissolving wall-tapestries are a child's imagination, as are animals speaking from them. (When Wilde was dying he had some lapses into childhood, including memories of taking the Irish Sea vessel *Munster*: his dying joke about being killed by the wallpaper may be a memory of Isola's death, his use of the wall-tapestry in 'The Canterville Ghost'.) At the heart is the idea of the little girl's redemptive power, and her love transcending the death she risks. That the story is introduced in high farce deepens the power of the girl's readiness for sacrifice.

If 'Canterville' is actually Oscar telling funny stories to Isola and Isola giving comfort to him, formal criticism is eavesdropping. We may sympathize, we may admire, we may deplore, but we do not *know*. Our work is extremely speculative. How far were his courtships of Florence Balcombe (who rejected him for Bram Stoker) or Constance Lloyd (who married him) in part a search for Isola? How far is Dorian Gray, the boy who never grows old as Isola never grew old, a male version? Isola was not a petulant nineteen-year-old Narcissus, but she may have inspired:

> his finely-curved scarlet lips, his frank blue eyes, his crisp gold hair. There was something in his face that made one trust him at once. All the candour of youth was there, as well as all youth's passionate purity. One felt that he had kept himself unspotted from the world.[17]

It is consistent with 'Requiescat', the fullest statement he made about her to have reached us. One obvious line of creative thought on a dead child is what they were spared by dying: had she grown old, could she have been corrupted, like Dorian?, or grown inhuman, like the Infanta?, or used humans as playthings, like Salomé? Or would she have been cruel in her innocence, like Lady Windermere, or ignorantly insensitive, like Hester Worsley in *A Woman of No Importance*? Or would she simply have remained a figure of captivating play and laughter, radiating charm and kindness, enjoying make-believe and yet brilliant in her diplomacy, as are Mabel Chiltern in *An Ideal Husband* and Cecily Cardew in *The Importance of Being Earnest*?

Her portrait has not survived. All we have are the lost hopes of her brother, and perhaps the portraits he developed from meditations on her. We have his portrait 'as a lad' from these years: wide-eyed, staring at something beyond the artist, lonely. Later likenesses are more sociable, but much more guarded.

VI

A set of examination papers administered by the Portora Royal School in Easter 1859 − five years before Oscar Wilde became a pupil there, but under the same headmaster, the Rev. William Steele MA − gives an impressive indication of the heights of education reached by its pupils. Twenty-seven papers cover subjects for the School Medals tested by eight dons of Trinity College Dublin. Some questions may appear risible ('Relate anything you know about John of Gaunt'), some incredibly ambitious ('Give some account of the origin of Trial by Jury in England'), some arcane ('Henry IV laid claim to the Crown as being a descendant of Henry III. For what purpose?'), some pursuing trivia ('Name all the Queens of the Kings of England from William I to Edward III, inclusive').

But in one respect they are consistent. Not one mention of Ireland is to be found. History is formally 'English History', but with all mention of the pre-Reformation Church excluded. Geography does include 'Aughrim' in a list of ten 'remarkable places' (including Marston Moor, Culloden Moor, Sedgemoor) whose counties are to be named, but nothing else. The population of 'England' is required: so is that of Norway (then part of Sweden), whence the question must extend to England minus Ireland, Scotland and Wales. Instances are demanded of Persian, Turkish, Arabic, Italian, Spanish and Dutch words 'naturalized in the English language' – but no Gaelic. The 'greatest pulpit orators of France' are to be named (without cause, and hence indicating official choice) and their epochs: these would have included Bossuet and Fénelon, presumably, and probably Calvin, but the nature of their discourses is ignored. Robertson is to be translated into French, Macaulay into German, Prutz into English and Thomas Arnold into Greek. Possibly the nearest the examination came to modern Ireland was a question in statistics on the natural labouring force of a labourer per day working for ten hours with twelve efforts per hour each of thirty pulls; certainly this did not presume research requiring participation by the youthful future master-class.

This explains clearly enough why the Union was doomed: any society which educates its future ruling class in ignorance of the country it rules has abdicated. The examination seems tailor-made for the future philippics of Daniel Corkery against what he termed 'The Garrison', and indeed *The Hidden Ireland* is eloquent on bogus internationalism and the imposition of 'the standards of a dead nation [which] killed in other nations those aptitudes through which they themselves had become memorable'.

Since the Renaissance there have been, strictly speaking, no self-contained national cultures in Europe. The antithesis of Renaissance art in this regard is national art. . . . The Renaissance may have justified itself, but not, we feel, either on the plane of genuine Christian art or genuine pagan art. It is not as intense or as tender as the one, nor so calm, majestic and wise as the other.

Thus Corkery in 1925. He added a remarkable footnote:

When writing this I had forgotten that Wilde had more brilliantly said the same thing: 'To me one of the things in history the most to be regretted is that the Christ's own renaissance, which had produced the Cathedral at Chartres, the Arthurian cycle of legends, the life of St Francis of Assisi, the art of Giotto, and Dante's *Divine Comedy*, was not allowed to develop on its own lines, but was interrupted and spoiled by the dreary classical Renaissance that gave us Petrarch, and Raphael's frescoes, and Palladian architecture, and formal French tragedy, and St Paul's Cathedral, and Pope's poetry, and everything that is made from without and by dead rules, and does not spring from within through some spirit informing it' – *De Profundis*.[18]

Corkery was ruthless in his high cultural priesthood, purging what he called 'Garrison' literature from the citadel of Irishness. Yet, while others abided his question, Wilde was free. Why? It took guts — especially for a bachelor scholar seeking an academic chair in the most clerical of all Irish centres of higher education, University College Cork. To the new guardians of morality in the Irish Free State, Wilde was usually unmentionable. And Corkery may even have been homosexual, consciously or otherwise. As a degenerate scion of the Protestant ascendancy who left Ireland at twenty and hardly ever returned, Wilde provided a shining instance of the perils the new Ireland had fortunately lost. So reasoned many of Corkery's fellow purists in the ranks of the exclusive brethren of the cultural nationalists. Wilde's mother's patriotic verse, Wilde's own death-bed conversion to Catholicism — what value did these have to balance the advantage of proving the Garrison a nursery of perversion?

The explanation may lie in the context. Corkery as a patriot was sympathetic to prison writing, schooled on work such as Davitt's *Leaves from a Prison Diary* or Tom Clarke's *Glimpses of an Irish Felon's Prison Life*. Five paragraphs after the words he quoted, Corkery would have found this in *De Profundis*:

Of late I have been studying the four prose-poems about Christ with some diligence. At Christmas I managed to get hold of a Greek Testament, and every morning, after I have cleaned my cell and polished my tins, I read a little of the Gospels, a dozen verses taken by chance anywhere. It is a delightful way of opening the day. To you, in your turbulent, ill-disciplined life, it would be a capital thing if you would do the same. . . . Endless repetition, in and out of season, has spoiled for us the *naïveté*, the freshness, the simple romantic charm of the Gospels. We hear them read far too often, and far too badly, and all repetition is anti-spiritual. When one returns to the Greek it is like going into a garden of lilies out of some narrow and dark house.

And to me the pleasure is doubled by the reflection that it is extremely probable that we have the actual terms, the *ipsissima verba*, used by Christ. It was always supposed that Christ talked in Aramaic. Even Renan thought so. But now we know that the Galilean peasants, like the Irish peasants of our own day, were bilingual, and that Greek was the ordinary language of intercourse all over Palestine, as indeed all over the Eastern world. I never liked the idea that we only knew of Christ's own words through a translation of a translation. . . .[19]

Regardless of what psychological identification Wilde may have unlocked in Corkery, the linguistic kinship was evident. Garrison or not, Wilde knew about Irish peasant bilingualism, and identified it with Christ. Despite his arguing for the cosmopolitan language, he still asserted that Christ has come down to us in his own vernacular. Wilde, therefore, demanded what Corkery sought: a genuine, not a borrowed, culture. Corkery would have realized that, to hold such views, Wilde must have been in full rebellion against the educational institutions of his upbringing. And clearly he was.

Robert Harborough Sherard (too readily belittled by subsequent Wildean students) was perceptive enough about Portora, recognizing that Wilde's very Irish-conscious family background made for his hopeless alienation. It was not so much the politics of the thing. As we have noted, Irish Protestantism had had its share of nationalist eccentrics, among them Wilde's own parents.

But Portora simply obliterated Ireland, as in the fullness of time it would obliterate Wilde himself in retrospect. His parents' decision to send him there may have been induced by conventional solutions to commonplace situations; or perhaps the mother felt the father's manner of life offered a dangerous example to his sons, and it did. Finance may have prohibited the choice of an English school, but it seems probable that the Wildes' national cultural sense − far more vigorous in them than any politics − militated against such a denial of their sons' birthright. If so, they little reckoned with the almost *1984*-like obsession at Portora with proving the school more English than the English. In any event, Wilde's Irish identity, riveted on him by his parents from the first, was absolutely denied at his school; and he was therefore conditioned to a life of irrelevance to his own cultural being. His Irishness was not erased, but rendered invisible. Further cultural growth became its palimpsest. But Portora, having apparently no cultural life of its own, had no palimpsest to impose, apart from encouraging his Greek. The examinations suggest a purely arid demand for regurgitation of fact and opinion, with scarcely a thought of development of aesthetics. Catholic students at Newman's unchartered University in Dublin received what Wilde lacked until Oxford.

But what the aridity of Portora forced Wilde to conceal went much deeper than inheritance of his parents' antiquarian preoccupations (and that was deep enough: his first published prose was an appeal for support [in 1878] for a starving Irish antiquarian artist). Richard Ellmann concluded, I think correctly, that Jane Wilde had her sons baptized as Roman Catholics, roughly about 1860. Her motives are unclear, but the most likely one is that the Famine persuaded her to regard Protestants as insufficiently Irish. Her friend Aubrey de Vere had made the break in 1851. Sir William Wilde voiced little objection in reply to the celebrant, the Rev. L. C. Prideaux Fox SJ, himself a convert, who called on him later ('I don't care what the boys are so long as they become as good as their mother'). But Fox was transferred, Lady Wilde's enthusiasm does not seem to have transcended the symbolic act and the event survived only as a half-memory. For the Wilde brothers it was a half-memory to be repressed. Portora could receive Protestant sons of Catholic mothers, but would have been horrified by Catholic sons of Protestant fathers. So Oscar, like Esau, was deprived of his blessing no less than of his birthright. It partly accounts for the predilection towards Catholicism which remained throughout his whole life. But it also meant that what would be called affectation must have been an early practice with him. He had to invent himself to appear visible where his reality had become invisible.

Other realities had also to be covered up − scandals about his father including the publicized Travers Trial of 1864, financial crises involving bailiffs in occasional possession, Isola's death — and Irish Protestant insouciance would be the pose to carry them off. But what had to be concealed was that he was not, in anything save manner and birth, still an Irish Protestant. His places at Portora and Trinity depended on his fidelity to his caste, and his preoccupations were increasingly those of a Catholic and nationalist internally debating his intensity of commitment. Henceforward there was but one Church in his life — at odds with it though he frequently was.

This necessarily reawakens the changeling question in a new form, not to say the whole issue of the Divided Self. Wilde's fiction made so much of the changeling because Portora had imposed it on him, and had done so, moreover, in a starkly ethno-religious and socio-political context. Privileged youth at Portora in a smiling countryside where the school existed as a Laputa, denying existence to any Ireland outside itself, was obviously analogous to the Happy Prince and the Young King, whose sumptuous jewels contrasted with the poverty their guardians ignored. Portora at Enniskillen would also convey the varieties of poverty and exploitation so vivid in these stories: the little Portorans were taught to lie back and think of England in indifference to poor Presbyterians, poor Catholics and even poor Episcopalians (being the most unproductive land in Protestant Ulster, Fermanagh saw deprivation for all religious sects). The idea of a fisherman divided from his soul — the fisherman being by profession associated with Christ's disciples — would stem from Portora's division of boy from his identity; and it is important that Wilde saw such results as evil.

From this standpoint *Dorian Gray* seems analogous to the school photograph Wilde was probably too early to receive, or to the Oxford group, bowler-hatted, outfitted in checked tweeds, an unlovely male chorus, all of them empty representations of an official institutional style. Portora made its unreal Dorians: the realities remained in the attic. On the other hand, there is not the slightest reason to believe that Portora proved its Englishness as a public school by introducing Wilde to homosexuality. Lord Alfred Douglas recalled asking Wilde about that, no doubt with memories of the Winchester which had debauched Douglas himself, and said Wilde told him there had been nothing of the kind. Neither Wilde nor Douglas had any reason to lie about it. It is quite likely Portora had its secret lives, but that Wilde knew nothing of these; it is ironic that the board where his name was no longer carried, preserved in honourable mention persons infinitely more proficient from earliest adolescence in the sexual expression universally associated with Oscar Wilde.

Of all Wilde's stories 'The Star-Child' seems the most profoundly influenced by this enforced denial of identity. The Star-Child is adopted — fostered among poor parents: as the Wildes would have known, a practice existing in Celtic tradition even as late as Daniel O'Connell himself, although for story purposes the fosterage is caused by accident — and the child gives himself airs, as a chieftain's child among fosterlings might (though the young O'Connell, the fullest case on recent record, seems fully to have accepted his place in a poor family). Then the Star-Child discovers his mother is a beggarwoman, and repudiates her, only to become foul in appearance himself and, in turn, be repudiated by his despised playmates. The child's real parents, beggar and leper, who turn out to be king and queen, would typify Wilde's Irish heritage, including that of the Famine. The wicked magician who enslaves the child and beats him for giving alms to the starving leper could be England, or the headmaster of Portora, or the spirit of cosmopolitan sophistication. Above all the story comes back to the great theme of *De Profundis*: 'The supreme vice is shallowness. Whatever is realised is right.'

However painfully Portora may have eradicated Wilde's public expression of his Irish consciousness, it gave him a level of subtlety and taught him the use of masks. His masks became instinctive as well as artistic; when he implicitly involved, for instance, the fate of Parnell in 'The Soul of Man under Socialism', Wilde knew that every reader of the *Fortnightly Review* for February 1891 would know to whom he was referring. Yet revelation of his Irish heritage was automatically oblique, indirect, unexpected, mockingly awry with him now. Irish literati, who never stopped beating on the patriotic drums, orange or green, or festooning conversation from the tinker's pack of grievances, could be as repulsive to him as the obliterationists. His own ultimate fate, the sundering of his history from its Irish background, the over-specialization of his subsequent students, meant that his automatic, dramatic, exclusion of Parnell's name from his philippic against the press jackals – almost the product of fastidiousness in refusing to couple the name with its loathsome hired assassins – shrouded his meaning for posterity. But contemporaries would have understood his reference with more clarity than almost any other allusion he made:

In centuries before ours the public nailed the ears of journalists to the pump. That was quite hideous. In this century journalists have nailed their own ears to the keyhole. That is much worse. And what aggravates the mischief is that the journalists who are most to blame are not the amusing journalists who write for what are called Society papers. The harm is done by the serious, thoughtful, earnest journalists, who solemnly, as they are doing at present, will drag before the eyes of the public some incident in the private life of a great statesman, of a man who is a leader of political thought as he is a creator of political force, and invite the public to discuss the incident, to exercise authority in the matter, to give their views, and not merely to give their views, but to carry them into action, to dictate to the man upon all other points, to dictate to his party, to dictate to his country; in fact, to make themselves ridiculous, offensive, and harmful.[20]

VII

There is in my hallway a framed photograph of a sculptured head of Oscar Wilde by Patrick O'Connor, exhibited in the Victor Waddington Galleries in Dublin in 1954–55. Where the bust is now I do not know. Waddington left Dublin soon thereafter, to our great loss. Waddington and O'Connor were very kind to the schoolboy who came to the exhibition and so much admired the bust, inspired principally, I think, from the Ellis & Walery photograph of 1892, in Sherard's *Oscar Wilde: The Story of an Unhappy Friendship*. The face gazes out with slightly flared nostrils, appreciative rather than sensual, the lips almost scientifically pursed, the forehead high and noble, the head looking forward, seeking rather than speaking, a mouth that might say a great deal and yet guard its reserves with remarkable success.

It inhibits the frame of a photograph I obtained for sixpence when the Great House on our Dublin avenue, Clontarf Castle, was being sold and its contents distributed. The Vernon estate had of course been owned and administered by Unionist landlords — Vernon Avenue and Oulton Road proclaimed their might — and the photograph originally in the frame had been of a contemporary of Wilde's whom the Vernons and Oultons had every cause to revere, the most successful and perhaps the most ruthless of all later nineteenth-century Chief Secretaries for Ireland, Arthur James Balfour. I suppose it is still at the back of my print of the Wilde bust, so generously given me by Waddington and O'Connor. Wilde produced many shafts against the Balfour regime in Ireland, among which his review of Wilfrid Scawen Blunt's prison poems in the *Pall Mall Gazette* (3 January 1889) may have penetrated the Balfourian exterior rather more deeply than most Irish objurgations:

all the sonnets are worth reading, and 'The Canon of Aughrim', the longest poem in the book, is a most masterly and dramatic description of the tragic life of the Irish peasant. Literature is not much indebted to Mr Balfour for his sophistical 'Defence of Philosophic Doubt', which is one of the dullest books we know, but it must be admitted that by sending Mr Blunt to gaol he has converted a clever rhymer into an earnest and deep-thinking poet. The narrow confines of the prison-cell seem to suit the sonnet's 'scanty plot of ground', and an unjust imprisonment for a noble cause strengthens as well as deepens the nature.[21]

The 'noble cause' was the plan of campaign. Blunt called his book *In Vinculis*, probably inspiring E. V. Lucas of Methuen to suggest the title of *De Profundis*, adopted by Robert Ross for Wilde's own prison letter in 1905. Balfour did not send Wilde to gaol, though he was the true leader of the government which kept him there from the summer of 1895 to May 1897.

('What is your religion, Mr Wilde?' 'Oh, I don't think I have one, Mr Balfour. I am an Irish Protestant.')

I find the domesticity of my portrait of Wilde corresponds pleasingly with his own poetic cult of the Sphinx. The charm of that poem in part arises from his mingling of the Sphinx as some sort of domestic pet with its fabulous history across space and time. But, as she should in a story, a Sphinx may fascinate without having secrets; and Oedipus remains unmentioned in his catechism of its mythology. Nor is this likely to be psychologically revealing. 'I think God has dealt very hardly with us', wrote Wilde on his father's death, unlike the desperate attempts to accept the Divine Will with which his Isola envelope was festooned. Sir William had died before Wilde's First in Classical Moderations at Oxford was announced, and the conversations between two proven scholars could now never take place. As we have seen, Oscar was able to continue talking to Isola, and perhaps listening to her, or to his memories of her.

He loved his father's country: he called it 'Lotus Land'. In a poem written about 1876 at Illaunroe, the Connaught home, he thought much as Yeats would think of Innisfree.

And in the polished mirror of the lake
My purple mountains see themselves again.

O sad, and sweet, and silent! surely here
A man might dwell apart from troublous fear. . . .[22]

'My purple mountains.' 'My Isola's hair.'

Venus in Blue Jeans: Oscar Wilde, Jesse James, Crime and Fame

FINTAN O'TOOLE

I THE ATTRACTIONS OF WICKEDNESS

> EDWARD CARSON: Listen, sir. Here is one of the 'Phrases and
> Philosophies for the Use of the Young' which you contributed [to the
> *Chameleon*]: 'Wickedness is a myth invented by good people to
> account for the curious attractiveness of others.' You think that true?
> OSCAR WILDE: I rarely think that anything I write is true.[1]

We do not know quite when the attractiveness of wickedness first impressed itself
on Oscar Wilde, but his close encounter with Jesse James must have reinforced it.

On 11 April 1882, a week after the death of the notorious outlaw, the front page of
the New York *Daily Graphic* was given over to a cartoon called 'The Apotheosis of
Jesse James'. It shows an imposing gravestone with the inscription: 'Hic Jacet Jesse
James. The most renowned murderer and robber of his age. He quickly rose to
eminence in his gallant and dangerous profession and his exploits were the wonder
and admiration and excited the emulation of the small boy of the period.... He was
followed to his grave by mourning relatives, hosts of friends, officers of the law, and
the reverend clergy who united in paying extraordinary honours to his memory. Go
thou and do likewise!' Around the base of the monument, a legion of small boys, each
with a pistol, rifle or knife, does homage to the fallen desperado.[2] What Jean Genet
will call, in *The Maids*, 'the eternal couple of the criminal and the saint', is already
joined together in the apotheosis of Jesse James.

The themes of the cartoon − the glamour of wickedness and the corruption of
the young − would become, in due course, central to the fate of Oscar Wilde.
What the newspaper was noticing was one of the origins of a central aspect of
modernity − the erasure of the dividing line between fame and infamy. Jesse
James ascended into Heaven with all the trappings of the saint. He was betrayed
by a friend before being martyred. And, almost immediately after his death, his
relics became objects of worship. Just seven days after his killing, the *Missouri
Republican* reported thousands of people visiting the house he had occupied in the
town of St Joseph. The owner charged an entry fee of ten cents, though the fence

and the stables had been mostly demolished by relic hunters who carried away pieces of them to keep as souvenirs.[3] Their reaction to the death of a violent outlaw suggests that already, in the Wild West of the 1880s, fame had become a transcendent quality, overriding and overruling moral and legal distinctions between the good and the bad.

On 18 April 1882, just over two weeks after the execution of James, Oscar Wilde lectured at Tootle's Opera House in St Joseph as part of his American lecture tour. He noted, as he wrote in a letter to Helena Sickert, that:

> the whole town was mourning over him and buying relics of his house. His door-knocker and dust-bin went for fabulous prices, two speculators absolutely came to pistol-shots as to who was to have his hearth-brush, the unsuccessful one being, however, consoled by being allowed to purchase the water-butt for the income of an English bishop, while his sole work of art, a chromo-lithograph of the most dreadful kind, of course was sold at a price which in Europe only a Mantegna or an undoubted Titian can command![4]

Wilde may have considered his own performance in America to be original, but in fact it was a replay of a familiar role. To take just one example of an educated Irishman arriving on the western frontier to civilize the natives, there is another Oscar and Trinity College Dublin graduate, Oscar J. Goldrick, who electrified the town of Auroria (now Denver) with his arrival in 1858. Goldrick was driving a wagon drawn by oxen, whom he instructed in loud Latin and Greek. He was dressed in 'a shiny plug hat, polished boots, an immaculate linen shirt, lemon-coloured kid gloves, a Prince Albert coat, and a waistcoat embroidered with lilies of the valley, rosebuds, and violets'.[5] With this costume, he attracted attention for his educational mission, and founded a school and a library, the Denver and Auroria Reading Room Association. Though he may not have known it, Wilde did not invent the role of Irish dandy as American reformer.

What he did do, though, was to recreate that role in the dawning age of mass media and advertising. Wilde arrived as an advertisement. He was the 'original' of Reginald Bunthorne in Gilbert and Sullivan's *Patience*, and his lecture tour was conceived as a way of drumming up publicity for the operetta's American production. Wilde was playing a version of a theatrical exaggeration of himself. And, like one of Andy Warhol's paintings of Marilyn Monroe, this 'Oscar Wilde' was itself capable of almost infinite and mechanical reproduction. Before Wilde arrived in Denver in the footsteps of Oscar J. Goldrick, the humorist Eugene Field carried through a successful hoax in which, dressed as 'Oscar Wilde', he was received with ceremony and driven through the streets. Just as versions of Jesse James, and of Billy the Kid, were being 'sighted' all over America, Wilde himself became a transferable icon, an image of dandified civility which was the other side of the coin of the image of outlaw derring-do which attached itself to the notorious desperadoes. Jesse James, Billy the Kid and Oscar Wilde may well be the first human figures to have become 'stars – like Marilyn Monroe – who are themselves commodified and transformed into their own images'.[6]

Much later on in Oscar Wilde's career, the shape of these events would become central to his aesthetic. *The Importance of Being Earnest*, in particular, juggles with roles, with disguises, with the art of the impostor and with the slipperiness of surface. Wilde's explorations of flatness, depthlessness and superficiality – which cannot but have been influenced by his American experiences – are perhaps the first coherent expression in art of the emergence of a commodified world, a world in which not objects merely, but also the human personality, can be reproduced and sold in limitless quantity. This is one of the reasons why, in the post-modern culture of the 1990s, Wilde still seems strikingly contemporary.

That Oscar Wilde and Jesse James should have come into such close proximity seems, at first, to fit in well with the official narrative of Wilde's tour of America. He arrived with the mission of civilizing America. He was an emissary of the world of civilization to the world of barbarism. And what could be more demonstrative of the need for such a mission than the Apotheosis of Jesse James? Even to respectable America, the image of a generation of wild children about to be raised on the myth of an outlaw's daring deeds seemed to express its worst nightmares. Wilde's own letter, with its playful comparisons of European culture, which values Mantegna and Titian, and American incivility, which values doorknockers, dustbins and the hideous lithographs of a murderer, is part of the script for that narrative.

Yet, if you read on in the same letter, the distinctions begin to blur. Wilde tells how, after St Joseph, he went on to Lincoln, Nebraska, where he lectured to a 'charming' audience of university undergraduates. After the lecture, he was driven out to see the state prison:

Poor odd types of humanity in hideous striped dresses making bricks in the sun, and all mean-looking, which consoled me, for I should hate to see a criminal with a noble face. Little whitewashed cells, so tragically tidy, but with books in them. In one I found a translation of Dante, and a Shelley. Strange and beautiful it seemed to me that the sorrow of a single Florentine in exile should, hundreds of years afterwards, lighten the sorrow of some common prisoner in a modern gaol. . . .

This passage is, of course, among the most haunting that Wilde wrote because we cannot help seeing it as a prefiguration of his own tragedy. Wilde himself stares out at us from prison as a criminal with a noble face. For him too the works of Dante, which he read in their entirety in Reading Gaol, would lighten sorrow. In his own life, he would cease to be the tourist of such places and become the native, cease to be the spectator and become the player. The distinction between civilization and barbarism, between the artist and the outlaw, on which his American tour is posited, would collapse.

II THE FURNITURE OF SIN

CARSON: Did his [Taylor's] rooms strike you as being peculiar?
WILDE: No, except that he displayed more taste than usual.
CARSON: There was rather elaborate furniture in the rooms, was there not?
WILDE: The rooms were furnished in good taste.
CARSON: Is it true that he never admitted daylight into them?
WILDE: Really! I don't know what you mean.[7]

But distinctions such as those between the civilized and the barbarous, the artist and the outlaw were not, in any case, as rigid as they might have seemed. The behaviour of the mob which flocked to secure the household relics of Jesse James was not all that far removed from the urgings of Oscar Wilde in his lectures to American audiences. One of his lectures was on 'The House Beautiful'. It was concerned with the aesthetics of household furnishings: why wallpaper should not be hung in entrance halls, why heating stoves should be of Dutch porcelain, why secondary colours should be used on walls and ceilings. Why blown glass was to be preferred to cut glass. Making a fetish of domestic goods, giving a charge to everyday objects beyond their functional value, venerating doorknockers and dustbins, was as much a habit of well-to-do consumers as of crazed relic-hunters. For each, functional objects could become imbued with an aura somewhere between the artistic and the religious. Household goods could take on, just as they do in modern advertising, the properties of things touched by magic. They could be, in themselves, suggestive of a moral, or an immoral, ambience.

At Wilde's trial, Edward Carson cleverly used the furnishings in the apartment of Alfred Taylor, one of his gay friends, to hint at a whole world of unspeakable decadence. Carson was playing on an obscure but powerful link between criminality and décor, one which was articulated later by Walter Benjamin:

The furniture style of the second half of the nineteenth century has received its only adequate description and analysis in a certain type of detective novel at the dynamic centre of which stands the horror of apartments. The arrangement of the furniture is at the same time the site plan of deadly traps, and the suite of rooms prescribes the fleeing victim's path. The bourgeois interior of the 1860s to the 1890s, with its gigantic sideboards distended with carvings, the sunless corners where palms stand, the balcony embattled behind its balustrade, and the long corridors with their singing gas flames, fittingly houses only the corpse. . . . The soulless luxuriance of the furnishings becomes true comfort only in the presence of a dead body.[8]

Nor was the Wilde who passed through Missouri a man entirely outside the world of the outlaw. Outlaw culture was concerned not merely with violence, but with ways of codifying violence. The Code of the West, by which the likes of Jesse James and Billy the Kid understood themselves to be living, was a code of manners. The outlaw saw himself as a gentleman. Gentlemen were permitted, as Wilde permitted himself, whoring and carousing and a life beyond the law. But the price for these pleasures was the ability to maintain a disdain for compromise and pragmatic calculation. The code imposed on its followers 'personal courage and pride and reckless disregard of life, it commanded practitioners to avenge all insult and wrong, real or imagined'.[9] It was, in its own way, a kind of democratized etiquette.

Wilde may have shot from the lip rather than from the hip, and his duels may have been conducted across a dinner table, rather than at high noon on a dusty and deserted Main Street, but his public persona had all the hauteur and recklessness of the outlaw. It is well to remember that Wilde's most important predecessor as Irish social comedian in England, Richard Brinsley Sheridan, had to announce his public presence in 'society' through two physical duels, fought against Captain Mathews in Bath and London in 1772. By the time of Wilde's assault on English society, such physical confrontations had been sublimated into wit and dandyism, but the underlying code is little different. In one of his most quoted epigrams – 'My wallpaper and I are fighting a duel to the death; one of us will have to go' – he plays on his own comic transformation of the code of the outlaw into the code of 'taste'. Likewise, in his duel to the death with Carson, his six-gun is loaded with the good taste of the furnishings in a den of iniquity.

And Wilde, of course, came to understand and be fascinated by this connection between the artist and the outlaw in himself. In his essay on the murderer and forger Thomas Wainewright, 'Pen, Pencil and Poison', published in the *Fortnightly Review* in 1889, Wilde draws Wainewright as himself: 'Of an extremely artistic temperament, [he] followed many masters other than art, being not merely a poet and a painter, an art-critic, an antiquarian, and a writer of prose, an amateur of beautiful things, and a dilettante of things delightful, but also a forger of no mean and ordinary capabilities. . . .' He says of Wainewright that 'His crimes seem to have had an important effect upon his art. They gave a strong personality to his style, a quality that his early work certainly lacked.' And he concludes that 'there is no essential incongruity between crime and culture'.

Even when he arrived in the Wild West, Wilde had as the principal purpose of his American tour the idea of getting a production of his first play, *Vera, or The Nihilists. Vera*, whose heroine is a Russian nihilist intent on assassinating the Czar, is just as awestruck by the glamour of guns as is any mythic penny chapbook account of the deeds of Jesse James. In it, Wilde's attraction to the outlaw life, even to the lone act of violence, is clear. If he is trying to make America more refined in his lectures, the play that he wants to stage there has no such intentions.

Wilde's visit to Lincoln prison took place just nine months after another strange parable of Ireland and America, of fame and infamy, had played itself out there. A young Irishman, born twenty-one years earlier in a tenement in New York to a woman, Catherine McCarty, who had fled the Famine in Ireland, was gunned down by a sheriff named Pat Garrett. By the time Wilde arrived in Lincoln, no fewer than five biographies of the young man, Henry McCarty, better known as Billy the Kid, had appeared. They included such titles as *The Cowboy's Career or*

The Daredevil Career of Billy the Kid, the Noted New Mexico Desperado; Billy the Kid and His Girl; and Pat Garrett's own account, *The Authentic Life of Billy the Kid, the Noted Desperado of the Southwest, Whose Deeds of Daring and Blood Have Made His Name a Terror in New Mexico, Arizona, and Northern Mexico.* Garrett's book appeared at the time of Jesse James's similar excursion into the new realms of fame and of Oscar Wilde's parade through America declaring his genius and staking his own claim to fame. While Wilde was preaching the interpenetration of art and life, American popular culture, especially on the frontier, was already practising it.

The blurring of the distinction between fame and notoriety which is so much a part of the afterlife of Jesse James and Billy the Kid, and which would become so much a part of the life of Oscar Wilde, also explodes the distinction between civilization and barbarism, and indeed between art and life, which was meant to be central to Wilde's American tour.

Long after his return to London, Wilde himself admitted that he was attracted to the 'barbarism' of the Wild West. He enthusiastically welcomed the arrival of Buffalo Bill's Wild West Show in London in 1887. In a typical reversal of accepted wisdom, and in a direct reflection of his own experiences in America, he noted that:

> English people are far more interested in American barbarism than in American civilization. . . . The cities of America are inexpressibly tedious. The Bostonians take their learning too sadly; culture with them is an accomplish-ment rather than an atmosphere; their 'Hub', as they call it, is the paradise of prigs. . . . Better the Far West with its grizzly bears and its untamed cowboys, its free open-air life and its free open-air manners, its boundless prairie and its boundless mendacity! That is what Buffalo Bill is going to bring to London; and we have no doubt that London will fully appreciate his show.[10]

As always, when a journalist says 'people', he means 'I'. American barbarism was indeed of far more use to Wilde than American civilization could ever be.

And indeed Wilde himself enacted this growing identification with the heroes of the Wild West on his American tour through the most obvious of outward signs – dress. He appeared at first as dandy and aesthete, in long green coat trimmed with seal or otter, turban-like hat, Lord Byron collar and sky-blue tie. But, as he progressed through the frontier, he adopted more and more the style of the cowboy and the miner: corduroys and wide-brimmed hat at first, then adding a cowboy neckerchief and tucking his trousers into his boots. Not only did he tell the silver miners of Colorado that they were the best-dressed men in America, but back in London he preached what they practised. Having himself shocked his American audiences by wearing his own theatrical knee-breeches, he ended up, after his Wild West tour, writing to the editor of the *Pall Mall Gazette* in 1884 to recommend broad-brimmed hats, short cloaks, leather boots and 'short loose trousers' which are 'in every way to be preferred to the tight knee-breeches which often impede the proper circulation of the blood'.[11]

Wilde, in effect, tried to do what Levi Strauss managed to do in the latter half of the twentieth century – to make the working clothes of the American West into a universal consumer fashion for city sophisticates. Contemporary advertisements for Levis and Wranglers, with their fetishization of cattle-wranglers and manual workers, are following where Wilde led. Tom Wolfe noted in the 1970s that the dress of the wealthy American young now consisted of:

> long-distance trucker warms, sheepherder's coats, fisherman's slickers, down-home tenant-farmer bib overalls, coal-stoker strap undershirts, fringed cowpoke jerkins, strike-hall blue workshirts, lumberjack plaids, forest ranger mackinaws, Australian bushrider mackintoshes, Cong sandals, bike leathers, more jeans, jeans, jeans, jeans, jeans, more prole gear of every description than you ever saw or read of in a hundred novels by Jack London, Jack Conroy, Maxim Gorky, Clara Weatherwax and any who came before or after . . . so that somehow the sons of the slums have become the Brummels and Gentlemen of Leisure, the true fashion plates of 1973. . . .'[12]

The proletarian dandy, spawn of Oscar Wilde's encounters with the Wild West, remains a central figure of present-day consumer culture. If, as Susan Sontag has suggested, modern camp is 'dandyism in the age of mass culture',[13] Wilde's encounter with the obsequies of Jesse James may well mark its point of origin.

III   CIVILIZING THE COMMUNITY

> CARSON: Did you know that one, Parker, was a gentleman's valet, and the other a groom?
>
> WILDE: I did not know it, but if I had I should not have cared. I didn't care twopence what they were. I liked them. I have a passion to civilize the community.[14]

The great American myth, of course, is the myth of the taming of the wilderness, the conquering of the uncivilized Indian by the civilized white man. The Irish played more than their fair part in this process. (It was an Irishman, General Philip Sheridan, who actually said, 'The only good Indians I ever saw were dead.') But that role remains crucially ambivalent. The ambivalence comes from the fact that the Irish are not, in this dichotomy, either/or, they are both/and. They are natives and conquerors, aboriginals and civilizers, a savage tribe in one context, a superior race in another.

At the same time as the West of America is being opened up, British colonial language is using the savagery of the Indian tribes as a convenient analogue for the native Irish. In 1844, an English traveller in Ireland remarks that 'The murders of this country would disgrace the most gloomy wilds of the most savage tribes that ever roamed in Asia, Africa, or America.'[15] In 1865 an editorial in *The Times* links the genocide of the American Indian with the emigration of the Irish, in a spirit of glee rather than outrage: 'A Catholic Celt will soon be as rare on the banks of the Shannon as a Red Indian on the shores of the Manhattan.'[16]

As the language of the Wild West and the Indian Wars becomes generalized through popular fiction and journalism – the one generally indistinguishable from the other – it becomes easy to apply this language to the wild Irish. A British visitor looking at Tuam in County Galway in the late nineteenth century thinks immediately of the Red Indians: 'Not only are the cabins in this district aboriginal in build but they are also indescribably filthy and the conditions of the inmates . . . is no whit higher than that obtaining in the wigwams of the native Americans. The hooded women, black-haired and barefooted, bronzed and tanned by constant exposure, are wonderfully like the squaws brought from the Far West by Buffalo Bill.'[17] For reactionary Britain, the Irish are the Indians to the far West, circling the wagons of imperial civilization.

Once in America, of course, the Irish cease to be the Indians and become the cowboys. They are the Indian killers and the clearers of the wilderness. They are the mythic outlaws. Jesse James's grandfather comes from Kerry; Billy the Kid is a child of the Irish Famine. According to some contemporary reports, Billy was born in Ireland, according to others, New York, and the ambivalence itself is perfect. In his legend, as it grows, Billy the Kid becomes a prodigious killer of Indians. He kills three Apaches in Sonora, rescues Texans from Apaches with the James gang. He takes on twenty 'well armed savages' in the Guadalupe Mountains with only his six-gun and his dirk.[18] But in reality, or as much of reality as there ever can be in this kind of legendary terrain, Billy the Kid fought not Indians but Irishmen. In the Lincoln County Wars he fought against the Murphy–Dolan–Riley ranching combine. The first murder he was charged with was that of the Murphy–Dolan–Riley sheriff, William Brady, who had emigrated from Ireland at the age of twenty.[19]

And, of course, Billy himself was killed by another Irish-American, Pat Garrett. In this seminal American myth the struggle of Irishman with Irishman in the New World is transmuted into a struggle of white man against native. Billy the Kid is Irish and American. His victims are Irish and Indian. The Irish are the killers and the victims, the civilizers and the wild men, the good guys and the bad guys. An important part of the American psyche, the ambivalence of the desperado as dangerous outlaw and rugged individualist, arises out of the ambivalence of the Irish in America. This is Ireland inventing America. And the Billy the Kid myth is itself crucially ambivalent. The transformation of Billy from foot soldier in an economic war into hero of the war against the Indians is an acceptance of the Irish as part of the governing American myth. But the ease with which Billy's Irish antagonists can become Indian antagonists shows how close the Irish remain to the Indians in the 'civilized' mind. This tension between acceptance and exile, between being insiders and outsiders, liberates a set of images that is enormously influential in the development of American culture and therefore on the development of global consumer culture.

Billy the Kid is the wild Irish savage but also the rugged white American, and in the development of his legend this tension is eventually resolved by dealing with Billy in conjunction with his father, his direct Irish antecedent, and splitting one off from the other. In Walter Wood's 1903 play about Billy the Kid, it is the Kid's father who is the villain and who actually gets killed, having been mistaken for his son. Billy lives on, and starts a new life 'where the sun always shines'[20] in peaceful, civilized America. Thus the savage Irish part is punished and expunged, the good American part is civilized and domesticated.

This set of images is one which emerges always in a curiously self-referential way: something that may be taken as a feature of the Irish-American cultural construct right from the start. The whole myth of the American West is one in which life and art imitate each other with dizzying speed. Buffalo Bill's Wild West Show has cowboys and Indians re-enacting their wars as theatre almost as soon as they have ceased to be wars. Far from being the originator of a myth, Billy the Kid himself grew up in the mythological shadow of Jesse James. Theatricality, Irishness and the Wild West intertwine with abandon in the James story.

In one of several letters from St Joseph, Wilde mentions Bob Ford, the Irishman who killed Jesse. He subsequently took a job with the repertory companies which were playing dramas about the James boys, appearing at the interval to tell the story of how he shot Jesse. Jesse's brother Frank, meanwhile, got a job in another theatre company playing a cowboy in Wild West shows.

The meaning of this self-conscious and intricate theatricality is close to the centre of Wilde's career, because it is the meaning of exile itself. Exile is a form of self-dramatization, the assumption of a role, the tailoring of one's personality to an alien audience. Exile makes things that are unconscious − language, gesture, dress, the accoutrements of nationality − conscious. It forces the exile to become a performer. And that performance involves ambiguity. It involves being who you are while being who you are playing. It involves, for the Irish in America, playing the white man and remembering the savage native that is left behind. And so the notion of play-acting itself becomes an inextricable part of the Irish ambivalence, an essential image of the doubleness of the exile's condition.

Wilde went to America as an Englishman. The letters sent to booking agents by D'Oyly Carte, who organized the tour, described Wilde as 'the new English Poet'.[21] Wilde's original lecture for the tour was on the English Renaissance. But the attacks on Wilde by the East Coast establishment take a form that is possible only on the assumption that he is not an Englishman but an Irishman. For what the most serious of those attacks do is to make Wilde a native, a savage, a black man.

The most remarkable of the attacks is a cartoon published on the front page of the *Washington Post* on 22 January 1882, shortly after Wilde's arrival in America. Entitled 'Mr Wild of Borneo', it shows an ape-like humanoid creature holding a coconut in its left hand, and, below it, Wilde holding a sunflower in his left hand. The text reads, 'How far is it from this [the ape-man] to this [Wilde]?' The caption notes the 'citizen of Borneo, who, so far as we have any record of him, is also Wild, and judging from the resemblance in feature, pose and occupation, undoubtedly akin'.[22]

The second attack in which Wilde is explicitly depicted as a black man came at one of his lectures in Rochester, New York, a fortnight later. Halfway through the lecture, as arranged by some of the students there, an old black man 'in formal dress and one white kid glove to parody Wilde's attire, danced down the centre aisle carrying an immense bunch of flowers and sat in a front seat'.[23]

These identifications of Wilde with blacks are in fact repeated in England at the height of Wilde's success. In April 1893 *Punch*, reviewing the opening of *A Woman of No Importance*, referred to its 'Christy Minstrel epigrammatic dialogue' and carried a cartoon called 'Christy Minstrels of No Importance', at the centre of which sits Wilde with the caption 'Massa Johnson O'Wilde'.[24]

These jokes depend on a set of connections between Irish ambivalence (civilized or barbarian?) and theatricality, which also work themselves out in the legends of Jesse James and Billy the Kid. However, much as he wanted to present himself as a civilized Englishman, Wilde was vulnerable to being read as a simian Irishman. And the Irish, in American theatre, were close to the blacks. In popular plays like James Pilgrim's *Katty O'Sheal* (1854), the Irish are 'coloured people', unsuitable for marriage to authentic whites. In James Macready's *The Irishman in London* (1853), Murtoch Delaney falls hopelessly in love with his perfect match, the humanoid 'grinning Cuba'.[25]

By insisting on wearing knee-breeches in the early part of his tour, Wilde, perhaps inadvertently, identified himself with the stage Irishman, who was always dressed in them. But the caricatures go far beyond such a casual identification, and the *Washington Post* cartoon in particular draws most explicitly on the nineteenth-century image of the Irishman as ape. Its politics and that of *Punch*'s strange identification of Wilde with blacked-up minstrels are spelled out in *Punch*'s version of Darwinism: 'A creature manifestly between the Gorilla and the Negro is to be met with in some of the lowest districts of London and Liverpool by adventurous explorers. It comes from Ireland, whence it has contrived to migrate; it belongs, in fact, to a tribe of Irish savages; the lowest species of the Irish Yahoo.'[26] Wilde, after his fall, was transformed into an ape-man, 'exhibited like an ape in a cage',[27] the caricature becoming reality; life, in its blackest joke, imitating art.

Being Irish meant that Wilde could never civilize America. His own persona was always open to being annexed to powerful racial images of barbarism, and therefore could never be a stable image of European cultivation. But the Irish ambivalence which made him ultimately incredible as an icon of English civility also allowed him to appropriate American barbarism in the forms which would prove, in the late twentieth century, to be most durable as aspects of mass consumer culture. He learned to make a virtue of ambivalence, to combine fame and infamy, proletarian egalitarianism and aesthetic dandyism. He learned how to be criminal and saint, artist and outlaw. He learned how to have it every way. And even though his career took on the logic of his identification with outlaws, the connections which he made between European style and the American frontier remain central to the mass culture of the closing years of this century.

Thirteen years after the auction of the household effects of Jesse James came the auction of the household effects of Oscar Wilde. A hundred years after that came the apotheosis of Oscar Wilde, when his name was inscribed inside Westminster Abbey. In the meantime, the distance between the two men as images of modern fame has narrowed almost to nothing.

The Wilde Irishman:
Oscar as Aesthete and Anarchist

JERUSHA McCORMACK

In the summer of 1893, a minor poet, visiting Oscar Wilde at his summer cottage, made some slighting remark about Home Rule. A small boy (whom the poet guessed to be Wilde's son Cyril), flushing with anger, asked whether the poet was not a Home Ruler. The poet was saved a reply only by the entry of Oscar. 'Ah!' said he. 'My own idea is that Ireland should rule England.'[1] Like much that is spontaneous in Wilde, the remark had a long history, not merely political but, in Wilde's case, an intimate one as well. His mother, Jane Francesca Elgee, had, under the pen-name of 'Speranza', gained a reputation for writing patriotic poetry and 'inflammatory' prose. Born of middle-class Protestant stock – the 'gentry' that traditionally supported the British government – Jane embarrassed her respectable Protestant relations with her anti-British stance.

Jane, however, felt no such divided loyalties. Anglo-Irish by class, she insisted on living as a hybrid. On the Anglo side, she pursued the distractions of a society belle while residing sedately with her mother on Leeson Street. On the Irish side, Speranza wrote as a revolutionary, a poet of the people whose verses were set to music by the street-singers of Dublin. During the revolt led by the Young Irelanders in 1848, Speranza wrote (anonymously) a notorious leader (entitled 'Jacta Alea Est' – 'The Die is Cast') for Charles Gavan Duffy's *Nation*: a trumpet-call to insurrection that caused the paper to be shut down and the article to be entered against the editor as proof of a charge of sedition.

As a woman, and a member of the leading class, Speranza herself was immune from such retribution. While Charles Gavan Duffy languished in gaol, Speranza attended a state ball at Dublin Castle. 'I went to the last Drawing room,' Jane reported to a friend, 'and Lord Aberdeen smiled very archly as he bent to kiss my cheek, which is the ceremony of presentation. I smiled too and thought of *Jacta Alea Est.*'[2]

Being kissed on the cheek by the agent of the government she publicly attacked only amused Speranza. Of a class which embodied contradictory allegiances – more Irish than the Irish themselves, at the same time the obvious support of an imposed and increasingly embattled English regime – Speranza herself thrived on contradictions and, as these multiplied, revelled in their patent irony. A fervent revolutionary, she predicted a popular revolt in Ireland, but distrusted democracy as mob rule, writing of the Fenians that 'it is a decidedly *democratic* movement and the gentry and the aristocracy will suffer much from them'.[3] Although (strictly speaking) Speranza was neither aristocratic nor middle-class, she lived with her husband, the eminent doctor William Wilde, in one of the houses on Dublin's Merrion Square abandoned by the ascendancy after the Act of Union. Just as they lived between the old class lines, so the Wildes flourished on both sides of the Irish cultural divide: lavish hosts to the new professional classes in Dublin, they spent much time also in the remote West of Ireland, among the Irish-speaking peasantry, whose folk-tales Sir William Wilde delighted in collecting.

Speranza's emotional commitments proved equally contradictory. As a young woman she had dedicated herself, as a writer, to freeing Ireland from the oppressor's wrong. After her marriage, her ardent nature found a new outlet in husband and children. Motherhood was a turning point. 'With this duty lovingly laid upon me,' she wrote a friend, 'what to me are Revolution or the struggle of an uprising Humanity?' After the birth of her second son, Oscar Fingal O'Flahertie Wills Wilde, she confessed to a friend (quoting a French writer, Jean Paul): '"a woman cannot live for her country and her children"'.[4]

Oscar inherited not only his mother's politics but her taste for living life at cross-purposes. Certainly Speranza, in the full glory of her contradictions, served as the model for the revolutionary heroine of his first play, *Vera, or The Nihilists*. In a reversal of Speranza's presentation at Dublin Castle, Vera appears in ball dress among the Nihilists, having come to their secret rendezvous straight from a masked dance at the Czar's Palace — a melodramatic enactment of her own divided loyalties: she had fallen in love with the Czarovitch. Although that love puts Vera at odds with herself, Wilde dramatizes it as having a single, concentrated source. In Speranza's own upholstered rhetoric, Wilde describes Vera's fervour as 'that Titan cry of the peoples for liberty, which in the Europe of our day is threatening thrones, and making governments unstable from Spain to Russia, and from north to southern seas. But it is a play not of politics but of passion.'[5]

In the end, that passion which fired Speranza's poetry also silenced her, as she willingly sacrificed herself on the altar of husband and children. Describing the ideal she sought in a man, she declared that 'in love I like to feel myself a slave — the difficulty is to find anyone capable of ruling me. I love them when I feel their power. . . .'[6] In like manner, Wilde's Vera is torn between revolutionary ardour and amorous submission. Unable to choose, she destroys herself, sacrificing her life simultaneously for a man and for Fatherland. Passion, and the contradictions into which it drives her, prove the cross of her martyrdom.

I

Wilde wrote *Vera* as his first bid for fame as a dramatist. In the event, his play never reached its London audience. When Wilde started to write (some time during 1880), Nihilism was still exotic; anarchism was not yet a byword; and the last Russian Czar to be assassinated was almost eighty years dead. But in true Wilde fashion the drama provided a script for history ('Literature always anticipates life,' Wilde later quipped[7]): on 13 March 1881, Alexander II, Czar of Russia, was assassinated by Nihilists. The fact that the Prince of Wales was himself married to the sister of the new Czarina gave cause for official concern. Emigrés were particularly suspect as agents of social unrest; another London exile, an anarchist by the name of Johann Most, published an article enthusiastically supporting the assassination. Under pressure from the Russian and German governments, the British authorities found Most guilty of incitement to murder heads of state and sentenced him to eighteen months' imprisonment.[8] A less direct route, it seems, was taken by the establishment in Wilde's case; apparently as the result of unofficial but influential representations, *Vera* was withdrawn from the English stage in November 1881 − the month it went into rehearsal.[9]

Wilde's prescience about the course of Russian history may be ascribed to instincts sharpened by his experience as the son of an Irish landlord. While Oscar was still a schoolboy, Sir William Wilde had bought a substantial estate on the shores of Lough Corrib in County Mayo, where he built Moytura House. After his death and her removal to London, Speranza depended on the rents from this property to augment a meagre income. But in 1880, the year Wilde wrote *Vera*, agitation among tenant farmers for reduced rents and ownership of land reached such a pitch that the *Pall Mall Gazette* commented: 'We have really to face in Ireland a social revolt of formidable magnitude.'[10] That revolt, organized by the Irish National Land League under Michael Davitt, and espoused by the new leader of the Home Rule Party, Charles Stewart Parnell, constituted nothing less than a land war. In rural areas of Ireland, 'Captain Moonlight' (a generic term for the murder squads that operated under cover of darkness) was notorious for his atrocities against the agents of the English absentee landlords. Speranza wrote that year to a friend: 'Ireland is in a very unquiet state − I fear the people will now refuse to pay rents and whoever enforces payment will be assuredly shot − I despair of my beloved Irish at last. . . . .'[11] The violence was to spread to Dublin itself. In 1882, within months of *Vera*'s withdrawal and following almost three years of agrarian agitation of an intensity unusual even for Ireland, two high-ranking officials of British rule were murdered in Phoenix Park. One of these, Lord Frederick Cavendish, had once dined with Wilde's parents at Merrion Square. The other, T. H. Burke, a Catholic and nephew of Cardinal Wiseman, had been active in seeking a Civil List pension for Speranza.[12]

Given their connection with his own history, Wilde's response to the assassination by the Irish nationalist Invincibles was, predictably, ambivalent. 'When liberty comes with hands dabbled in blood, it is hard to shake hands with her.' Then he added: 'We forget how much England is to blame. She is reaping the fruit of seven centuries of injustice.'[13]

By this time a resident of England for eight years, Wilde was careful to express such bald nationalism within the context of its counter-truth. This was not merely diplomacy, but the actual character of Wilde's intelligence. 'A Truth in art', he was to write, 'is that whose contradictory is also true.'[14] By this definition, art – and his status as an artist – permitted Wilde to test the divided allegiance of his own contradictory fate. If his family in Ireland, being Anglo-Irish, had been in fact a queer kind of English people, in England, Wilde himself was a queer kind of Irishman, at once more English than the English themselves, an Oxford graduate, a dandy, a figure with a public who came to recognize in him a parody both of the Irishman and the proper English gentleman. The Irishman was straight out of the Celtic stereotype – wild, anarchical, imaginative, witty, passionate and self-destructive. The Englishman, a straight aristocratic prototype – cool, elegant, contemptuous, manipulative, obsessed with position and its signs in dress and manner. At some point, both colluded: the Irishman was lazy, the aristocrat leisured; the Irishman paradoxical; the aristocrat, systemically rude – contradicting others as the Irishman contradicted himself – the Irish bull rendered as an English snub.

Wilde's genius lies in his creation of himself as a figure who was a terrorist by another name, a dandy who chooses not to nail himself to a cross but to nail others with his cross-talk, to expose the shoddy half-truths and double standards by which they operate: in other words, an *agent provocateur*.

A shift away from direct political action – for Wilde, almost always idealistic and self-destructive – to indirect political engagement may be marked in Wilde's very first play, in which the focus of the drama obviously shifts from the martyr to the dandy. Vera may be its sacrificial heroine (martyred on the cross of her own dilemma) but Prince Paul, as dandy, defines the play's artistic strategy. He is the truest of all Nihilists: playing traitor to both Czar and revolutionary, he exposes the political manoeuvres of both sides as a game, an elaborate performance dictated by a debased and empty rhetoric. His wit attacks every value on which the drama is based: love, family, loyalty, sacrifice. Disbelieving equally in both sides, Prince Paul plays off one against the other: an absolute Nihilist in that he believes nothing and in nothing. Or as Wilde defined him elsewhere: 'The Nihilist, that strange martyr who has no faith, who goes to the stake without enthusiasm, and dies for what he does not believe in, is a purely literary product. He was invented by Tourgenieff, and completed by Dostoieffski.'[15]

Being a literary invention, the Nihilist could not exist outside art, or rather he imported the values of art into political action. In the history of anarchism, the Nihilist's appearance coincided with an aestheticizing of terrorism. During the 1880s and 1890s, especially in England and France, the anarchist became a recognized literary character: from R. L. Stevenson's 'The Dynamiter' in his *New Arabian Nights* (1882) to Henry James's *Princess Casamassima* (1886) and Joseph Conrad's *The Secret Agent* (1907) – not to speak of the comic saboteur in Wilde's own 'Lord Arthur Saville's Crime'. Conversely, in France and (less frequently) in England, aesthetes became anarchists who regarded acts of political terrorism, such as bombing, as art-acts (one recalls Félix Fénéon's description of the 'intimate charm' of a bomb which exploded at a police station).[16] Alternatively, these new-style anarchists devised art-forms which employed a kind of terrorism: a trend which one might date from Rimbaud or Alfred Jarry and which culminated in Artaud's theatre of cruelty or the art-acts of Dadaism.

In short, during the closing decades of the century, the distinction between political action and political speech-acts had eroded to the point where Wilde could declare that 'talk itself is a sort of spiritualised action'.[17] The assertion came easily to Wilde, originating as he did from a country where words had the force of deeds.[18] Conversely, in the politics of the day, action could now be identified with a form of discourse. By means of the 'propaganda of the deed', anarchism entered a realm of cultural semiotics, whereby acts might be read as signatures of specific political agendas. Moreover, from the 1880s until after the Great War, these agendas were themselves spelled out in a tide of manifestos (particularly in France) – aesthetic and political and aestheto-political.

Wilde entered the fray with one immortal piece, 'The Soul of Man under Socialism'. Published in the *Fortnightly Review* in February 1891, it is one of the only Wilde essays that is usually read 'straight', as sincere and from the heart. But in the guise of a gentle literary essay on socialism, mischief is afoot. It soon dawns on the attentive reader that what is advocated is not socialism at all, but pure anarchy, once defined by Arnold in a famous essay under that rubric, as 'doing as one likes'.[19] Wilde argues for nothing less than the abolition of all authority, since 'all authority is quite degrading. It degrades those who exercise it, and degrades those over whom it is exercised.'[20] Thus, Wilde argues, 'Disobedience . . . is man's original virtue. It is through disobedience that progress has been made, through disobedience and through rebellion.'[21]

Why were Wilde's words not taken as words of sedition? He was now (after Parnell) one of London's more famous Irishmen and Irish issues had always played an important part in the programme of British anarchism, which, in 1891, manifested the first signs of organizing itself independently of the socialist and Fabian movements.[22] Like his fellow London exile George Bernard Shaw, Wilde had moved freely in radical circles during the 1880s, befriending such prophets as William Morris and Prince Kropotkin and participating in or otherwise supporting their causes. In 1886, for instance, Wilde signed George Bernard Shaw's petition supporting the American anarchists credited with instigating Chicago's Haymarket Riots. And yet there is every indication that Wilde's essay was not (certainly in terms of policy) taken seriously.[23] Its political fate was to belong to a future in which 'The Soul of Man under Socialism' was read eagerly by the young revolutionaries of China and Russia (who would not have been alerted, in translation, to its various modes of irony).[24]

Paradoxically, its Irish context may have in fact acted on this occasion against readers taking it in earnest. In the actual issue of the *Fortnightly Review*, 'The Soul of Man under Socialism' was placed alongside an essay by Grant Allen on 'The Celt in English Art'. Is it possible that, in writing his article, Wilde himself was simply living up to his name – and to the stereotype of the Celt? According to Matthew Arnold, the Celt is 'undisciplinable, anarchical, and turbulent by nature . . . just the opposite of the

Anglo-Saxon temperament, disciplinable and steadily obedient within certain limits . . .'.[25] Within that paradigm, Arnold located the Irish as the unacknowledged and rejected shadow-self of the English: the origin of that self-delighting Hellenic consciousness suppressed by the English in their mistaken self-identification with a stern Hebraic/Teutonic racial inheritance.[26]

Arnold went on to argue that instituting a Chair of Celtic Literature would be an important step in restoring Britain's Celtic, or better, self. But Grant Allen did Arnold one better, by identifying the anarchical Celt with the very source of the artistic. 'The great and victorious aesthetic movement,' he observed, 'is a direct result . . . of the Celtic reflux on Teutonic Britain, and of the resurgence of the Celtic substratus against Teutonic dominance. . . . The Celt comes back upon us with all the Celtic gifts and all the Celtic ideals – imagination, fancy, decorative skill, artistic handicraft; free land, free speech, human equality, human brotherhood.'[27] Like Arnold – and Wilde – Allen believed that race was the determinant of culture and that the case of the Celt was (to quote their master, Renan) an example of 'that great law by which the primitive race of the invaded country always ends by getting the upper hand'.[28]

Finally, to emphasize the 'connexion between the decorative revival and the Celtic upheaval of radicalism and socialism', Allen points specifically to William Morris and Oscar Wilde. 'Mr. Oscar Wilde,' he wrote, 'whom only fools ever mistook for a mere charlatan, and whom wise men know for a man of rare insight and strong common-sense, is an Irishman to the core'.[29] Framed by such a declaration, how could Wilde's essay be read other than as performative, a part of Wilde's own definition of himself to an English public, as an Irish artist – and *provocateur*?

Wilde's mode of attack would underwrite such a reading, for what Wilde sought to subvert was not a political programme but the cant by which his English public justified their politics. If the Englishman, as Arnold defined him, lived by the phrase – 'those formulas which . . . he has always at hand in order to save himself the trouble of thinking'[30] – then Wilde is determined that he should die by it: almost every shibboleth about the values of property, family and altruism is systematically detonated by following it to its logical (and absurd) extreme. If Wilde's attack was rhetorical, it took this route because it aimed to expose a corruption not of institutions, but of language itself: 'one of the results of the extraordinary tyranny of authority', he writes in a crucial passage, 'is that words are absolutely distorted from their proper and simple meaning, and are used to express the obverse of their right signification'.[31]

Such radical estrangement from the English mother-tongue may be traced to Wilde's Irish origins. He came to manhood in a colony where, as he once observed, the 'peasants' were bilingual[32] and living under pressure to adopt a foreign tongue. From his prolonged stays with his family in County Mayo, Wilde had learned a little Irish himself (his own son, Vyvyan, recalls Wilde singing him a lullaby in Gaelic[33]). Wilde was also, in his own style, aware of 'Celtic' deviations in occasional turns of phrase.[34] For Wilde, it was the issue of language which sealed his sense of displacement; as he wrote to Edmond de Goncourt (in his stepmother tongue): 'Français de sympathie, je suis Irlandais de race, et les Anglais m'ont condamné à parler le langage de Shakespeare.'[35]

More significantly, having come to the centre from the periphery, he arrived as an outsider, attuned to the double-speak of the empire at home. Empire-speak mirrored its master. Just as the Englishman prided himself on his integrity, empire-speak presented itself as single, insistent and sincere. It was spoken in one tone, without nuance or irony; and it was the voice of passion, commitment and command – the voice, if you wish, of Vera – and of what passes as truth. It speaks the big words that men die for – God, King, Country. And it presumes unanimous consent.

To this single, passionate voice, Wilde proposes another, that of Prince Paul: one that speaks double, in the ironical and self-cancelling wit of the dandy. The dandy's style has often been described as 'paradoxical'. Wilde, versed in classical literature, frequently does deploy paradox; but, as he developed his own style, he occasionally jettisoned paradox for a native Hiberno-Irish speech form called the Irish Bull. The Irish Bull sounds like paradox, but is, in fact, its empty mime. It keeps the form of logic, while outraging reason and bringing it to a violent halt. As Wilde once quipped (in a different context) this idiom hits below the belt of intellect. If language is the agent of authority, the Irish Bull is a verbal bombshell, exposing the arbitrary nature of the speech-act itself.[36] In terms of Wilde's own divided linguistic allegiances, the Irish Bull might be seen as the colonist's revenge on the imperialist father-tongue.

In speech, then, Prince Paul is an honorary Irishman. His wit is fatally attuned to the double standard implicit in big words such as family, loyalty, property. None of these words survives his barrage; they implode by virtue of their own emptiness, exposed as the shams they are, the counterfeit currency of bankrupt values in which no one really any longer believes. At first this may seem merely destructive; for all his glorious cynicism, Prince Paul cannot in fact save Vera from dying for the big words, 'love' and 'Fatherland'. He is a mere saboteur, throwing verbal grenades to no great effect. Vera's 'sincerity' overwhelms him – her futile sacrificial gesture subsuming his own futile wit. It took Wilde all of fifteen years to incorporate that form of futility into a really lethal instrument, for which the icon is the dandy.

II

As a term, the dandy may be taken as a kind of shorthand for a political phenomenon which Wilde perfected on the stage: he represents the transactions by which the powerless, the nobodies, assume power and importance. As was said of that great English dandy, Beau Brummell: 'He was nobody, who had made himself somebody, and gave the law to everybody.'[37] He is the perfect nonentity who is made over into a compelling popular image: perhaps the precursor of the modern mass-media politician. The dandy is more than a man of fashion. His importance is inscribed by Charles Baudelaire, as 'an institution outside the law'.[38] He sees that the dandy's pursuit of style is not a mere act of homage to fashion but, in fact, a passionate revolt against convention itself.

Revolt is not repudiation. Its potency relies on the force of what it repudiates. As another exponent of dandyism, Barbey d'Aurevilly, observed: 'Dandyism, while still respecting the conventionalities, plays with them. While admitting their power, it suffers from and revenges itself upon them, and pleads them as an excuse against themselves; dominates and is dominated by them in turn.'[39] It is this reciprocity of turn and counter-turn, the implicit structure of an act of provocation and revenge, upon which I wish to focus in the performance of Wilde's dandyism.

Politically, Baudelaire notes, 'dandyism appears especially in those periods of transition when democracy has not yet become all-powerful, and when aristocracy is only partially weakened and discredited'.[40] At such a time of insecurity, conventions become elevated into ideals, deriving their authority from a kind of communal team-think which masks pervasive double standards.

Such a scenario graphically describes what was known as 'society' in late Victorian England. Constructed as a veritable cathedral of bourgeois denial and double-think, its unparalleled degree of conformity was enforced by a policy of exclusion. Given over to the tyranny of niceness and order, it was an airless world built on the rejection of all that threatened – or seemed to threaten – its uneasy security. As Wilde's heroines are eloquent testimony, ostracism from such a society constituted a fate worse than death.

Into this scenario the dandy arrives: a leisured outsider who conceives of himself (in the words of Baudelaire) as 'establishing a new kind of aristocracy'. Despising the society into which he seeks initiation, the dandy takes his revenge by creating himself in its image, miming its clothes, its manners and mannerisms. ('Imitation', as Wilde observed, 'can be made the sincerest form of insult.'[41]) Inherently exaggerated, such mimicry exposes the fissures of its own performance: the double standards on which it rests. What the dandy performs is a kind of psychic jujitsu – he 'throws people' by using the force of their attitude to defeat them. In effect, by means of his performance the dandy gets his audience to share his contempt for itself.

Arriving in Oxford from Dublin, Wilde became more English than the English themselves: he abandoned his Irish accent and beat the scholars at their own game, scooping a Double First. Although born of the 'gentry', he, like Baudelaire's dandy, assumed the status of an English aristocrat, leisured, extravagant, charming and mannered. If these virtues were slightly exaggerated, it was only to give a double edge to the performance, parodying as well the stereotype of the Irish: lazy, improvident, charming and witty. As Arnold trenchantly observed, the Irish had, by their very nature, more in common with the virtues of the English upper class than either had with the hard-working, thrifty and dour English middle class.[42]

That conspiracy of the dandy with the aristocracy to undermine middle-class values defines the action of Wilde's only other political play, *An Ideal Husband*. Staged in 1895, the play's title is shadowed by the scandal of Charles Stewart

Parnell, whose flawed private life caused him to be deposed (in 1891) as leader of the [Irish] Home Rule party. It is generally agreed that Parnell was crucified on the cross of bourgeois sexual hypocrisy; his political agenda of Home Rule sacrificed to the middle-class ideal of Home Life.

In *An Ideal Husband*, Wilde rewrites Parnell's fate as comedy. Here, Parnell's dilemma is inverted: it is a flaw of public honesty which dooms the politician's private life. But in Wilde's version, he is rescued from the cross of middle-class hypocrisy by that master of cross-talk, the Wildean dandy.

In brief its hero, Sir Robert Chiltern, flourishes in his wife's belief that his apparent political integrity qualifies him also as an 'ideal husband'. A mysterious woman appears to shatter this cosy illusion: Mrs Cheveley, who has secret information about Robert Chiltern's past. She attempts to blackmail him; when this fails, Mrs Cheveley tells her dirty secret to his wife, who then confronts him:

LADY CHILTERN: You sold a Cabinet secret for money! You began your life with fraud! You built up your career on dishonour! Oh, tell me it is not true! Lie to me! Lie to me! Tell me it is not true.

SIR ROBERT CHILTERN: What this woman said is quite true. But, Gertrude, listen to me. You don't realise how I was tempted. Let me tell you the whole thing. (*Goes towards her.*)

LADY CHILTERN: Don't come near me. Don't touch me. I feel as if you had soiled me for ever. Oh! what a mask you have been wearing all these years! A horrible painted mask! You sold yourself for money. Oh! a common thief were better. You put yourself up to sale to the highest bidder! You were bought in the market. You lied to the whole world. And yet you will not lie to me.[43]

Lady Chiltern here falls into the rhetoric of shocked virtue. Believing − in womanly fashion − that 'One's past is what one is', she finds her husband guilty of gross deception, of wearing a 'horrible painted mask'. But, in the same breath, she begs him to tell her that the information is not true, even though she believes it to be so ('Lie to me! Lie to me!'). On close reading, the rhetoric confesses to a double standard: that Lady Chiltern is concerned not so much with the morality of the deed as with the painful feelings that it arouses in her. As a woman, she is apt to become the victim of her feelings ('Women represent the irrational', as her husband remarks). She now asks to be released from them. Significantly, it is the dandy, Lord Goring, who comes to the rescue.

His critical intervention occurs in Acts III and IV under the banner of dandyism. To reinforce his otherwise hollow performance, Wilde's stage directions for Act III invoke the image of the perfect dandy: 'He is a mask with a manner. Of his intellectual or emotional life, history knows nothing. He represents the dominance of form'.[44] These lines serve to define the double mission of Lord Goring: to neutralize the effect of the history embodied in Mrs Cheveley and thus preserve the dominance of form implicit in Lord Goring's performance as an ideal husband (privately) and politician (publicly). To achieve the first, Lord Goring must intervene in the plot, the agent of history. This he accomplishes in Act III by turning the tables on Mrs Cheveley; through sheer coincidence he succeeds in blackmailing the blackmailer, thus bringing the potentially tragic train of events to a halt.

To achieve the second objective, the preservation of Sir Robert's political 'image', Lord Goring must convert his wife to the creed of dandyism. She represents a threat to it because she is herself ostensibly 'sincere', a believer that appearance must match actuality. Lord Goring subverts such a simple-minded view by pointing out that different standards must be applied to men: 'A man's life', he tells her, 'is of more value than a woman's. It has larger issues, wider scope, greater ambitions. A woman's life revolves in curves of emotions. It is upon lines of intellect that a man's life progresses.'[45] In accepting this sexual double standard, Lady Chiltern is persuaded that her insistence on integrity should not interfere with Sir Robert's success. Repeating Lord Goring's formula to her husband, she remarks: 'I have just learnt this, and much else with it, from Lord Goring. And I will not spoil your life for you, nor see you spoil it as a sacrifice to me, a useless sacrifice!'[46] Sir Robert Chiltern's career has been preserved and home rule re-established — although at some cost to dramatic probability and moral probity. (One wonders if this similar formula could not also have rescued Parnell?[47])

Lord Goring is able to save Sir Robert precisely because he understands that the single, integrated 'moral' self is a fiction. Those who demand it, and represent its standards of absolute purity, are women. But the women, as Lord Goring perceives, are in fact playing a double game: Mrs Cheveley had herself a guilty secret; Lady Chiltern does not really care about the truth of the matter (she does, after all, beg her husband to lie to her). As a dandy, Lord Goring's power depends on an open acknowledgement that all selves are fabricated by a kind of duplicity, whether that of moral hypocrisy (such a Lady Chiltern's) or by conscious double-dealing (such as Mrs Cheveley's). Operating on a double standard himself, he exposes the duplicity of others. It is by virtue of this action that Lord Goring 'stands in immediate relation to modern life, makes it indeed, and so masters it'.[48]

Here for the first time, Wilde perfects the dandy as one with the power of exposing empire-speak so as to reveal its forked tongue and the actual spiritual anarchy on which it rests.

III

Unlike Yeats or Joyce, Wilde never devised a new style. What he did invent, however, was an instrument to blow up the old style of Victorian high seriousness — one so lethal that when he came to employ it himself, in the letter from prison to Robbie Ross (later published as *De Profundis*), it blew up in his own hands: as in this passage about his boy companions:

People thought it dreadful of me to have entertained at dinner the evil things of life, and to have found pleasure in their company. But they, from the point of view through which I, as an artist in life, approached them, were delightfully suggestive and stimulating. It was like feasting with panthers. The danger was half the excitement.[49]

While Wilde intended here to be writing at his most sincere, the very style prevents us from taking him seriously. (One can see why Shaw dismissed the whole letter as 'comedy'.[50]) People found it 'dreadful' (that is, they half envied him) that he had entertained 'evil things' (boy prostitutes) to 'dinner' − that wonderful note of propriety! The second sentence merely explicates the double-talk of the first: clearly the audience found Wilde's conduct 'suggestive and stimulating', as he found that of his company. Wilde's 'artistic' point of view in a way calls their bluff; it is of course not aesthetic but sexual. In this passage the language operates so that audience and writer engage in an unspoken complicity to exonerate the action.

Such exoneration is possible because Wilde uses the language of his audience. The last lines of *Lady Windermere's Fan* and of *The Importance of Being Earnest* may demonstrate how language has been cut adrift and set afloat; and what distance key words such as 'good' and 'earnest' have travelled from their dictionary meanings. Wilde begins not with dictionary meanings, however, but with a language which is already faithless, the language of common double-talk. In Wilde, Thomas Mann discovered much of the essential Nietzsche, his 'furious war against morality', and his transvaluation of moral into aesthetic values.[51] But Wilde may not have read Nietzsche (who was not translated into English until 1896): nor did he need him. Victorian hypocrisy was in itself a transvaluation of values. Thus 'evil' does duty in the above passage not in a metaphysical or even strictly moral sense, but in the sense of vice, scandal or even foible. It sails perilously close to the implication of 'naughty', a lovable vice − precisely the type of self-cancelling oxymoron which distinguishes the dandy's style.

Wilde employed this language in order to expose the public's double standard, its purely manipulative use of such words. 'Wickedness', he once wrote, 'is a myth invented by good people to account for the curious attractiveness of others.'[52] In other words, 'good' people often try to discredit attractive people (presumably for the threat they pose to their goodness) by calling them 'wicked'. In doing so, 'good' people of course also discredit themselves as 'good'. The strategy of such a statement is not aesthetic, but political − if 'political' may be taken in the wider sense as the art by which others are manipulated. In *An Ideal Husband*, Wilde was perhaps the first to acknowledge openly the importance of style in politics. At the end of the play, Robert Chiltern's career survives his disgrace because his wife is persuaded, against the facts, to adopt the public's attitude towards him − to maintain what is now called a politician's 'image'.

That image is, of course, in turn constructed by the politician from what he imagines to be the expectations of his audience: a mental image constantly present to him as a model by which to represent himself: literally, to present the public to itself again. Or, as Wilde observed, 'It is the spectator, and not life, that art really mirrors.'[53]

Such a performance, therefore, requires not merely collaboration but complicity on the part of the audience. That actor implicates his audience, forcing them to recognize themselves in his own transparent dissembling. What Wilde asks of his public is exoneration. He gains it by means of a kind of blackmail, by threatening to expose their double standards, their hypocrisy, their necessary duplicities. The public, in response, treats the play as a work of art, thus denying the charges. Yet they are, by their laughter, which is both recognition and assent, implicated. As in blackmail, both parties emerge discredited. But as in blackmail, it is not credit but power that is at stake.

In a review of *An Ideal Husband*, George Bernard Shaw caught the acute discomfort of Wilde's audience. 'They laugh angrily at his epigrams,' he wrote, 'like a child who is coaxed into being amused in the very act of setting up a yell of rage. . . .' Shaw understands the rage as the inevitable outcome of the cultural divide between the Irish playwright and his English public:

All the literary dignity of the play, all the imperturbable good sense and good manners with which Mr Wilde makes his wit pleasant to his comparatively stupid audience, cannot quite overcome the fact that Ireland is of all countries the most foreign to England, and that to the Irishman (and Mr Wilde is almost as acutely Irish an Irishman as the Iron Duke of Wellington) there is nothing in the world quite so exquisitely comic as an Englishman's seriousness. It becomes tragic, perhaps, when the Englishman acts on it; but that occurs too seldom to be taken into account, a fact which intensifies the humour of the situation, the total result being the Englishman utterly unconscious of his real self, Mr Wilde keenly observant of it and playing on the self-unconsciousness with irresistible humour, and finally, of course, the Englishman annoyed with himself for being amused at his own expense, and for being unable to convict Mr Wilde of what seems an obvious misunderstanding of human nature. He is shocked, too, at the danger to the foundations of society when seriousness is publicly laughed at. And to complete the oddity of the situation, Mr Wilde, touching what he himself reverences, is absolutely the most sentimental dramatist of the day.[54]

As this perceptive review makes clear, the strategy deployed by Wilde's dandies is a kind of ritual provocation that effectively hands control over to the audience. He did so by dealing literally on the audience's own terms, constructing the dandy as a kind of mime of ritual cant which exposes it as cant. By its laughter, Wilde's audience betrays recognition while denying implication. In making Wilde's dramas a success, his audience (as Wilde pointed out in his curtain speech to *Lady Windermere's Fan*) declared itself a success. When it turned on Wilde, his audience did so with the ferocity of those betrayed by a figure of their own making. To use Wilde's own phrase in another context, their reaction was the 'rage of Caliban seeing his own face in a glass'.[55]

Such strenuous, potentially lethal, interaction between the dandy and his audience is the logical consequence of its intimacy. By accepting the conventions of his audience even while subverting them, Wilde's witty despots operated within a closed circle of response. How many of Wilde's texts – from *The Picture of Dorian Gray* through *Salomé* to *The Ballad of Reading Gaol* – may be construed as variations of this cycle of reciprocity: of murder becoming, in effect, suicide? In *Vera, or The Nihilists*, Wilde demonstrated how paradox operated as the verbal equivalent of suicide, cancelling out any allegiances by which the self might be sustained. How fair is it to say that Wilde ensured the equivalent fate in flinging verbal detonations from the dock? A great deal of the Wilde mythos tacitly or explicitly invokes the concepts of 'victimization' and 'martyrdom', implying an act of unprovoked violence against him. Wilde himself never underestimated the rage of the artist or the force of his scorn, even while acknowledging it to be predicated upon a reciprocal and answering violence. Until his dandyism is interpreted in terms of protest and provocation and even in terms of larger political dissent, it may not be possible to understand the full implications of Wilde's claim that he stood in symbolic relation to the art and culture of his age.

Wilde and Parnell

W. J. McCormack

I take it for granted that you are all familiar with the story called 'Silver Blaze'. That is the first narrative in the *Memoirs of Sherlock Holmes*, published in 1894, in which the great detective solves the mystery of a racehorse's disappearance by noting that the guard dog had not barked in the night. In other words, the thief was well known to the dog, who remained suspiciously silent. If you think that horses and dogs have little to do with Oscar Wilde, let me remind you of his definition of fox-hunting – 'the unspeakable in pursuit of the uneatable'. My concern is not so much with what is unspeakable – the English squirearchy in pinks, or the love that dares not speak its name – but rather with something which remains very oddly unspoken in Wilde's words as they are available to us today.

But in order to make sense of this curious omission from Wilde's recorded words, this non-barking dog, I have to introduce two additional interrelated themes. The first of these is quite simply politics. Traditionally, anyone interested in Wilde's politics was referred to 'The Soul of Man under Socialism', which was first published in the *Fortnightly Review* in February 1891. Some objected that 'The Soul' was an unconvincing blend of attitudes which Wilde derived from the two major influences of his Oxford days – those of John Ruskin and Walter Pater. Contradictory or not, Wilde's affirmation of an anarchistic and individualistic version of socialism undoubtedly contributed to the maintenance of his reputation on the Continent in the first three decades of the twentieth century. In other words, his survival as a writer of serious import largely depended on this understanding of his radicalism.

Since the World War II, and especially since the 1960s, notions of political radicalism have changed and nowhere more strikingly than in academia. In the post-modern discourses of the present, sex rather than socialism, homosexuality rather than the dialectic of human labour, sets the agenda. Consequently, 'The Soul of Man under Socialism' is a title wholly unrecognizable to the English undergraduate of the late 1990s, the centenary of what Chris Baldick has reasonably described as Wilde's martyrdom. Other priorities reign. With little regard for the eleventh-hour nature of the announcement, Alan Sinfield has renamed the age we live in the Wilde Century, and Richard Ellmann's comprehensive, if also rather error-haunted, biography has been challenged by a specifically gay life of Wilde.

Yet there is an important stage between the forgetting of the socialist Wilde and the discovery of PMO − Post-Modern Oscar. Twenty-five years ago Richard Ellmann published a collection of reviews and articles by Wilde, which he called *The Artist as Critic*. From this selection of casual writings, we have been able to discover a man with determined political opinions on the issues of his day and with a determination to express these opinions even in difficult circumstances and on unexpected occasions. For example, in an unsigned article in the *Pall Mall Gazette* of 17 February 1887, Wilde brusquely dismissed the obscurities of contemporary verse, and insisted that:

> The struggle to live in all parts of Western Europe, and perhaps especially England, is so fierce that we are in danger of having all that is idealistic and beautiful crushed out of us by the steam engine and the manipulations of the Stock Exchanges. We were never in greater need of good poets, and never better able than in this practical age to do without literary medicine men and mystery mongers.

In local terms this could be read simply as an early statement of the basic contradiction elaborated in 'The Soul of Man under Socialism', a contradiction between the utilitarianism of Ruskin (art improves the world of ordinary people) and the aestheticism of Pater (in Wilde's summary, 'all art is entirely useless'). But in broader, European terms, the attitudes revealed in the *Pall Mall Gazette* could be assimilated to what is known as romantic anti-capitalism, essentially a protest against the manifest violence and ugliness of contemporary society which nevertheless failed to identify the underlying connection between causes and effects.

What is striking in Ellmann's presentation of these articles and reviews is the relatively little attention he pays to 'The Soul of Man under Socialism'. Yes, of course, it occupies more pages than any of the miscellaneous writings which precede it. But in his introduction Ellmann refers to it only twice − and on both occasions he takes up the issue of crime. Crime is the second of my preliminary themes in approaching the relationship between Wilde and Parnell. And to a large extent Ellmann as both editor and biographer is concerned to examine in the complex case of Oscar Wilde the implications of a late-romantic notion in which crime and art are seen as complementary activities, comparable values. In his first allusion to the essay of 1891, Ellmann quotes the remark that 'Crime . . . under certain conditions, may be said to have created individualism.' In the second, he cited as an anticipation by Wilde of his own fate the remark that 'even in prison a man can be quite free'. Thus summarized, Wilde's major political statement is transformed into a series of epigrams on the topic of crime, epigrams in which the value of crime as a resistance to existing social arrangements is approved. It hardly needs to be added that, in his fiction, Wilde explored the tortuous avenues opened up by this topic — comically in 'Lord Arthur Savile's Crime', tragically in *The Picture of Dorian Gray*.

It is very difficult to say anything original about Wilde's novel, and so I will stick to a few seemingly unimportant crude facts. The origins of the work lie close together with plans made by an American publisher, J. M. Stoddart, to recruit British contributors to *Lippincott's Monthly Magazine*. In pursuit of this scheme, he organized a dinner party in London on 30 August 1889, at which Wilde was an honoured guest together with Arthur Conan Doyle and the Irish member of parliament T. P. Gill. The occasion was a great success, Stoddart buying rights on two as yet unwritten novels, *The Picture of Dorian Gray* and the second of Doyle's Sherlock Holmes novels, *The Sign of Four*. From the outset, Wilde's only novel was contextualized by a concern with crime and detection. It appeared in *Lippincott's* issue for July 1890. Immediately hostile reaction set in, as evidenced in the *Scots Observer* review, which accused Wilde of writing for 'outlawed noblemen and perverted telegraph-boys', a reference to a scandal of the previous year. Wilde sustained public debate of his work by replying to such criticism, by publishing a 'preface' to the novel in the *Fortnightly Review* in March 1891, and finally by extensively revising and augmenting the fiction for publication as a book in April. W. B. Yeats favourably reviewed the novel in *United Ireland* in September 1891.

It is now time to retrace our steps and to consider a different set of occurrences among the Irish notables who were so prominent in London society at this time. Writing as a Wicklowman, I do not have to emphasize the extent to which British politics in the 1880s was dominated by another man from Wicklow, Charles Stewart Parnell. In 1880, the leader of the Irish Party was tried with others on charges of conspiracy arising out of Land League activities, and, though the jury disagreed in this case, he was rearrested the following year. For nearly seven months, Parnell conducted his political campaign from a — rather comfortable — suite of cells in Kilmainham Gaol. Four days after his triumphant release, Chief Secretary Cavendish and his under-secretary were murdered by 'Invincibles' in the Phoenix Park.

Though Parnell was in no way implicated or compromised by this incident, an association between Irish politics and crime was powerfully established in the British public mind. Yet it was not only in the public sphere that such associations were dangerous: in November 1884, the bearer (probably self-appointed) of a message from Parnell to Chamberlain on the topic of renewal of a Prevention of Crime Act was Captain William Henry O'Shea. The indelicacy of this mediation — O'Shea was already well aware of his wife's affair with Parnell — was nicely matched in the general election of exactly one year later, Parnell's followers exactly equalling in numbers the Liberal majority over the Conservatives in the House of Commons. Even before the election, Katharine O'Shea had also acted as political go-between for her lover and Gladstone, the Prime Minister. In 1886, the government fell, Gladstone became Prime Minister once again, and at a by-election in Galway O'Shea was imposed as Parnell's candidate against the internal opposition of many in the Irish Party. On 24 May 1886, the *Pall Mall Gazette* published a paragraph entitled 'Mr Parnell's Suburban Retreat', the first public allusion to his cohabiting with Mrs O'Shea. In the same month Wilde signed George Bernard Shaw's petition supporting the American anarchists at the centre of Chicago's Haymarket Riots; throughout the year he contributed to the *Pall Mall Gazette* and, at some not exactly identified date, was initiated into homosexual practice by Robbie Ross, whose seventeenth birthday fell on 25 May.

In the public domain, the following year was dominated by a number of specially commissioned articles originally published in *The Times* and reissued in pamphlet form. The accusation levelled against Home-Rulers, that under Parnell they were complicit in murder and other outrages, was sustained into 1888 and in August a Special Commission of judges was appointed to investigate what was familiarly known as 'Parnellism and Crime'. At a hearing in February 1889, the journalist Richard Pigott was exposed as a forger and the evidence against Parnell discredited. In April and May, a vindicated Parnell himself testified before the Commission and on 19 May Mrs O'Shea's wealthy aunt died, leaving a legacy sufficient to liberate wife from husband. On Christmas Eve, Captain O'Shea filed for divorce.

It would be fatuous to attempt any parallel chronology of Wilde's doings at this time, for he occupied a far inferior place in the public's awareness of its own critical condition. Yet there is something to be said of a shift in his journalism, away from the largely *belle-lettriste* reviews of 1885–6, towards a more aggressive stance. The article already quoted, emphasizing the difficulty of living conditions in Western Europe generally, appeared in February 1887 in the *Pall Mall Gazette*. In May, 'Lord Arthur Savile's Crime' began to appear in the *Court and Society Review*, just as *The Times* renewed publication of the 'Parnellism and Crime' series of articles. At the beginning of 1888, Wilde gave a lecture in Bournemouth on the eighteenth-century boy-poet Thomas Chatterton, who fabricated impressive fifteenth-century poems but committed suicide in poverty and despair. On 1 March 1889, Richard Pigott committed suicide following the exposure as forgeries of the letters allegedly written by Parnell. In April, Wilde wrote to the publisher William Blackwood offering a story in dialogue, 'The Portrait of Mr W. H.', in which an enthusiastic critic of Shakespeare's sonnets forges a portrait of an untraceable young man to whom he is convinced the poems were addressed; like the real-life forger, once discovered in his fabrication, the critic responsible for the false portrait commits suicide. 'The Portrait of Mr W. H.', published in July 1889, is directly followed by the Stoddart dinner-party in August, at which *The Picture of Dorian Gray* was effectively conceived. When news of O'Shea's divorce broke over Christmas, Wilde was at work on his novel or, rather, he was stalled in the middle of it.

By the time the divorce was heard in November 1890, *Dorian Gray* had been published in its magazine but not in its book version. 'The Soul of Man under Socialism' had also appeared in the *Fortnightly Review*, and work had begun on the first of the social comedies (*Lady Windermere's Fan*). As I have suggested, Wilde's response to hostile reviews of his *Lippincott's* story was to extend its central theme into a veritable philosophy of art and literature. In April 1891, W. H.

Smith's (the railway-station booksellers and arbiters of suburban taste) refused to stock the book version because it was, in their word, 'filthy'.

All that was taking place in England. In Ireland, the furious conflict between Parnell's supporters and the majority of the Irish Party who required his resignation was fought out in terms no less extreme. On the surface, the two crises differ in every important respect: the one arising from the publication of a short novel, the other from a vote of confidence in a political leader. Yet the common denominator was the recurrent and pervasive Victorian phenomenon of a double life. Parnell was both a bachelor and an undeclared sexual partner of a woman whose husband was politically sustained by the rival. Dorian Gray was an unblemished figure and a hidden icon of corruption and depravity. Moreover, the creator of Dorian Gray was himself living a double life, as the husband of Constance Lloyd and father of her children, and as the undeclared sexual partner of Robbie Ross, John Gray and – from June or July 1891 onwards – Alfred Douglas also. Less than four months after the likely beginning of a homosexual relationship between Wilde and Douglas, Parnell suddenly died – on 6 October 1891. On 16 October, the publisher William Heinemann lunched with Wilde and was surprised to find him in mourning – it was his thirty-seventh birthday.

As the discrepancy between these dates clearly dramatizes, no neat correlation of Parnellite and Wildean chronologies can be tabulated. What is at issue is not any mechanical impact of the earlier career upon the latter, but rather the degree and nature of Wilde's unquestionable awareness of Parnell's fate. And here we return to the story of the racehorse and the dog that did not bark in the night. A scrupulous but hardly infallible examination of the public and printed record indicates that, throughout the entire decade of the 1880s, throughout 1890 and the critical months of 1891, Wilde never recorded the name of Parnell – not in any of the many reviews in which he proclaimed the Irish cause, or espoused socialist ideas, or praised William O'Brien by name, or generally poked fun at the conservative parties in Britain. The absence of Parnell's name from these reviews is remarkable enough; its non-appearance in Wilde's correspondence for the same period – at least in so far as the letters have been published to date – is even more remarkable. For Wilde is known to have attended the Special Commission on Parnellism and Crime; he actually possessed the volumes which comprised the Commission's report, perhaps because his brother William was even more closely involved as a reporter at the Commission's sessions for the *Daily Telegraph*. In his 1992 book on *The Parnell Split*, Frank Callanan has argued that Wilde, in 'The Soul of Man under Socialism', had approved of Parnell just as much 'as a man of political thought as . . . a creator of political force'. Be that implicit identification as it may, the fact remains that Parnell is not explicitly named.

It is worth pausing to consider the full significance of this omission, even if we have also to admit that there is still a great body of Wilde's surviving correspondence as yet unpublished. Throughout the best part of a decade, Parnell and Wilde were (in their different spheres) each regarded as the most eminent or notorious

Irishman in London society. If their spheres were different — the one parliamen-
tary, the other literary and bohemian — there were points of intersection. Wilde's
mother, for example, was a zealous Irish patriot who fancied herself even in old
age as a political hostess of some consequence. Wilde's brother, as we have just
noted, was stirred to uncharacteristic activity by the proceedings of the Parnell
Commission and covered it as a journalist. On the other hand, the Parnellite party
had its literary wing, both before and after the split of 1890. When the young W. B.
Yeats wrote favourably of Wilde as an author, he published in the strongly
pro-Parnellite *United Ireland.* Less than two weeks later, Parnell was dead. Thus,
in noticing with Sherlock-Holmes-like keenness that the name of Parnell is never
to be heard in Wilde's journalism or in his available correspondence, we must
surmise that what has occurred here is nothing less than a forceful repression.

Affinities between the two can be reinforced in a brief consideration of
significant resemblances. As both men were living double lives, the younger was
able to observe the risks which his senior ran in maintaining an alternative
establishment in Mrs O'Shea's house. That is to say, he was also well placed to
judge the vindictiveness of public opinion in other, unconnected scandals: such as
the divorce case which ruined the political career of Sir Charles Dilke or the
scandal connected with a gay brothel in Cleveland Street, which forced a prominent member of the nobility, Lord Arthur Somerset, into exile from England.
Moreover, Wilde's intellect was keenly attuned to doubleness, as in his reverence
of both Pater and Ruskin, and his inclinations towards both freemasonry and
Catholicism. At a deeper psychological level, both Parnell and Wilde survived by
the projection of exceptional personalities through public performances in which
outrage played its part. Both walked the razor's edge.

Thus, when Parnell is publicly cited at the end of 1889 for an offence against
conventional sexual morality, is rejected by many of his supporters and is
hypocritically condemned by political leaders who had long known of his double
life, Wilde cannot be other than alert to the implications. Coming between the
magazine publication of *The Picture of Dorian Gray* and its expansion in book
form, the Parnell crisis initially has the apparent effect of urging Wilde towards
an even clearer defiance of public opinion. But, as I hope to show in a moment,
there were complex consequences in other aspects of Wilde's activity.

Before turning to these, we should note also the marked contrast between the
two men, not only in their sexual orientation but also in their intellectual attitudes.
Wilde was steeped in the exotica of all the arts — book-binding, dress, music,
painting, poetry; Parnell was a thorough philistine, with no time for literature.
Wilde's sexual needs involved risk as a defining characteristic; Parnell craved
domestic banality. Wilde's verbal range was astonishing in its resourcefulness and
its relaxed formality; Parnell wrote pathetic schoolboyish letters to his 'Dear
Queenie'. Apart from the question of sexual contrast, there is also one of simple
political differentiation. If Wilde and Parnell shared a profound concern with the
fate of their homeland and its people, they disagreed about methods, indeed
differed philosophically.

Though the terms of the distinction are rare enough in the heavily repressed courtesies of Irish political discourse, Parnell's entire programme was based on notions of private property. Even as a slogan, Home Rule proclaimed this bourgeois priority, and the campaign for tenant proprietorship also preferred individual ownership over any kind of collectivity. Wilde genuinely detested private property, and repeatedly mocked its magical power over the individual and society alike. Like Joyce's Aunt Dante in this one regard, he was, with Michael Davitt, more likely to favour nationalization or public ownership than the owner-occupier schemes of Parnell and his reluctant British allies. Wilde therefore looked on the fallen Parnell as a figure at once like him and unlike him, as someone with whom it was impossible to avoid symbolic identification and equally impossible to acknowledge as a soul-mate.

The intensification which characterized Wilde's revision of *Dorian Gray* cannot be read simply as his response to the Parnell business. There were other pressures and other reactions. In particular, Wilde was to turn away from fiction towards drama, away from a literary form in which some kind of narrative singularity must be maintained into the multi-voiced, pluralistic medium of the theatre. A good deal of *Dorian Gray* finds itself re-employed in the plays; Wilde never missed the opportunity to reuse an effective witticism. But as the corpus of the social comedies grows from the solitary and rather awkward success of *Lady Windermere's Fan* (February 1892) towards the climactic triumph of *The Importance of Being Earnest* (February 1895), a very different thematic priority emerges.

In *Dorian Gray*, a guilty double life cannot be ultimately concealed. Even when external threat is removed through the murder of Basil Hallward and the accidental shooting of James Vane, there remains evidence which cannot be ignored. This evidence, judged against its model, is a forgery; it is not an accurate representation of the immaculate being who lives in the world. But, in truth, it is the original which is a forgery. In the end, the bogus Dorian attacks the true Dorian, only to kill the former and to restore the latter to an ironic, detached perfection. In the plays, however, guilty double life is repeatedly absorbed to the preservation of surface and serenity. Mrs Erlynne's abandonment of her child, her later bullying and blackmailing of her daughter's husband, is conceded, because the alternative would be to destroy the child, Lady Windermere. The succeeding two plays explore the same theme in sexual and political terms, with the same ultimate denouement – the absence of a denouement. The double life of a politician who has done something shabby in his past, something shameful, even traitorous, can be preserved by the development of a finer surface, a more articulate speech.

As he was working on *The Importance of Being Earnest*, Wilde's own double life became even more complicated. From August to October 1894, Wilde with his wife and children stayed at Worthing in Sussex, during which period most of the new play was written. But Lord Alfred Douglas was often a guest, unloved and loved; the two sides of Wilde's sexual existence were dangerously converging, like the magnetized plates of an infernal electrical device. John Worthing is one of the principal characters of the play, but his address is in Hertfordshire – a displacement which renders wholly formal the tension between the world of domesticity and the world of dramatic action. And, in this play above its predecessors, action is formalized; questions of guilt and identity are transferred into a nominalist dialogue and the abandonment of a child treated in a manner of refined farce. Wilde has finally been able to parody Wilde, and thus wholly to master the disruptive elements which threaten the existence of leading characters in the three earlier comedies.

But *The Importance of Being Earnest* was not always thus. For a start, the crucial name was originally George, and the happy choosing of 'Ernest' established the essentially punning style of the action. Then, there was (briefly) a Grimsby incident in which Algernon is very nearly arrested for debt and taken to Holloway Gaol, a scene in which a solicitor admits to using two names, much as Ernest has been used by Algy. In cutting the scene, Wilde not only improved the dramatic structure of the play, he also avoided a public preview of his own fate. W. H. Auden called the play a verbal opera, the only verbal opera in English. Perhaps an even better description would be verbal ballet – for it is hard to know what a *non*-verbal opera might be like – in which movement and action are identical and in which content has been drained to reveal in all its purity a crystal structure. The name of Miss Prism is striking, indicating not just a personal hardness of heart, comically exploited, but also a more generalized redirecting reflectiveness in the play – so that Worthing may be in Hertfordshire and Algy may be Ernest.

It could not last. Richard Ellmann stressed the extent to which Wilde was prescient of his crisis, confirming his insight by engineering his own doom. This is, in a strict sense, a Satanic interpretation, but it makes more sense if one recognizes in Charles Stewart Parnell an objective correlative whose career Wilde observed and suppressed, just as the plays progressively exhaust themselves of gross plot to become a kind of subjectless emancipation. But when – to borrow Betjeman's not wholly accurate terms – it came to the arrest of Mr Oscar Wilde at the Cadogan Hotel, the Grimsby incident restored itself, and the self-destructive hubris of Parnell took possession of an apt and prepared victim.

The Journey to Reading Gaol: Sacrifice and Scapegoats in Irish Literature

BERNARD O'DONOGHUE

There is a general feeling, derived partly from nineteenth-century stereotyping, that sacrifice, linked to violence, is somehow natively Irish. Indeed, sacrifice as an idea pervades the Irish cultural tradition. It is, however, a complex idea which has often been taken too simply; it has several senses which come from different sources and traditions. What I want to do first is to separate those senses, arguing that some of them are much more applicable to the Irish tradition than others. In particular I want to argue that the criteria assumed in Irish notions of sacrifice are broadly to do with a culture of shame rather than guilt. These distinctions are crucial in order to read properly texts such as Yeats's play *The King's Threshold* or Heaney's Bog poems in *North*, for example, as well as some less obviously related texts such as Wilde's plays. The scapegoat in several of these contexts is an important metaphorical device which can be used to absolve a society of its guilts by freeing it from marks of shame.

Clarification is necessary because the idea of sacrifice has been associated with Irishness in the same unquestioning way as other aspects of the Celtic stereotype: Arnold's revolt against the despotism of fact; defeatism; a taste for violence; fecklessness; Kuno Meyer's 'the half-said thing to them is dearest'; Chesterton's 'all their wars are merry and all their songs are sad', and so on. It is striking that three writers with very different histories and views of the world – Thomas MacDonagh, Bernard Shaw and Louis MacNeice – concurred in rejecting these stereotypes on exactly the same ground: that they attributed to the Gaelic/Irish tradition a fondness for unrealism which is directly opposed to the pragmatism of Celtic literature and thought. This is to propose what Yeats would call 'a counter-truth', of course – the Celt as pragmatist rather than romantic – but it fits in with a figure of romantic, naive Englishness encountering an Irish rationalism, a reversal which occurs particularly in drama.

Before examining the literary evidence, I want to look at Richard Kearney's important essay 'Myth and Terror' to see how centrally sacrifice has been placed in characterizations of the history of ideas in Ireland.[1] Kearney's convincing thesis about the connections between terror and myth begins by noting that three motivations of terrorism have traditionally been recognized: constitutional (a demand for shared power), economic (a demand for shared wealth), and historical (a demand for shared identity). He then proposes the addition of a fourth motivation: the mythological, which demands a share of symbolism. In defining this symbolism, Kearney quotes Chesterton on 'Pearse and his colleagues' before going on to say of 1916, 'indeed we need only recall the incredible transformation which their martyrdom effected to realize how deeply-rooted in the Irish national psyche is this mythological cult of sacrifice'.[2] At this point in his essay, Kearney goes along with the view that he attributes to Conor Cruise O'Brien, Ruth Dudley Edwards and Augustine Martin — that there is an established link between 'Irish nationalism and the whole mythic ideology of sacrificial blood-letting, martyrdom and the ancestor cult'.[3] But Kearney proceeds to a different though equally sweeping generalization about sacrifice: 'It is important to note here that the oblation myth which underpinned the consciousness of the 1916 leaders sprang as much from the pagan myths of seasonal rejuvenation as from the Christian myths of salvation-through-sacrifice, which in turn stemmed largely from the ancient Hellenic mystery rites'.[4]

The reason that literary evidence is important in considering this history is obvious. At least since the nineteenth century, there have been close connections between romantic literature and cultural nationalism throughout Europe, not least in Ireland. The 1916 Rising was a rebellion led by poets; Yeats wonders in a late poem whether 'that play of mine' (*Cathleen Ni Houlihan*) sent out 'Certain men the English shot'. I will argue later on against Kearney's view that Pearse's notion of sacrifice was in any way pagan or Hellenic. Like Wilde's, it was almost totally founded in Christian imagery and terminology.[5] But more crucially I want to review the evidence for seeing 'blood-letting and the ancestor cult' as connected with Irish nationalism (it is representative of the discussions of stereotyped nationalism that martyrdom is lumped together with the other two in this catalogue, even though, as I have been suggesting, it is logically and historically quite distinct from blood-letting).

First of all, though, I am concerned with the Arnoldian Celtic generalizing here, as in the list of clichés noted above. The one I am most concerned with is blood-letting as the toleration of violence, which is important in this context because, if self-sacrifice is defined as violence against the self, then the distinction between violent ritual sacrifice and passive sacrifice, like hunger-striking, disappears. Support for the connection between the Irish literary tradition and violence came from an unlikely source in 1995, in Dick Spring's opening address to that year's Kerry International Summer School (I am quoting from Katie Donovan's report in *The Irish Times* of 1 August), in which he noted 'that Irish writers have tended to focus on violence'. After a number of caveats, Spring went on to deplore the 'school of thought, epitomized by Pearse's definition of bloodshed as "a cleansing and sanctifying thing", which depicted violence in a heroic light'. Nobody is going to disagree with the ethics of any of this, but I am concerned about the ease with which it domiciles ideas of violence and blood-sacrifice in an Irish tradition. This has made it natural for even well-disposed commentators to take violent sacrifice as an Irish norm. For example, in the first week of its life, the London *Independent* carried an unattributed profile of Gerry Adams in which the IRA's success was attributed to 'the traditional Irish toleration of violence'.

There are, in fact, at least three senses of the term 'sacrifice' which are crucially different but tend to get vaguely linked together: self-sacrifice (as in hunger-striking); ritual sacrifice, involving violence towards other people or creatures (which is where scapegoats come in); and the rather curious symbolic sense of the term in the phrase 'the Holy Sacrifice of the Mass' where the root-notion of sacrifice has more or less disappeared. I want to concentrate on the first two, where the word 'sacrifice' is used in normal dictionary senses, and leave the Mass out of it here, though I will return to Christian notions of sacrifice briefly in discussing Pearse and Wilde.

To start with sacrifice of self, it might be argued that there is no point in distinguishing this from outward-directed forms of sacrifice by ritual, since all involve some kind of damage against the body. Is self-sacrifice appropriately regarded as *violence* against the self? In many circumstances it seems not. For example, hunger-striking as practised by Gandhi is more often seen as a measure *against* violence than violent in itself.[6] Tibetan monks and Jan Palach in Prague in 1968 are other cases. The haunting photograph in the *Guardian* of a Bosnian girl who hanged herself as an act of despair in a context of rape and violence was a horrifying reminder that violence against the self can be a protest against inflicted violence.

Turning now to review the literary evidence, the obvious place to start is with Yeats. The most familiar text is this much quoted passage in 'Easter 1916':

Hearts with one purpose alone
Through summer and winter seem
Enchanted to a stone
To trouble the living stream.

 . . .

The stone's in the midst of all.

Too long a sacrifice
Can make a stone of the heart.
O when may it suffice?[7]

This has been a very influential passage of late. The lines are drawn on by Edna Longley for the title of her second collection of essays on Irish poetry, *The Living Stream* (1994), which is much concerned with the destructiveness of sacrifice. She develops the contrast of the vivifying 'living stream' with the repeated 'stone' which symbolizes the anti-life destructiveness of sacrifice. Again, in an important essay in his book *Minotaur: Poetry and the Nation State*, Tom Paulin suggests that, although this poem was written shortly after the Rising in 1916, it was officially published as a response to the death of Terence MacSwiney over four years later, so that the 'sacrifice' attained a new specificity in application to hunger-striking.

It comes as something of a surprise, given the familiarity of this passage, to learn from the Parrish and Painter *Concordance* to Yeats's poems that this is one of only two occurrences of the word 'sacrifice' in Yeats's poetry (the other is 'What is this sacrifice?', the famous question in 'Parnell's Funeral', another poem urgently concerned with responsibility).[8] Strikingly, the word occurs nine times in the *Plays*, and its derivatives twice. Five of those eleven occurrences are in the Greek world of *Oedipus at Colonus*, where the idea of ritual sacrifice and determinism is of course central.

Before turning to the play *The King's Threshold* (1904), the second most familiar sacrifice text in Yeats, a further distinction needs to be made: between suicide, as the active killing of the self which, as Dante grimly reminds us, is in itself a highly culpable act of violence, and the passive acceptance of death. In some circumstances this might seem a fine distinction, but it is crucial in the Irish tradition. Sacrifices there, as in *The King's Threshold*, are passive protests rather than acts of violence. This distinction does not seem to be made fully in two sympathetic and insightful discussions of the 1981 Long Kesh hunger-strikes: in a poetry review the critic Tim Dooley referred to the hunger-strikers as 'the IRA suicides', and, in a more extensive context, Maud Ellmann referred to them as 'the serial suicides' in her brilliant book *The Hunger Artists*.[9] These terms do not sound quite appropriate in an Irish context because of the Christian guilt associations of the term suicide. The distinction is clear in *The King's Threshold*, where the poet Seanchan, 'a mere man of words', uses not words but willed self-starvation to shame King Guaire, who has denied him admission to the authority of 'the great council of the State'. The message of this play is somewhat confused (perhaps because it shifts from a comic to a tragic resolution with no other textual changes) in that it implies a power in the poet which he cannot deliver. 'Those that make rhymes have a power from beyond the world', one of Seanchan's pupils says, but in the end Seanchan has to fall back on what he sinisterly calls 'The victim's joy among the holy flame'.[10]

The significant point, though, is that Seanchan's protest makes sense only in what has been termed 'a shame culture'. The classic statement of shame culture in an Irish context was Terence MacSwiney's proposition that the victors are 'not those who inflict most but those who endure most'. King Guaire in Yeats's play recognizes the threat that '[Seanchan] may bring disgrace upon me'. The dilemma for the King is:

> While he is lying there,
> Perishing there, my good name in the world
> Is perishing also. I cannot give way
> Because I am king.[11]

And Yeats does localize the dilemma as an Irish one, as the King explains:

for there is a custom,
An old and foolish custom, that if a man
Be wronged, or think that he is wronged, and starve
Upon another's threshold till he die,
The common people, for all the time to come,
Will raise a heavy cry against that threshold,
Even though it be the King's.[12]

In the original version of the play, Seanchan gets his way and survives; later Yeats changed it, in keeping with the post-1916 centrality of sacrifice that he saluted. Indeed it was argued by Thomas McGreevy that Yeats changed the play to a tragic ending in reaction to the death of MacSwiney in 1920 (just as Paulin suggested that the publication of 'Easter 1916' was also in response to that death). The implication is that the shaming triumph of sacrifice has come to seem more effectual than winning the argument (this is Ruth Dudley Edwards's view of 1916, indicated in the title of her biography of Pearse, *The Triumph of Failure*). In one way the moral issue (the question of guilt, as against shame) remains the same: the King's intransigence is wrong, and Seanchan is right to make a stand for the poet's political rights. Indeed the shame culture aspect of the story is more pronounced in the original comic version as paraphrased by Lady Wilde (printed in Jeffares – Knowland's *Commentary* on Yeats's plays)[13] where Seanchan protests at St Kieran's saving of him from the giant king of the cats because it reflected all the more ill on King Guaire that it was in response to a slight by him that Seanchan, the chief poet, had come to be in this disgraceful condition on a cat's back. It is abundantly clear here that the moral issue is not *the* issue; it is a question of shame.

A similar exercise in shame culture comes, very much in passing, in a vastly different context, Wilde's *Lady Windermere's Fan*, where the Duchess of Berwick says in words that sound eerily prophetic in an Irish context: 'It was only Berwick's brutal and incessant threats of suicide that made me accept him at all.'[14] As so often, Wilde's satire encapsulates a complex issue almost imperceptibly: the idea that the threat of suicide is a 'brutal' act towards people other than the self is a kind of trope of the phrase 'violence towards the self' and, it might seem, a telling satiric answer to the argument that killing the self is as 'brutal' as killing someone else. In fact, this kind of reciprocal brutality is crucial to a number of Wilde's works (Dorian Gray intends murder but commits suicide; Bunbury is invented and then dispatched with heartless haste, in order to maintain an entrenched social order). Nor has their casual cruelty been adequately addressed by critics.

Clearly, ritual sacrifice – the second major sense of the term – is altogether another matter morally, where the sacrificial victim is an unwilling one. The classic case of the ritual sacrifice in our tradition is the biblical story of the scapegoat which comes in Leviticus (c. 1500 BC). God instructs Moses about what Aaron must do on the Day of Atonement:

After he hath cleansed the sanctuary, and the tabernacle, and the altar, then let him offer the living goat. And putting both hands upon his head, let him confess all the iniquities of the children of Israel, and all their offences and sins. And praying that they may light on his head, he shall turn him out by a man ready for it, into the desert. And when the goat hath carried all their iniquities into an uninhabited land, and shall be let go into the desert, Aaron must return and wash and burn his clothes.[15]

The brutality and injustice involved here clearly do imply violence, though it is still presented as a violence tolerated in the service of a higher cause, rather than as an end in itself.

Although the idea of the scapegoat as victim is crucially present in Irish writing (and I will return to it at the end with the drama), this notion of sacrifice by ritual is largely absent from the Irish tradition. The only instance is the story of the brutality of Crom Cruach in the Dinnseanchas section of the Book of Leinster. But it is important to realize that this was a Christian document, observing the ill-practices of a pagan enemy, not those of the observer's own race. In fact it is a strikingly consistent feature of accusations of ritual sacrifice. Who practised ritual sacrifice? According to Caesar, his enemies the Gauls; according to Tacitus, the Germans; according to Lucan, Rome's enemies in Marseilles; according to the Christian Adam of Bremen, the pagan Vikings (the horrific human and animal sacrifices at Uppsala). Evidence for the Druids' 'Wicker Man', the towering wickerwork figure in which enemies were allegedly immolated, derives from Caesar. Likewise, it has been questioned whether the apparent sacrifice on the Gundestrup cauldron represents a Gaulish/Celtic subject (for that matter, it is not certain that it does depict a human sacrifice at all). In summary, ritual sacrifice was practised by barbarians, regarded from the viewpoint of the civilized (like cannibalism, which Montaigne said was practised only to express 'an extreme and inexpiable revenge'). We might recall in this connection a proposition by Adorno and Horkheimer, quoted by Maud Ellmann: 'The history of civilization is the history of the introversion of the sacrifice.'[16] It is only among pre-civilized barbarians that sacrifice is performed externally. The Greek sense of sacrifice – Iphigenia sacrificed for a wind, for example – does not occur in the Gallo-Celtic tradition.

This is an important point because the fatalism of Greek tragedy (as in Yeats's *Oedipus at Colonus*, which contains nearly half of Yeats's uses of the term 'sacrifice' in his plays) has been read into Irish literary contexts where it does not apply: in Kearney's 'Hellenic' background to 1916, and interpretative responses to Heaney's Bog poems in *North*. Wilde again offers an enlightening instance of the more specialized way in which the sacrificial victim occurs in Irish writing. The language is unmistakably Christian. For example, this is part of the story 'The Young King', with sacrificial and scapegoat terminology italicized:

the body of the Princess was being lowered into an open grave that had been dug in a *deserted* churchyard *beyond the city gates*, a grave where it was said that another body was also lying, that of a young man of marvellous and foreign beauty, whose hands *were tied behind him with a knotted cord*, and whose breast *was stabbed with many red wounds.*[17]

The evocation of representations of the Christian passion is unmistakable here, as is the terminology of the desert place beyond the city gates into which the scapegoat was driven. Sacrifice is clearly a theme in Wilde's stories generally; the sacrifice (for no very clear purpose beyond a vague service of virtue) of the swallow and the Prince in 'The Happy Prince' is representative, as is the double sacrifice in 'The Nightingale and the Rose'. What is equally clear is that the inspiration for the ethics of these stories is a sentimental Christian one (it is made explicit in 'The Selfish Giant'); the text is 'greater love hath no man than that he lay down his life for his friend'. The idea can be illustrated very readily from the less wholly comic plays: Lady Windermere says: 'Nowadays people seem to look on life as a speculation. It is not a speculation. It is a sacrament. Its ideal is Love. Its purification is Sacrifice.'[18] In the same play, Mrs Erlynne herself embraces sacrifice when she consciously ruins her own reputation to save that of her child, knowing that the price to be paid is to be cast into the desert (the world outside London society). Her justification is similarly Christian: 'As for me, if suffering be an expiation, then at this moment I have expiated all my faults.'[19]

This is the kind of sacrifice that Pearse invokes too. Nora in 'The Roads' witnesses Christ's passion; three of the stories ('Eoinin na nÉan', 'The Keening Woman' and 'Iosagán') end in death. Most remarkably, Barbara ends with the death and burial of the doll: 'Nothing would convince Brideen that Barbara wasn't killed, and that it wasn't to save her she gave her life. I myself wouldn't say she was right, but I wouldn't say she wasn't. How do I know? How do you know?'[20] I am not concerned to comment on the pathology of this, beyond noting that it is very akin to Wilde's sentimental (as against his satirical) mode, and that both recognizably belong within popular Christianity. Both are a long way from the determinism and austerity of Greek tragedy's version of sacrifice. It is curious too that both Pearse and Wilde are often accused of bringing upon themselves their own destruction: Wilde by his legal challenge to Queensberry and Pearse by the 1916 Rising. What I would suggest is that both behave like Yeats's Seanchan, by challenging the world to be ashamed of its wrongs: Wilde asks the Victorian world to be ashamed of its hypocrisy; Pearse asks England to see the shame of unjust rule over Ireland. By now it is a historical curiosity that shame culture, it seems, *has* justified them; few now would take Queensberry's side against Wilde, and the idea of English misrule in Ireland is a truism. Pearse's blood-sacrifice may be thought unwise or unnecessary; but it is not exactly seen as shameful in the way that the execution of the 1916 leaders sometimes is.

The bizarre end of Brideen's doll is not ritual sacrificing either; yet there is a clear sacrificial victim in question, even if, as with Wilde's nightingale, it is not entirely clear what the sacrifice is for. I want to turn finally to a version of the scapegoat which I think developed as an expression of impatience with the unchallengeable, self-righteous vantage-point of these narratives. The texts I want to consider briefly (and I can be brief because they all turn on exactly the same victim-figure) are Boucicault's *The Shaughraun*, Frank O'Connor's 'Guests of the Nation', Behan's *The Hostage* and Friel's *Translations*. Boucicault and Friel both take us back to the point made at the outset: both challenge the stereotype of the merry, ineffectual Gael (and Boucicault brilliantly puts him into his play while questioning him: what, after all, *is* a shaughraun?). Both Boucicault and Friel personify the maker of the stereotype as an English romantic – an innocent soldier – who suffers grimly for his misconception. In each case, the soldier falls in love with a local Irish girl (it is hard to avoid the word *cailín*) with terrible consequences. Similarly, both 'Guests of the Nation' and *The Hostage* feature English soldier hostages who are shot. (O'Connor accused Behan of plagiarizing his plot; in fact both are operating with the same literary counter-stereotype.) We could adduce Somerville and Ross's *Irish R.M.* and Shaw's *John Bull's Other Island* for further English gulls in Ireland, but the victims there, though clearly related to the other figures, retain the ultimate political power.

What all these writers are doing is refusing to abide by the stereotype of the Irish victim who dies passively for a cause, by replacing it with a proposed harder-headed reality. In the texts, believers in the victim-stereotype pay a terrible price for not seeing the Celtic realism noted by MacDonagh, Shaw and MacNeice. Wilde also was one of its exponents. In his only overtly political play, he demonstrates how the interests of *realpolitik* overturn the imperative of a career sacrificed for mere 'moral' concerns. 'An Ideal Husband' is neither ideal nor a good husband, but a hard-headed political hack. Such realism begets its Yeatsian counter-truth elsewhere in the theatre: the oppressor as victim, like Yolland in *Translations*. But I want to conclude with Seamus Heaney's Bog poems, particularly 'Punishment', a poem that I think represents beautifully the complexities involved here and refuses to reach a conclusion. It is perhaps not accidental that its author paid a harsh price for *not* abiding by either stereotype: the wild Irish sacrificer or the Christian pacifist.

Something must first be said about the context of the Bog poems themselves which draw heavily on a tradition of Germanic cult sacrifice, linked clearly with the 'tribalism' of the Northern Celts. Again, this ritual cult is described by a hostile classical commentator, Tacitus in *Germania*, where the votive service to the mysterious male-named female goddess Nerthus is described. How it becomes translated into the cult of a feminine Ireland requires a separate and extensive discussion elsewhere. But the image is firmly rooted in the Irish psyche by the time of Wilde's earliest play. *Vera, or The Nihilists* ends with Vera killing herself for the sake of an ideal Mother Russia, a barely suppressed political correlative for Mother Ireland. It leaps from the page into a new century and a new Ireland, won by acts of blood-sacrifice.

Some commentators were critical of what they felt was the determinism of the Heaney poems in *Wintering Out* and *North*, seeing a suggestion that violence such as that in present-day Northern Ireland was fated and inevitable as a kind of 'sacrifice to the goddess'. It is not a reading, in my view, that will bear much literal scrutiny; indeed, it might be felt that the poems' message that violence breeds violence, metaphorically speaking, has proved grimly true. But the possibility of giving the poems in good faith a determinist misreading — that is, that 'blood will have blood', or the goddess must have her victim, irrespective of human agency or volition — was surely a product of the kind of stereotyping of violence and sacrifice I have been partially unravelling here.

'Punishment' begins with an extended, strangely personal reflection on the Windeby girl as she is depicted and described in P. V. Glob's *The Bog People*, accepting Glob's speculation that she was a victim of the ritual punishment inflicted for adultery. The most controversial part of the poem is its closing lines:

My poor scapegoat,

I almost love you
but would have cast, I know,
the stones of silence.
I am the artful voyeur

of your brain's exposed
and darkened combs,
your muscles' webbing
and all your numbered bones:

I who have stood dumb
when your betraying sisters,
cauled in tar,
wept by the railings,

who would connive
in civilized outrage
yet understand the exact
and tribal, intimate revenge.

Much of the discussion of this controversial poem has centred on the word 'understand': does an understanding of this revenge involve to any degree a qualification of the 'civilized' disapproval of it, on the principle *tout comprendre, c'est tout pardonner*? The poem argues that dishonesty lies in the connivance: everyone has baser emotions that are vengeful and cruel, but they are suppressed by a civilized compact of silence. In political terms, it implies that violence cannot be ended while it is claimed to be only the actions and inclinations of other people.

This is strikingly reminiscent of the attitude to violence of civilized societies: violence is characteristic of barbarism, which is the behaviour of aliens, looked at from the perspective of the civilized. In fact the narrative attitude in this poem is close to another kind of civilized conniving that I have been tracing here, which is the kind of non-negotiating passivity of those who believe they are absolutely right — Yeats's Seanchan, for example. By adopting a posture of self-sacrificing Christian virtue, Wilde and Pearse are open to the same charge. Their outrage appeals to a shaming notion based on a sense of a superior civility. Boucicault, Shaw, O'Connor and Behan undermine this attitude by placing the figure of the innocent — in Yeats's scenario — on the King's side, as though the poet's pupils should attack a soldier of the King.

Something similar is suggested by the curious endearment at the start of the Heaney passage quoted: 'My poor scapegoat'. The 'My' here is not only the fond possessive as in 'my dear'; the phrase also means 'scapegoat for me' and for my understanding of the barbarity that surrounds us but which the Irish tradition of passivity disowns. It is an attempt to recover the sense of guilt which a shame culture ignores by its employment of scapegoats.

So does the scapegoat effect some kind of bringing together in a post-violence era? It has been fashionable recently to note that the scapegoat was expelled on the Day of Atonement and — by the employment of strict etymology in a Derridean way — to link that to the end of violence: atonement as at-one-ment. This is a dubious procedure, both linguistically and strategically. The expulsion of figures of shame as a way of escaping responsibility may satisfy the demands of civilization, but it is necessary to understand and face the vengefulness and potential violence that it asks for. This is the truth that the literary opponents of the two stereotypes — the cheerful defeated Celt and the triumphant pacifist who rouses shame in his oppressor — keep insisting on, from Boucicault to Wilde and O'Connor and on to Heaney and Friel. Perhaps the text to end with is Wilde's *De Profundis*, which sees his own systematic shaming as a barbaric act by society, one for which he owns no responsibility. To be precise, Wilde fails or simply refuses to share Heaney's 'understanding' of a barbarous revenge, as the only way of appeasing guilt.

Oscar Wilde's mother, Jane Elgee Wilde, known as the poet 'Speranza',
as a young woman. From a photogravure by Stephen Catterson Smith.

Oscar Wilde's father, William Wilde, as a young man.
From a drawing by J. H. McGuire, 1847 (National Library of Ireland).

Sir William and Lady Wilde as caricatured by Harry Furniss (British Library).

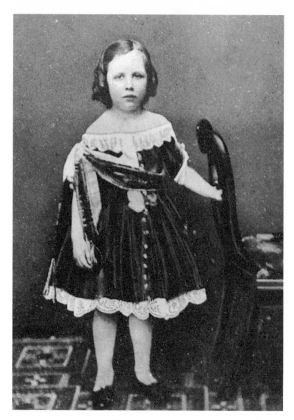

Oscar Wilde as a young child.

Oscar Wilde's home as a child, One Merrion Square,
as it was at the beginning of the twentieth century.

The envelope decorated by Wilde when he was twelve containing a lock of hair of his sister, Isola, which he kept until he died.

Oscar Wilde as a young boy (William Andrews Clark Library).

Moytura House, the holiday house built by William Wilde on the shores of Lough Corrib, County Mayo. Oscar Wilde spent several holidays there as a child and teenager.

Illaunroe, the Wildes' fishing lodge on the shores of Lough Fee, County Galway, where Wilde came on at least one memorable holiday with an Oxford friend, the painter Frank Miles, in 1876.

Portora Royal School, Enniskillen, County Fermanagh.

'Wilde on *US*: Something to "Live Up" to in America', by Thomas Nast in *Harper's Bazaar*, 10 June 1882. A cartoon celebrating Wilde's tribute to the Western miners as the 'only well-dressed men I have seen in America'.

Mr Wilde of Borneo: Oscar Wilde compared to 'The Wild Man of Borneo'.
The Washington Post, 22 January 1882.

'The Aesthetic Monkey', engraved from a painting by W. H. Beard in *Harper's Weekly*, 28 January 1882.

Maquettes submitted by finalists in the competition for the Guinness Oscar Wilde Sculpture Commission for Merrion Square. Photographs courtesy of Guinness Ireland Group.

Sculptors clockwise across both pages from above:
Danny Osborne, Louise Walsh, Cathy Carman, Don Cronin, Brian King, Benedict Byrne.

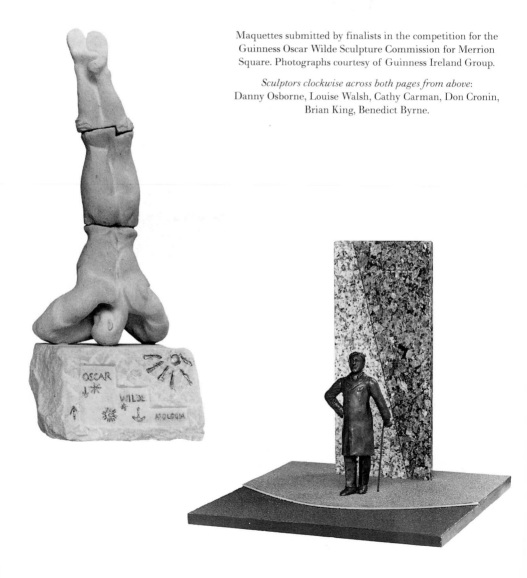

Head of Oscar Wilde by Patrick O'Connor.

Oscar Wilde attending the hearings of the Parnell Commission, 1889.
From a drawing by S. P. Hall (National Portrait Gallery, London).

Against Nature?
Science and Oscar Wilde

JOHN WILSON FOSTER

I

Late and soon, W. B. Yeats identified science as a culprit standing in dangerous opposition to art and imagination. In 1897, in 'The Celtic Element in Literature', he welcomed a widespread reaction 'against the rationalism of the eighteenth century' which was mingling 'with a reaction against the materialism of the nineteenth century', a reaction he identified in literature as 'the symbolical movement'.[1] In 1900, he told Shaw in debate that Shaw belonged 'to a bygone generation − to the scientific epoch − and was now "reactionary"'.[2] (Shaw was not amused.) In 1921, Yeats recalled his detestation of T. H. Huxley and of the famous (Irish-born) physicist John Tyndall, who had deprived him of 'the simple-minded religion' of his childhood.[3] His 1934 essay 'Louis Lambert' put the nineteenth century's most famous scientist in the dock for 'what our instinct repudiates, Darwin's exaltation of accidental variations'.[4] Given such sentiments, one detects approval in Yeats's 1936 remembrance of Lionel Johnson as a Rhymers' Club-man who asserted that 'science must be confined to the kitchen or the workshop, that it could discover nothing of importance'.[5]

Ireland, Yeats believed, provided the most fertile and hospitable ground available for the counter-Renaissance and counter-Enlightenment. Science was particularly uncongenial as a way of engaging with Irish nature (landscape and its creatures), which is by turns magical, dreamlike, mysterious, spiritual and symbolic, something inspiring local and national patriotism, subjective yet ancestral, most suitably expressed in poetry and art. Long after the Celtic Twilight (which promoted such an idea of Irish nature), Yeats's hostile attitude to science remained influential in Ireland. Of course, the exclusion of science from received 'native' Irish culture antedates Yeats, but the poet and his literary movement copper-fastened it.[6]

Yeats's dislike of science, if it owed something to Matthew Arnold's notion of Celticism (which helped to sponsor the Twilight), also flourished in the midst of the aesthetic movement of the close of the century. We might, then, expect it to have owed a debt to his fellow Irishman Oscar Wilde, whom Yeats first met at the house of the poet W. E. Henley in 1888. We can find in Richard Ellmann's *Eminent Domain* (1967) some of Yeats's other intellectual and artistic debts to

Wilde eloquently tallied as borrowed ideas: the superiority of the imagination (and 'lying') over reason and observation (and 'truth'); the inferiority of life beside art and the latter's capability of imposing its images upon the former, and life's imitation of art; the crucial significance for Western civilization of Hellenism, of 'the spirit that is Greek', as Basil Hallward terms it in *The Picture of Dorian Gray* (1890); the rejection of art as mere self-expression or mere fidelity to externalities.[7]

Although we might wish to ascertain the precise extent of Yeats's reading of Wilde and keep in mind how easy it is to confuse influence with affinity (many late-Victorian British writers, after all, fell under the sway of French Symbolism), we could, unsupervised, lengthen Ellmann's tally. For example, Yeats was to explore in his verse dialogues, and systematize in his prose, Wilde's distinction in 'The Critic as Artist' between the contemplative man and the man of action.[8] Secondly, Wilde's elaboration of the pose became Yeats's theories of the mask and the anti-self. Thirdly, if Wilde and Yeats shared the influence of Arnold, Wilde's acquaintance with the English poet's criticism predated Yeats's. It is true, of course, that by the time Wilde was endorsing Arnold's identification of the Celtic spirit in art, Yeats was already steeping himself in Celticism.[9] We cannot, then, claim Wilde's interest in Celticism as a fourth anticipation of Yeats – unless, that is, we broaden Celticism to include those attributes we now regard as amounting to a damaging stereotype of the Celt as lazy, imaginative and unrealistic (and most certainly unscientific), a stereotype that Wilde toyed with and that flourished before Yeats undermined it in his own peculiar way: that is, by retaining it while dignifying it and draining it of condescension.[10] Wilde proudly regarded himself as a Celt (in England at any rate), and thought, not wholly seriously perhaps, that he and Shaw spearheaded 'the great Celtic school'. Ironically, Wilde and Shaw are the two major writers who are normally excluded, for nationalist reasons, from the canon of the Irish Literary Revival.[11]

Fifthly, Yeats's 'artifice of eternity' is Wilde's early ideal of beauty writ (and thought) large. Nature – that is, the natural condition of things – is in human beings impossible: 'Being natural is simply a pose, and the most irritating pose I know', cries Lord Henry Wotton in *The Picture of Dorian Gray*. 'To be natural is to be obvious', says Gilbert in 'The Critic as Artist', 'and to be obvious is to be inartistic.' In another sense, nature is the *substance* of things, and decorative art is for Gilbert the highest art because it deliberately rejects nature as a model, in favour of that sense of *form* in which life is deficient and 'which is the basis of creative no less than of critical achievement'. 'The Decay of Lying' (1889) begins: 'The more we study Art, the less we care for Nature. What Art really reveals to us is Nature's lack of design, her curious crudities, her extraordinary monotony, her absolutely unfinished condition.'[12] Aestheticism, Camille Paglia remarks, 'is predicated on a swerve from nature', and by nature we might mean variously human nature, the subject of the natural sciences and the nature of things.[13]

None of this surprises, though I will return to it in an attempt to do just that. Nor does it surprise that Wilde praised Poe's 'Sonnet – to Science', in which science is humanized as a prying daughter of old Time (whose peering – in an interesting anticipation of Heisenberg – alters what it peers at), a failed muse; it is also animalized as a vulture feeding upon the poet's heart (like Prometheus' liver); in either guise it steals from the poet 'The summer dream beneath the tamarind tree'.[14]

Perhaps, if we wished to propose a case-study of Wilde's attitude to science, of which the study of nature is a branch, we might choose the role of flowers in Wilde's life and work. The conventional imagery and symbolism of flowers in poetry assume a certain hothouse association in Wilde's writing, and indeed in his life, in which what Ellmann calls 'Pre-Raphaelite' and 'talismanic' lilies were frequent, not just as items of personal affectation (like the green carnations), not even just as emblems of beauty (and therefore uselessness), but also (and ranking in this regard with sunflowers) as 'perfect models of design, the most naturally adapted for decorative art'.[15] It was design more than appropriate symbolism that Wilde was thinking of when he wrote to the Rev. J. Page Hopps in 1885, expressing both his regret at not being well enough to attend a meeting of the Funeral and Mourning Reform group and his agreement (couched in a solemnity that skirts humour) with the group's aims: 'The habit of bringing flowers to the grave is now almost universal, and is a custom beautiful in its symbolism; but I cannot help thinking that the elaborate and expensive designs made by the florist are often far less lovely than a few flowers held loose in the hand.'[16] Tongue more obviously in cheek, Wilde responded, in a letter that appeared in the *Pall Mall Gazette*, to a poet's botanically based correction of Wilde's pronunciation of the word 'tuberose':

Sir, I am deeply distressed to hear that tuberose is so called from its being a 'lumpy flower'. It is not at all lumpy, and, even if it were, no poet should be heartless enough to say so. Henceforth there really must be two derivations for every word, one for the poet and one for the scientist. And in the present case the poet will dwell on the tiny trumpets of ivory into which the white flower breaks, and leave to the man of science horrid allusions to its supposed lumpiness and indiscreet revelations of its private life below ground. In fact, tuber as a derivation is disgraceful. On the roots of verbs Philology may be allowed to speak, but on the roots of flowers she must keep silence. We cannot allow her to dig up Parnassus.[17]

Like Miss Prism, Wilde spoke horticulturally, his metaphors drawn from fruits and flowers, and nowhere more so than in *Dorian Gray*, whose eponymous hero has a 'rose-white boyhood' and a 'rose-red youth', who eats the moon-chilled cherries that life (no, artifice) offers him and for which he lives (no, dies) to pay the penalty. The novel opens with the rich odours of roses, mingling with the odours of lilac and thorn: nature's flourishes and fertilities are created to sustain a dangerous aesthesis – dangerous because it proves a moral anaesthesis – but that in turn is signified by nature's deficient form and threatening riot ('the sullen murmur of the bees shouldering their way through the long unmown grass') that is best turned from (it seems) in favour of human art and artifice. Almost immediately after this remarkable opening, nature is tamed into symbol and design before the reader eventually senses that the 'swerve from nature' – though, granted, not the nature of Basil Hallward's studio garden – is fatal.

II

We might expect such hostility to science from the man who, in Paglia's words, 'projected himself internationally as the ultimate aesthete'.[18] But on reflection the expectation seems shallow. To begin with, Wilde first knew that the 'marvels of design' achievable by decorative art were often absent from nature, not through studying Art (as he declares in 'The Decay of Lying'), but through reading students of nature.[19] He wrote in his Commonplace Book while a student at Oxford: 'We have outgrown the theory of design and talk easily of the "silly maladaptations of organic nature" (Clifford).'[20] The editors of the Commonplace Book do not offer a precise source in William Kingdon Clifford for Wilde's entry, and nor can I; but Clifford, in his lecture 'On the Aims and Instruments of Scientific Thought' (reprinted in an 1879 volume of Clifford's essays and lectures that Wilde read studiously), does discuss purposeless or defective adaptations in organic nature.[21] 'Design' was a word shared by decorative artists and pre-Darwinian espousers of natural theology, but among naturalists in Wilde's time it was being superseded by the word 'purpose' so as to uncouple natural processes from an intelligent Creator, and pull back on teleological explanations of the organic world.[22]

But Clifford was only one of the major scientific thinkers Wilde read assiduously while a student at Oxford; others included Huxley, Tyndall and Herbert Spencer. His career at Oxford was timely in this regard: he matriculated two months after Tyndall's challenging, pro-evolutionist 'Belfast Address' to the British Association in August 1874, which provoked, in the assessment of one historian, a controversy more important than the earlier Huxley–Wilberforce clash.[23] The thinkers young Wilde paraphrased and annotated in his Oxford Commonplace Book and College Notebook were grappling with the vexing issues of the day (often posed as disturbing oppositions), made more irritating by the recent intervention of the evolutionists: mind versus matter, idealism versus realism, imagination versus reason, individuality versus race, experience versus heredity, consciousness versus external reality, freedom versus necessity.

We discover in Wilde's Oxford notebooks a surprising pleasure in science; witness his delight in Shelley's 'passionate enthusiasm for science' (*pace* Yeats) and in the claim that Goethe, 'a devoted pupil of science', was the first Darwinian.[24] Ignorance of Darwin was enough to condemn a putative thinker in Wilde's eyes as late as 1889, the year in which he wrote to W. L. Courtney backhandedly thanking him for a copy of his *Life of John Stuart Mill*: 'As for Mill as a thinker – a man who knew nothing of Plato or Darwin gives me very little. His reputation is curious to me. . . . But Darwinism has of course shattered many reputations besides his.'[25] 'Unscientific' remained for the mature Wilde an indictment, 'scientific' a term of praise.[26] He had correspondents with scientific interests (for example, Grant Allen and Edward Heron-Allen), and of course his father was a practising scientist through whom Wilde would have absorbed to some degree the scientific element of Anglo-Irish culture and an implicit respect for it.[27]

Yet the early reading, the pondering of the weighty questions of the day and the respect for science were all inferable from the epigrammatic shorthand of the imaginative works. I say 'were', for I had so inferred before coming gratefully upon *Oscar Wilde's Oxford Notebooks* (1989), edited by Philip E. Smith and Michael S. Helfand, a product of strenuous scholarship which describes the bio-biblio-graphical base of that linguistic pyramid whose apex is the brilliant aphorism. The text of the notebooks, the provision of sources and the exhaustive and illuminating editorial commentary establish this book as the most important contribution to Wilde studies since the Hart-Davis edition of the letters in 1962. It is no longer possible to view Wilde as a supreme exponent of one, and only one, of what were once called the Two Cultures, as an artist blithely contemptuous of the other 'culture', or as a figurative inhabitant of Art, as Des Esseintes was a literal inhabitant of the sequestered artifice of his house at Fontenay-aux-Roses.

But even *A Rebours* (1884) (translated by Robert Baldick under the title *Against Nature*) can give us pause in this regard, should we take our cue from Wilde. To the hero of the book that poisons Dorian Gray, nature has had her day: 'artifice was considered by Des Esseintes to be the distinctive mark of genius'.[28] But if Des Esseintes rebuffs nature in this peremptory way (and how far is he the object of Huysmans' irony?), he does not so rebuff the modern sciences by which nature has been studied. The narrator of *Dorian Gray* tells us that Des Esseintes was one 'in whom the romantic and the scientific temperaments were so strangely blended': that is, unexpectedly blended and bizarrely blended, as they were more familiarly blended in, say, Goethe or (as we now know) the student Wilde. Wilde's novel, like Huysmans', is among other things a natural history of sensations, and includes (following Huysmans to the verge of plagiarism) a description and taxonomy of the hero's cabinets of collected exotica (strange perfumes, musical instruments, jewels), all reminiscent of both the Victorian collections of exotic natural specimens and the Victorian mania for cataloguing and classification. Dorian Gray also collects for a time stories about jewels, whereas Lord Henry Wotton collects epigrams; if Dorian's collection is secret, like Des Esseintes', Lord Henry's is for select public display. Moreover, the epigrams are Lord Henry's own: he collects, as it were, himself. And the aphorisms and epigrams themselves, Lord Henry's and the others', we might even see as Wilde's social version of scientific axioms and theorems, summations of long observation and experience analogous to physical laws.[29]

Dorian Gray's passing addiction to collection and classification is an aspect of the connoisseurship practised by Lord Henry: both the artistic connoisseur and the scientific collector meet in taxonomy and nomenclature. When writing *Dorian Gray*, Wilde remembered his 1885 letter to the *Pall Mall Gazette*, for he has Lord Henry complain that scientific names for flowers do not emulate the beauty of the plants: he entertains the idea of renaming the organic world on aesthetic principles. Again, scientific method (that of nomenclature) is borrowed and adapted, not dismissed. As a dramatist and novelist, Wilde paid close attention to his characters' names, and in his most famous play founded a plot upon a pun and the nominal betrayal of the nature of the (mis)named.

As well as collector, Lord Henry is an experimenter who 'had been always enthralled by the methods of natural science, but the ordinary subject-matter of that science had seemed to him trivial and of no import. And so he had begun by vivisecting himself, as he had ended by vivisecting others.' He jettisons the subject matter and retains the method: 'It was clear to him that the experimental method was the only method by which one could arrive at any scientific analysis of the passions; and certainly Dorian Gray was a subject made to his hand, and seemed to promise rich and fruitful results.'[30] 'He would be a wonderful study', Lord Henry tells Basil Hallward, choosing a word that suggests both pictorial composition and scientific inquiry (the case-study).

Like his literary forebears, Victor Frankenstein and Dr Jekyll (doubtful heroes in novels which, like *Dorian Gray*, exploit the *doppelgänger* theme), Lord Henry acknowledges that the price of treating one's life as a natural phenomenon is, at best, a hazardous project:

It was true that as one watched life in its curious crucible of pain and pleasure, one could not wear over one's face a mask of glass, nor keep the sulphurous fumes from troubling the brain and making the imagination turbid with monstrous fancies and misshapen dreams. There were poisons so subtle that to know their properties one had to sicken of them. There were maladies so strange that one had to pass through them if one sought to understand their nature. And, yet, what a great reward one received! How wonderful the whole world became to one! To note the curious hard logic of passion, and the emotional coloured life of the intellect – to observe where they met, and where they separated, at what point they were in unison, and at what point they were at discord – there was a delight in that! What matter what the cost was? One could never pay too high a price for any sensation.

'It often happened', he reflects, 'that when we thought we were experimenting on others we were really experimenting on ourselves.'[31] Shelley's Frankenstein, Stoker's Van Helsing and Wells's Time Traveller all learn this (while Jekyll learns its inverse), which might indicate a widespread cultural anxiety about science during the last century , not merely about the threatening illusion of its objectivity but also about its generative capability, which rivalled and therefore offended that capability exercised by God and nature.[32] 'To a large extent,' Lord Henry concludes, 'the lad was his [Lord Henry's] own creation.'[33]

III

Neither the suggestion of mock-science in *Dorian Gray*, nor the novel's moralistic, almost Christian conclusion (itself subverted beforehand by the celebrated Preface), nor the Faustian underpinning nullifies in my opinion the importance of science to the book's conception or to Wilde's world-view and artistic vision. Nor do any of these nullify the novel's 'Hellenic ideal', its 'new Hedonism' that Wilde pits against what he calls in 'The Critic as Artist' the 'new Puritanism' abroad in England. It is fascinating to discover that in his Oxford notebooks Wilde, drawing on Arnold, J. A. Symonds and others, thought it worth recording that 'the Greek attitude can only be gained by a recognition of the scientific basis of Life', that 'in early civilizations science is found intimately blended with poetry', that 'in modern science, the fourth dimension of space, infinity, eternity, &c are poetical conceptions', and that 'the early Greeks had mystic anticipations of nearly all great modern scientific truths'.[34]

Through Hellenism, Wilde associated science not with pessimism or glum materialism but with optimism and progress. Goethe, he wrote in his Commonplace Book, 'owed his sublime cheerfulness to his scientific training' and this was the heritage of his Hellenism.[35] But this did not entail emotionalism or sentimentalism. Lord Henry's belief that science is untouched by the emotions and therefore could enable us to solve social problems exacerbated by the nineteenth century's 'over-expenditure of sympathy' is repeated by Gilbert, Wilde's spokesman in 'The Critic as Artist': 'That Humanitarian Sympathy wars against Nature, by securing the survival of the failure, may make the men of science loathe its facile virtues.' Wilde's systematic antipathy to philanthropy stands opposed to Dickens and may help explain Wilde's dislike of that novelist.[36] Yeats shared the antipathy but not its Darwinian rationale.

The *a*morality of science, as Gilbert and Lord Henry (and Wilde) see it, is what some regard as its *im*morality, but Lord Henry interprets immorality as itself the occasion for individuality. Between morality and individualism, the latter 'has really the higher aim. Modern morality consists in accepting the standard of one's age. I consider that for any man of culture to accept the standard of his age is a form of the grossest immorality.' Later in the novel, Dorian sits in front of his portrait, filled at times 'with that pride of individualism that is half the fascination of sin'.[37] Again, the moral penalty Dorian pays for that pride does not nullify individualism, which is a perennial virtue in Wilde's writings, from 'The Critic as Artist' (1890) to *De Profundis* (1897), maintained as it was by his concept of the Greek attitude. 'The longer one studies life and literature,' Gilbert claims, 'the more strongly one feels that behind everything that is wonderful stands the individual, and that it is not the moment that makes the man, but the man who creates the age.'[38] If he jested that 'the whole of Japan is a pure invention. There is no such country, there are no such people',[39] Wilde seems quite serious in having Gilbert claim that Wilde's own century had been made by two men: 'The nineteenth century is a turning point in history simply on account of the work of two men, Darwin and Renan, the one the critic of the Book of Nature, the other the critic of the books of God.'[40] 'Progress in thought,' Wilde wrote in his Commonplace Book, drawing on Clifford, 'is the assertion of individualism against authority.'[41]

At times Wilde called individuality 'self-preservation', a term that Darwinism would have suggested. He wrote in his Commonplace Book: 'The instinct of self-preservation in humanity, the desire to affirm one's own essence': these are the engines of progress, whereas puritanism, philistinism, sensualism and fanaticism are forces that seek to inhibit 'higher freedom'.[42] 'Essence' I understand as 'being', or, more precisely, the potential or blueprint for a possible fulfilment in the absence of repression, deflection or blockade; it is in one sense an Aristotelian, teleological idea, in another sense a Darwinian, hereditarian idea. In a Wildean paradox, Lord Henry − practitioner of influence for whom the natural is the greatest pose of all − is a disbeliever in nurture and a believer in nature; he practises fervently, that is to say, what he does not believe in. (The Christian martyr, Wilde was fond of saying, died for what he did not believe in.) 'The aim of life is self-development. To realise one's nature perfectly − that is what each of us is here for.' When Dorian Gray at the end of the novel accuses Lord Henry of having poisoned him with a book (*A Rebours* or *Against Nature*), Lord Henry replies: 'You and I are what we are, and will be what we will be.'[43]

There is, then, the obligation to one's own nature, and Wilde never abandoned as a virtue what he called 'self-realisation'. This unwittingly aligned him in an Irish context with George Moore and (in the future) with James Joyce, both of whom championed self-realization against the counter-individualist claims of the Irish Catholic Church and the Irish nationalist revival.[44] In *De Profundis*, Wilde returns again and again to the desirability of self-realization. 'The supreme vice is shallowness', he tells Lord Alfred Douglas. 'Whatever is realised is right.'[45] 'I am far more of an individualist than I ever was', he writes. 'Nothing seems to me of the smallest value except what one gets out of oneself. My nature is seeking a fresh mode of self-realisation.'[46] If in his moving letter he courts hubris in his self-identification with Christ ('Christ was not merely the supreme Individualist, but he was the first in History'), he at least rescues it from its shallower guise as mere eccentricity, flamboyant self-exhibition, perverse uniqueness: 'People used to say of me that I was too individualistic. I must be far more of an individualist than I ever was.'[47]

It was by his Oxford reading that Wilde discovered the evolutionary foundation of his belief in individuality, thereafter lifelong. Having defined progress in thought in his Commonplace Book, he then defined progress in matter, using Clifford's analogy between organic evolution and cognitive evolution: 'progress in matter is the differentiation and specialisation of function: those organisms which are entirely subject to external influences do not progress any more than a mind entirely subject to authority'.[48] He derived this analogy from Clifford's 1868 lecture, 'On Some of the Conditions of Mental Development', in which the scientist defines individuality as differentiation from other organisms, and individuality in thought as differentiation from surrounding minds.[49] Clifford goes on to identify sharp mental differentiation as one of the characteristics of genius, which must have impressed the young Wilde. The evolutionary process of developmental differentiation ('the parts of the organism get more different'; 'the organism gets more different from the environment'; 'the organism gets more different from other individuals'), the evolutionary mechanism of natural selection, and the evolutionary concept of hierarchy in the organic kingdoms (arrangement in terms of organizational complexity) − all by analogy became Wilde's notion of cultivation, and gave a biological foundation to his aestheticism. Although in his Commonplace Book he joked that 'Nature kills off all those who do not believe in the Uniformity of Nature and the Law of Causation',[50] Wilde (like Lord Henry) practised artificial selection on himself. There is a suggestive analogy between Wilde's over-cultivation as an aesthete (a too great differentiation from his moral environment and other, hypocritically moral individuals) and the fate that natural selection visits upon those organisms that exhibit its counterpart in nature (unadaptable and self-damaging over specialization); the analogy is both suggested by, and rendered ironic as a result of, Wilde's own readings in evolution and its exploitation in his works. It is tempting to see Lord Henry as another specimen of over-cultivation but Dorian Gray as one of devolution; that is, of the descent, rather than ascent, of man – a sociobiological reversion such as Spencer might have explained.[51]

IV

Certainly Dorian Gray is a specimen of flawed heredity as well as of malign nurture. He is a 'son of Love and Death': 'A beautiful woman risking everything for a mad passion. A few wild weeks of happiness cut short by a hideous, treacherous crime. Months of voiceless agony, and then a child born in pain. The mother snatched away by death, the boy left to solitude and the tyranny of an old and loveless man.' Dorian Gray's parentage (the quarrelsome, mean grandfather, the beautiful, romantic mother, the socially insignificant father) is for Lord Henry a fascinating, tragic background for the decorative portrait of the boy he intends to 'paint': all pattern and 'symbolical value' after 'the new manner in art'. But it is also an influence, even a determinism, beyond Lord Henry's evil tutelage. What befalls Dorian Gray befell his mother, and what Lord Henry wishes to happen does, not just for reasons of sinister supervision (a self-fulfilling prophecy), but also for reasons of heredity: 'I hope that Dorian Gray will make this girl [Sybil Vane] his wife, passionately adore her for six months, and then suddenly become fascinated by some one else.' Along the way there is a mad passion; a hideous, treacherous crime; and voiceless agony. 'The men were a poor lot,' says Lord Fermor of Dorian's family, 'but, egad! the women were wonderful.'[52] Dorian has inherited only his mother's wonderful beauty; otherwise, he has inherited the character-poverty of his male forebears.

But at least he did not succeed to what the narrator calls 'the inherited stupidity of the race' – that is, of the English, which Lord Fermor himself has come into. It was that stupidity that, according to Wilde, produced the philistinism, rampant common sense and puritanism of the English to which aesthetes – and the Irish – were congenitally opposed (also the French, originators of aestheticism; Dorian's mother bears the surname Devereux).[53] Instead, Dorian has inherited tendencies from decadents and tyrants, exponents of a magnificent indifference portrayed in dramatic procession in the pages of Huysmans – Tiberius, Caligula, Domitian, Elagabalus – as well as tendencies inherited from writers, including Petronius and Gautier. We are told, in a sentiment of which Borges would later have been proud: 'Yet one had ancestors in literature, as well as in one's own race, nearer perhaps in type and temperament, many of them, and certainly with an influence of which one was more absolutely conscious.'[54] And, of course, there is the inheritance of the human race itself, for Dorian Gray re-enacts the fate of Eve and the fall of man into sin and pain. It is as if by virtue of his mother's beauty he has become female, or perhaps transvestite like Huysmans' Elagabalus, whom he imitates by attending a costume ball as Anne de Joyeuse, in a bejewelled dress. Like Des Esseintes, Dorian suffers from an inherited sickness, and both Wilde's novel and Huysmans' are studies in pathology, indeed of that pathological condition we call monstrosity and which so fascinated the Victorians in that age of moral and medical obsession.[55]

But the record of Wilde's reading at Oxford (1874–79) proves that his interest in heredity and pathology predated the publication of *A Rebours* in 1884. In one entry that might be a digest of Clifford, Wilde wrote: 'neither in the world of thought or in that of matter is the past ever annihilated'; and in another: 'the past is the key of the future'. From the pages of H. T. Buckle, Wilde thought it important to enter the names of William Cullen (1710–90) and William Hunter (1718–83), 'the earliest pathologists: their object was to show that there is a science of the abnormal'. And such a science is possible because 'even animal monstrosities', he writes down from Buckle, 'are now known not to be capricious but essentially natural; a new science is thus produced[,] that of Teratology'.[56] (Surveying his collection of fantastic musical instruments, Dorian Gray is delighted 'that art, like nature, has her monsters'.) If 'everything must come to one out of one's own nature', as Wilde wrote in *De Profundis*, 'there is no use in telling a person a thing that they don't feel and can't understand'. A refrain in *De Profundis* is the flawed heredity of the Douglases; he tells Lord Alfred: '[Your mother] saw, of course, that heredity had burdened you with a terrible legacy, and frankly admitted it, admitted it with terror: he is "the one of my children who has inherited the fatal Douglas temperament," she wrote of you'; 'Through your father you come of a race, marriage with whom is horrible, friendship fatal, and that lays violent hands either on its own life or on the lives of others'; 'the fact that the man you hated was your own father, and that the feeling was thoroughly reciprocated, did not make your Hate noble or fine in any way. If it showed anything it was simply that it was an hereditary disease.'[57]

Behind the allegation that Douglas betrayed a vicious mole of nature lay a contemporary idea, deriving from the theories of the Italian psychiatrist Cesare Lombroso, author of *Delinquent Man* (1875): that of degeneration.[58] Certain ironies attach to Wilde's belief in the power of heredity. If the biological concept of inheritance helped to sponsor the fashionable late-Victorian notion of degeneration, the notion was for many people exemplified in literary and cultural decadence, of which Wilde was regarded as a vivid, even lurid, embodiment. Also, seven months before he began *De Profundis*, Wilde petitioned the Home Secretary for release from Reading Gaol, on the grounds that his misdeeds were due rather to a curable sexual pathology than to criminality, citing in evidence Max Nordau, author of *Degeneration* (1892, translated 1895), a work which discussed Wilde as an example of 'a pathological aberration of a racial instinct ... a malevolent mania for contradiction ... the ego-mania of degeneration'.[59] *Degeneration* was dedicated to Lombroso, who had also written *Genius and Insanity* (1861), and in his petition Wilde professed his fear of losing his mind were he to remain in gaol (a rather *too* sharp mental differentiation, he might have added, remembering Clifford). Self-realization in the sense of fulfilment of the individual's heredity could, then, be deemed a vice, as it was in Douglas's case and – as Wilde was ironically and implicitly claiming by petition – in his own. Yet beyond his petition, and Douglas's behaviour, he preferred to consider it as a virtue.

In Wilde is argued out the comparative forces of nature (or heredity) and nurture (including self-nurture, or self-cultivation) that so preoccupied his contemporaries at that junction of culture and biology that was called sociology. Self-realization could be the product of either, and nurture was not necessarily superior in this regard. Whereas, for many of those contemporaries, the weight of the past known as inheritance was a bleak proposition, for Wilde it was, on the whole, just the opposite (perhaps in part because he was immensely fortunate in, and immensely proud of, his own parentage and lineage). 'By revealing to us the absolute mechanism of all action,' Gilbert says (as though fresh from Wilde's own scientific reading), 'and so freeing us from the self-imposed and trammelling burden of moral responsibility, the scientific principle of Heredity has become, as it were, the warrant for the contemplative life. It has shown us that we are never less free than when we try to act.' In compensation for our imprisonment in 'practical and external life' (though in *Dorian Gray* and *De Profundis* Wilde reinstated moral responsibility without endangering the imagination or minimizing heredity), we are at liberty 'to realize the experiences of those who are greater than we are': Leopardi, Theocritus, Pierre Vidal, Lancelot, Abelard, Villon, Shelley, Atys, Hamlet. As in *Dorian Gray*, literary-historical characters are – sociologically in Spencer's term, sociobiologically in present-day terminology – in a very real sense our forebears. They constitute in 'The Critic as Artist', as in the novel, a 'terrible shadow, with many gifts in its hands', yet seem less oppressive, more liberating in the dialogue than in the novel. They are, in the dialogue, at least in part the creatures of our own imagination; we are ordinarily more active in their summoning than was Dorian Gray, who seems merely to act out the consequences of Lord Henry's misguidance and (like Lord Alfred Douglas, as Wilde saw him) his own genotype. If the fate of Dorian Gray qualifies Gilbert's optimism, it still leaves his observation a considerable force: 'the imagination is the result of heredity. It is simply concentrated race-experience.'[60] For Wilde, Darwinism did not undermine the uniqueness of humanity or the freedom of the individual; rather, it sponsored both by explaining the origin and direction of art (the product of imagination or recessive contemplation) and thereby vindicated art and the aesthetic life against the deluded claims of practicality and progressivism. Wilde was the aesthete who, in one of the larger paradoxes of his career, gave aestheticism a scientific foundation.[61] Life, he thought, imitates previous life as surely as it imitates art.

The concept of hereditary descent could also have sponsored, had Yeats but allowed it, the race-membership and race-consciousness upon which his Celtic Revival ultimately rested. Indeed, the invisible life Yeats championed was surely reconcilable with the ancestral life that Spencer championed and that was inexplicable in the exclusive terms of an individual's own experience. Clifford was persuaded by Spencer, and Wilde by Clifford, that all human knowledge derives from experience but not solely *individual* experience.[62] Such a view enabled a resolution of the dilemma posed by the exclusive empiricism of Locke and Hume on one side, and the transcendentalism of Kant (with his theory of universal truths, innately known) on the other.[63] Wilde absorbed the view into his work dramatically as well as polemically. For example, Gwendolyn's ideal Ernest (she seeks to marry the embodiment of Ernestness) is realized by the hitherto hidden heredity of Jack's ancestral Ernestness. Such a view also balanced the role of accidental variation (of pure, contingent individuality) to which Wilde, no less than Yeats, objected.

But an interest in science, including evolutionary theory, an admiration for Darwin, a respect for the nature of things and the honouring of self-realization (even if he reconciled it with self-transcending imagination) – all distinguish Wilde from Yeats, who emulated him in so much else. It is possible to revise our perception of Wilde by demoting the Victorian aesthete in him and promoting the anti-English, wittily subversive feminist and anti-colonialist in him. This has recently been done for reasons of Irish cultural nationalism.[64] The revision is fine (if not dandy), but it threatens to backfire, since the case pursued reveals Wilde as a lifelong champion of that individualism that rejects the primacy of causes such as nationalism, Irish or otherwise. He is also revealed as an Anglo-Irishman who inherited the intellectual interests – scientific as well as artistic – of his tradition. And its outdoor pursuits as well; those included fishing and shooting – encounters with nature in the flesh, so to speak. It is amusing to read the early and unexpectedly knowledgeable and enthusiastic letters about the action from the Wilde lodge at Lough Fee, County Galway.

> The fishing has not been so good as usual. I only got one salmon, about 7½lbs. The sea-trout however are very plentiful; we get a steady average of over four a day and lots of brown trout, so it is not difficult to amuse oneself and as no fish are going in any of the neighbouring lakes I am fairly pleased. . . . One week more of this delightful, heathery, mountainous, lake-filled region! Teeming with hares and trout! Then to Longford for the partridge, then home.[65]

Of course, Wilde soon after underwent a serious conversion to aestheticism, but nature and its scientific understandings stayed with him, translated rather than dispatched. No attempt at a recuperation and rehabilitation of natural history and nature writing in Irish culture, or in late-Victorian literary history, for that matter, need shrink from enlisting at some juncture the works and philosophies of this still surprising genius of Irish literature.

Part Two
CONTINUITIES

Part Two
CONTINGENCIES

The Quare on the Square:
A Statue of Oscar Wilde for
Dublin

PAULA MURPHY

> Good people, belonging as they do to the normal, and so, commonplace, type,
> are artistically uninteresting. Bad people are, from the point of view of art,
> fascinating studies. They represent colour, variety and strangeness. Good people
> exasperate one's reason; bad people stir one's imagination.[1]

Oscar Wilde numbered himself among the 'bad', and as early as 1878 he had even
referred to himself as such.[2] Transmuting the meaning of good and bad, he
advocated, most particularly in the opening stages of *The Picture of Dorian Gray*,
a hedonistic lifestyle, which with wilful error he located in the Hellenic ideal,
rather than in Hellenistic decay. Colour, variety and strangeness feature in
abundance throughout Wilde's short life, and are at the very root of the public
sculpture that has been erected in Dublin to commemorate him. The sculpture,
commissioned by Guinness Ireland,[3] is the work of Danny Osborne[4] and was
unveiled in Merrion Square in October 1997.

It has been a long time coming. While the public scandal surrounding Parnell
did not prevent a statue being erected in his honour in Dublin at the beginning
of the twentieth century — in fact the Parnell statue was very actively sought —
it has taken nearly one hundred years for an Irish body, public or private, to risk
suggesting that we might consider Oscar Wilde worthy of such commemoration.[5]
But then it has taken the same length of time for Ireland to awaken, reluctantly,
to the existence of sexuality and the reality of the way in which it dictates a
lifestyle. We are now, at the close of the century, in a position to pay homage to
the man of letters, while also demonstrating acceptance of his homosexuality.
The varied elements, sometimes contradictory, that created the wholeness of the
man can all be explored — the kind father, the obsessed lover, the racy *bon
viveur*, the camp homosexual, the arrogant intellectual, the sharp wit, the
sensitive creator. Dublin has already made Wilde one of its own. Knowing, before
the event, that the commemoration was intended for Merrion Square, across the
road from the house in which Wilde spent his youth, Dubliners, with their
traditional sense of irreverence and familiarity, instantly dubbed the work 'the
quare on the square'.

Wilde would surely have been delighted by the idea of a lasting commemoration,[6] but perhaps fearful of the outcome. As a devoted admirer of Greek art, he was particularly aware of the way in which the late-Victorian period marked a distancing from Greek universality in public monuments in favour of what became known as the 'coat and trousers' style.[7] The Greek style, revived in Neoclassicism in the late eighteenth century, had promoted a form of classical heroization, symbolized in the unspecific toga or realized in nude representation. The Victorians, however, favoured the faithful likeness, a portrait image, representative of its time rather than transcending it. Sir Joshua Reynolds was the first president of the Royal Academy and one of the earliest English artists to address the theory and practice of sculpture. In a lecture to students and academicians towards the end of the eighteenth century, advocated the use of classical attire in sculptural work. 'The desire of transmitting to posterity the shape of modern dress must be acknowledged to be purchased at a prodigious price, even the price of everything that is valuable in art.'[8] Reynolds's theories were studied and adopted by academic artists in the nineteenth century. Oscar Wilde concurs with Reynolds's view on the use of contemporary fashionable dress in art works and is even more affronted by it because of his general hatred of modern styles of dress. Indeed, to be commemorated in such fashion seemed to Wilde the final insult: 'To see the statues of our departed statesmen in marble frock-coats and bronze, double-breasted waistcoats', he quipped, 'adds a new horror to death.'[9]

The limitations of such public sculptures are evident in their lack of expression, or as Wilde puts it, 'atmosphere'.[10] In a speech at the unveiling of a monument to Shakespeare at Stratford-upon-Avon in 1888, Wilde was critical of the way in which English sculptors confined themselves to the more imitative processes.[11] He considered sculpture in the late nineteenth century largely incapable of representing the complex nature of contemporary life, and it is certainly true that facial portraits and period dress are scarcely revealing of the life and personality of the 'sitter'. This inadequacy was addressed in Wilde's day by Alfred Gilbert[12] in his commemoration of the Earl of Shaftesbury, unveiled in Piccadilly Circus in 1893. Gilbert chose a functional fountain topped by a statue of Eros to 'symbolize his [the Earl's] life's work'.[13] Similarly, in his Wilde commemoration, Danny Osborne has chosen to explore beyond the portrait likeness of the man, in an attempt to represent the internal complexity, the destructive passion of Wilde's soul.

In Osborne's statue, Wilde is displayed languishing on a large white quartz rock,[14] clutching a green carnation to his breast, exotically attired. His garments are carved in coloured stones: the trousers in blue pearl granite, the jacket in nephrite jade with pink thulite lapels and cuffs, the socks and shoes in black granite. Small details, such as the carnation, the button cords and the shoelaces are cast in bronze with a green patination. The polychrome echoes the rich and precious materials, and their exotic, heady colours, described in Wilde's fairy stories. Even the extensive journeys to distant and remote places (such as were undertaken in 'The Fisherman and his Soul') have their counterpart in the context of the monument. For while the two granites, blue pearl from Norway and black from Zimbabwe, were available from stone-yards in Ireland, Osborne had to travel to Norway to choose the thulite and to Vancouver for the jade.

The use of polychrome in this monument is of particular interest. While we have become familiar with painted metal abstract works in the twentieth century, the use of colour in sculpture in the past has been controversial. Increased knowledge of ancient Greek sculpture in the nineteenth century brought with it the discovery that the marble, which for so long had been assumed to be pure white, was in fact originally highly coloured. Such had been the influence of sculpture in its pure white state, it was difficult for classically inspired artists and theorists readily to accept this (relatively) shocking information. The debate raged across the century between those for and against coloured marble. The Professor of Sculpture at the Royal Academy in mid-century, Sir Richard Westmacott, thought that sculpture should remain pure and unadorned, dismissing the use of colour as ornate, and therefore decadent. John Ruskin, on the other hand, saw the use of colour as symbolic, with inherent spiritual connotations. The controversy was played out in Ireland as well. In the context of the most significant monumental commission in the nineteenth century – the national monument commemorating Daniel O'Connell for the centre of Dublin – the competition instructions detailed that coloured marbles were not to be employed.

Wilde himself generally supported the use of colour in sculpture, which is perhaps not surprising for a writer who employed colour so extensively in his own creative work. He even proposed the idea that the absence of colour in contemporary dress had 'almost annihilated the modern sculptor'.[15] In one particular incident, Wilde actively advocated the use of colour. When in Rome in 1877 he visited the tomb of Keats in the Protestant Cemetery and, while moved by the experience, he was critical of the actual monument, especially the inclusion of a white marble profile bust of the poet, which he found wanting.[16] Wilde thought that a tinted bust would be more appropriate and cited the example of the sculpted portrait of the Maharajah of Koolapoor which he had seen in Florence. The Indian Prince had died in that city in 1870 and is commemorated by a monument in the Cascine, the work of Charles Francis Fuller,[17] erected in 1874. While the monument has lost much of its colour today, a description of the unveiling reveals the extent of the polychrome and identifies the jewelled effect of the colours that Wilde would have seen just a year later.[18] In the case of Osborne's Wilde monument, the sculptor has employed coloured stones to express a colourful personality. In doing so, Osborne has also positioned the work within an interesting art-historical framework.

Somewhat unusually for a large scale public monument, Danny Osborne has chosen to execute the face and hands of the portrait statue in unglazed porcelain, since this material does not age in the manner of marble.[19] This seems curiously appropriate for the author of *The Picture of Dorian Gray* and for a man as absorbed as Wilde in artistic representation of ageless and beautiful youth. It is also particularly representative of turn-of-the-century Symbolist art. The image of face and hands projected with glistening clarity amidst a surfeit of rich and beautiful materials calls to mind the paintings of Gustav Klimt and, perhaps less well known, the figures on Alfred Gilbert's Clarence Tomb.[20] It is of interest that in 1994 Danny Osborne made a seemingly prophetic study trip to Britain to examine late nineteenth-century sculpture and in particular the work of Gilbert. Within this context, Osborne's Wilde monument might be considered a late twentieth-century variant of *fin de siècle* Symbolist sculpture.

In its final form, Osborne's sculpture is a three-piece sculptural work, expanding across space; situated in front of the figure of Wilde are two further smaller sculptures, positioned on black granite plinths as though presented for his contemplation. One plinth supports the bronze figure of a nude woman, representing Constance pregnant with their second child: an image that disgusted Wilde. The second supports a male torso, also executed in bronze and loosely based on a Hellenistic fragment of a figure of Dionysus.[21]

This sculptural group is in the tradition of many images in the history of art that represent decision-making, among which the figure of Hercules at the crossroads, choosing between vice and virtue, is perhaps the best known.[22] Other representations include the choice between comedy and tragedy or art and life. In such imagery, it is more usual for the protagonist to seem troubled by the choice; however, Wilde appears rather to reflect on a decision already taken. Such an interpretation might be further supported by the great quartz boulder on which Wilde is positioned. The employment of such a rock is more usually symbolic of achievement, a difficult task overcome, with the protagonist depicted successfully surmounting the stone.[23] However, this is not a triumphant representation of Wilde, who appears to recline halfway, acknowledging the less publicly acceptable choice of vice over virtue and, ultimately, tragedy over comedy.

Art and life are also at issue here, as represented in the bronze figurines. Wilde is presented with, on the one hand, the reality of life, the earthiness of which is depicted in the image of his pregnant wife, and, on the other hand, the spiritual beauty of art, as witnessed in the otherworldly perfection of the Greek statue. The selection of Dionysus, who in his wild, irrational and sensual behaviour ultimately symbolizes creativity and passion, to represent art at this particular moment of choice, is clarified in Wilde's *De Profundis*. In a discussion of the Greek gods, he identifies what he considers to be the two most suggestive figures of Greek mythology: 'for religion, Demeter . . . and, for art, Dionysus, the son of a mortal woman to whom the moment of his birth had proved the moment of her death also'.[24] Ultimately the bronze figurines represent the triumph of art over life. Wilde's theorizing on the interrelationship between art and life promotes the superior nature of art and the way in which art has the power to inform, to correct and even to obliterate life. 'Life by its realism is always spoiling the subject-matter of art. The supreme pleasure in literature is to realize the non-existent.'[25] Wilde had no desire for art to mirror life, rather he preferred, in his pursuit of androgynous and beautiful youth, to see life mirror art.[26]

In honour of Wilde's famous wit, quotations from his writings are presented in graffiti fashion, incised into the black granite plinths. While graffiti have become an independent art-form in the late twentieth century, in the case of the Wilde commemoration the sculptor anticipates this particular form of public interaction with the work. The inclusion of fragments of text in visual works of art has been popular throughout the century and the significance of the fragment in this instance seems to highlight the fact that Wilde's writings are more widely known in quotation than in their completed form. Wilde, who might almost be considered the creator of the 'soundbite', also writes to inform. His work is always replete with message, despite his admiration of art for art's sake.[27]

Danny Osborne was offered the commission for the Wilde monument as a result of a competition open to artists living and working in Ireland and to Irish artists working abroad. On the basis of an open submission at the initial stage in April 1995, at which point over fifty artists made application, six sculptors were shortlisted by the selection panel:[28] Cathy Carman, Don Cronin, Brian King, Melanie le Brocquy, Danny Osborne, Louise Walsh. Their work represents an interesting variety of talents. However, shortly after the selection was made, Melanie le Brocquy withdrew,[29] to be replaced by Benedict Byrne. Each sculptor was invited to submit a maquette[30] within six weeks. The only artistic guideline given suggested that the work be 'broadly figurative'. Not all the artists were happy with the idea of presenting a maquette, since several of them favour working their ideas through in the full-size, large-scale image. In the case of the winning entry, for example, given the dimensional restrictions of the maquette, it was not possible to project any real idea of the impact of the completed work on to the tiny scale of the sketch model.

In common with the Osborne monument, the remaining five works reflect the concerns of the sculptors through a variety of issues: from portrait likeness and symbolism to duality and sexuality. Two worked very specifically with the portrait image. Oscar Wilde was rarely the subject of painted or sculpted portraits in his lifetime. This can be considered the result of a relatively short life which ended in such a tragic fashion, but must also be related to the fact that the Victorian age saw a growing interest in photographic portraits. Consequently, there exist many photographs of Wilde, from the famous childhood image in a dress to the photographs taken in Rome in the year of his death. His life and physical decline are well documented in photographs. Sketch portraits and caricatures of him were executed by many artists, most famously by Toulouse Lautrec. Wilde's character was perhaps best expressed in this particular technique and his physique lent itself to rapid line drawing. There can be no doubt that the late nineteenth-century fashion for posing was most successfully captured by the graphic arts. There are, however, few known formal portraits. Ellmann records that a portrait by Harper Pennington hung in the drawing-room in Wilde's house in Tite Street.[31] Pennington, an American portrait painter, had been a pupil of Whistler and exhibited often in London in the 1880s.

In creating a posthumous portrait there is a requirement to encompass the whole person, rather than, in the case of a live sitter, capturing a moment in time or a personality at a particular age. The posthumous likeness obliges the artist to work with a photograph or another portrait or, as is possible in the case of Wilde, a memory of same. Don Cronin[32] was wholly committed to the idea of a real portrait likeness, 'a three-dimensional photograph',[33] and to this end he studied photographs of Wilde in his mid-twenties. He presents him casually seated, slightly decadent and overblown, and intended, in a completed state, to be life-size and cast in bronze. The sculpture represents a mature variant of the image of Wilde in New York in 1882, posing on an elaborately draped sofa and photographed by Napoleon Sarony. There is something comfortably familiar about Cronin's portrait of Wilde, devoid of message, literary or sexual, and revealing its artistic dynamic in what the sculptor proposed would be the abstract and textured treatment of the garments. This is a simple uncomplicated work, capturing a suggestion of the 'Celtic laziness' that Wilde identified in himself,[34] and which would probably have had immediate appeal for the general public.

Among his writings on art, Wilde left little comment on portraiture, except to criticize the extent to which nineteenth-century portrait artists concerned themselves with likeness and were thus 'doomed to absolute oblivion'.[35] His requirement centred on style over fact, and imagination over realism, dismissing the century as dull and prosaic. While *The Picture of Dorian Gray* does not theorize about portraiture, beyond suggesting that a portrait painting reveals more of the painter than of the sitter, it does have the portrait image at its core, and inevitably the duality in this text served as an important source of inspiration for the sculptors in the preliminary stages of their work. This influence remains most evident in the second of the two specifically portrait images, the work of Brian King.[36]

King chose a life-size standing bronze portrait likeness because he believes that there should be a portrait statue of Wilde, not some abstract or symbolic work.[37] Wilde is represented as a confident, arrogant figure, projecting his ego. The sense of presence and self-promotion is palpable even in the small scale of the sketch model. The Dorian Gray variant in the image is manifest in the placing of a young head on an old body, the body likeness to be worked from a photograph taken in the year of Wilde's death. This is in the style of 'the marble frock-coats and bronze, double-breasted waistcoats' mentioned earlier, an image of Wilde that might have been created in his own day.[38] The duality, as represented in the contrasting face/body in the statue, is echoed and emphasized in the tall granite backdrop, cut through at a diagonal and executed in two colours: blue and red. King intended that the granite wall would carry a text, either the inscription on Wilde's tomb monument in Paris, or an excerpt from the John Gray poem[39] of 1931 which appears to be written as Wilde's elegy.

The dual personality of Wilde continues to be the central focus of inspiration in the maquettes of both Cathy Carman and Louise Walsh, both of whom became very emotionally engaged with the complexity and contrariness of the man. Carman,[40] in a symbolic interpretation of Wilde the writer, makes use of a mask,[41] a deconstructed variant of the popular nineteenth-century portrait bust, and ultimately, in the face/mask image, drawing a parallel with the theatrical comedy and tragedy. The mask is two-faced, to project the inner spirit and personality of the man, rather than simply the identifiable facial details. The left side conveys the heavy, rounded, slightly bulging features of the sensual man, and dissolves on the right side into a play of distorted abstract form to indicate the dark mystery and, inevitably, the tragedy in his life. The image is at once figurative and abstract, formed and deformed, looking out and retreating inwards. A series of voids across the work combined with the shifting planes of the sculptural form suggest instability, which is further projected in the rich but unpredictable play of light and dark. Duality has been a constant concern in the work of Cathy Carman and she has explored the two-faced image before, inspired on a previous occasion by the primitive island sculptures in County Fermanagh.

Carman's submission is the most original of the six maquettes in that she tackles only the face. The impact of this proposed monumental bronze mask, with its tactile quality and its rhythmic forms, would likely have been awesome and certainly controversial. The maquette strikes a melancholy note and, in its finished state, standing eight feet high, the sadness might have been overwhelming − or perhaps lost altogether. It is certainly the case that this sculpture would have worked more successfully on an open and raised site. In the intended, rather enclosed, space the mask might have been rendered invisible, which would have been an unsatisfactory outcome in the case of this particular public commemoration.

The most moving among the maquettes is that executed by Louise Walsh,[42] one in which Wilde is portrayed as a standing figure, wrists bound, holding a mask, which in turn sprouts lilies. If Wilde looks somewhat contrite in the bronze model, this was not the intention of the artist for the full-size work, in which she proposed that he would appear more flamboyant and more majestic.[43] Her aim was to contrast the artificial façade that he built around himself, with the inner pain, as represented in the mask positioned over his heart. The mask has the appearance of a severed head and therefore refers also to John the Baptist, while the bound wrists connect the representation to St Sebastian, homosexual icon, and refers to a favourite painting of Wilde executed by Guido Reni. Lilies, more usually employed as a symbol of purity in art, are here emphatically sexual, with their phallic thrust. While their compositional arrangement suggests the possibility of encagement, the flowing lines of the display create a link with Victorian decorative design. The sculptor further intended that some of the lilies would metamorphose into arrows, therefore continuing the identification of Wilde with St Sebastian. In the multi-layered readings of this image, Walsh reveals the depth of the relationship that developed between the sculptor and the writer in the course of the work. While particularly interested in exploring Wilde's sexuality and the way in which he is now being reclaimed, Louise Walsh expressed a desire 'to do something for him', to comfort and amuse him.

Benedict Byrne[44] was alone among the six shortlisted artists to present a purely symbolic work. Byrne believed that Wilde's biographical details and sexuality were not important concerns in relation to the proposed monument. Nor was he interested in his prose writing. Ultimately Byrne found Wilde in his poetry and was inspired particularly by the poem 'Apologia', in which he feels that Wilde anticipates his imprisonment. Working with the idea of a fallen angel, the figure, naked, youthful, idealized and, somewhat unusually, upturned, is not intended as a portrait of Wilde, but rather, in its connection with the poem, is intended to represent the image of a humanized spotted hawk in flight. The sculptor intended that the final work would be inscribed with the relevant lines from 'Apologia'. However, while torment and pain are expressed, the symbolism remains obscure and it is of interest, therefore, to know that Byrne was adapting a sculptural work that he had already submitted for an earlier unrelated competition, and that the sculpture in its original conception had no connection with Wilde. The monumental image, over nine feet, and carved in granite, while expressing a silent statuesque strength, nonetheless reveals a certain awkwardness. The maquette figure submitted for the Wilde competition is a reduced copy in Portland stone of the already completed statue, thus reversing the more usual practice whereby the sculptor moves from small sketch model to full-scale finished sculpture. In its small scale the image is strikingly acrobatic.

Wilde's writing, both literary and critical, formulated a theory of art, if sometimes a contradictory one. He was dogmatic in the manner in which he addressed artist, art work and observer and, although an early admirer of Whistler's art and a continuing admirer of art for art's sake, his dogma was more usually academic. There can be no doubt that he had a lifelong interest in sculpture, but his writings on the subject are fragmentary and largely based on his deep commitment to the art of the Greeks, in whose sculpture he admired 'the beauty of form, outline, and mass, the grace and loveliness of design, and the delicacy of technical treatment'.[45] This interest was nurtured in his early surroundings in Dublin, where his father, William Wilde, took an active role in sculptural commissions. Wilde's earliest sculptural memory must have been the classical works in the family home in Merrion Square, copies of ancient sculptures, such as the Dying Gladiator,[46] and copies of relief roundels by the Danish sculptor Bertel Thorvaldsen.[47] Thorvaldsen was the leading Neoclassicist in Rome in the 1820s and 1830s after the death of Antonio Canova. His work lacks the spiritual dimension of Canova and, though linear in style, exudes a control that is often at once dry and chilling. The carving of the original roundels, however, is exquisitely beautiful and attains a level of refinement that is highly sophisticated.

Close to the house, not a hundred yards away on Merrion Square, stands the National Gallery of Ireland, opened in 1864 in the aftermath of the Great Industrial and Art Exhibition held in Dublin in 1853. While there was little original sculpture on exhibition in the Gallery in the nineteenth century, there was an extensive display of plaster casts of ancient works. In keeping with the Neoclassical theorizing of J. J. Winckelmann[48] and with academic teaching, which considered that a study of ancient sculpture offered the most perfect way of learning about art, aesthetics and taste, copies of Greek and Roman works proliferated in eighteenth- and nineteenth-century collections. This sculptural display in the National Gallery had great prominence, arranged, as it was, in the Front Hall and in the Sculpture Hall (now the Shaw Room), and accompanied by an informative catalogue. Yet again the sculptural work most immediately available for the young Oscar Wilde to study was largely classical or classically inspired.

The Irish expression of the severe Neoclassical style is to be found in the sculpture of John Hogan,[49] who had spent the most significant part of his career working in Rome, but who returned to Dublin in 1849. Hogan became a friend of the Wilde family and a patient of William Wilde, who attended him in his illness in 1855. William Wilde's active participation in issues related to public sculpture in both Ireland[50] and England[51] resulted in his chairmanship of the memorial committee that commissioned Hogan to execute a statue of Thomas Davis after his death in 1845.[52] Davis is portrayed draped *à l'antique* over contemporary costume. Oscar Wilde would have been too young to have made Hogan's acquaintance before the sculptor's death in 1858, and, though work by him was to be seen in Dublin and elsewhere in Ireland, much of it was either in private collections or in Catholic churches. His first encounter with a carving by Hogan may have been the marble relief of John Brinkley, Bishop of Cloyne, in Trinity College. Brinkley, who had been Professor of Astronomy and was buried in the College chapel, was portrayed by Hogan seated at work wearing his academic robes. The garments give a linear flow to the monument, but the relief presentation forces a certain awkwardness in the compositional arrangement.

If Hogan's was a rather academic example of Neoclassicism, Wilde had an opportunity to view a particularly fine variant of the style in another, earlier work in the university. After the death of Provost Richard Baldwin, who left an important sum of money to Trinity College Dublin in his will, the authorities commissioned a tomb monument to commemorate his generosity. The commission was offered to Christopher Hewetson,[53] an Irish sculptor working in Rome, and the work, portraying the Provost at the moment of death accompanied by an angel and a muse (symbolizing science), was erected in Trinity College in 1784. Intended for the College chapel, which was at the time incomplete, the monument was positioned in the examination hall, where it can still be seen. Its positioning in this particular location afforded Wilde the opportunity of being distracted in the course of examinations by a quietly emotional sculptural work, simple and clear in its composition and rhythmic in its linear flow. An inspirational and classical calm is revealed in the work of this sculptor who, at the time of the completion of the monument, was working in the aura of Canova.

From these early classical beginnings, Wilde would continue to be inspired by the classical style and its subject matter. Descriptions of his house in London reveal the presence of a small number of sculptural works.[54] A bust of Augustus Caesar, which was awarded to Wilde for winning the Newdigate Prize for Poetry at Oxford in 1878, was placed in the corner of the drawing-room, while a bronze figure of Narcissus was positioned on the mantelpiece. It seems probable that this was a copy of the bronze Narcissus discovered at Pompeii in 1862 and subsequently displayed in the National Museum at Naples. The statue was immediately acclaimed as a masterpiece and widely copied.[55] In Wilde's bedroom stood a plaster cast of the famous Hermes of Olympia, a work of greater archaeological interest than the Narcissus. This statue had a special significance for Wilde, positioned as it was in his bedroom, for he also presented a copy of it to Harvard for the gymnasium.

The original marble group of Hermes holding the infant Dionysus was found in the Temple of Hera at Olympia shortly after Wilde's visit there in 1877. It was identified as the work of Praxiteles, from the writings of Pausanius, and acclaimed as the only extant authenticated work by the hand of this sculptor.[56] Seen to reveal the less impersonal and new individualistic style of the fourth century BC, the figure of Hermes is typical of the late classical period in its soft modelling and graceful pose. Winckelmann considered that 'The beautiful style of art begins with Praxiteles.'[57] Even the introductory text to the 1868 catalogue of sculpture in the National Gallery of Ireland indicated that 'Praxiteles was perhaps the greatest' sculptor in the period after Phidias.[58] However, because of the lateness of this find, neither Winckelmann nor any of the authorities on ancient sculpture to date had been in a position to consider this statue, nor was it exhibited among the already formed collections of copies of antique sculpture. The contemporary nature of the find and the fact that Wilde was almost, but not quite present for the uncovering (a mere month intervened), must have persuaded him to adopt the work. The presence of a copy of this statue in Wilde's bedroom, which eventually became the children's nursery, reveals his active pursuit of improvement through art. His theory is based on that of the Greeks, who, as Wilde pointed out in 'The Decay of Lying', placed statues in their bedrooms to inspire the conception of beautiful children.[59] Wilde believed that life gains spiritually and in beauty from the presence of great works of art and, in placing a copy of an ancient statue in his bedroom, he was echoing the actions of a late-eighteenth-century German enthusiast of ancient art. Goethe, in Rome in 1788, reflected on the importance of acquiring good plaster casts. 'Then,' he writes, 'every morning, when one opens one's eyes, one is greeted by perfection; one's whole thinking becomes permeated by their presence, until it becomes impossible ever again to relapse into barbarism.'[60] In the same vein, Wilde sees life reproducing 'the grace of Praxiteles'.[61]

Oscar Wilde delighted in ancient sculpture in formalist terms, admiring the surface rhythms, the sensuous forms, the flawlessness of the marble. His experience is similar to that of Winckelmann and in his descriptions of the calm that is to be found in the work of the ancients, 'the calm which comes not from the rejection but from the absorption of passion',[62] the influence of the German theorist in Wilde's aesthetic education is evident. Wilde, like Winckelmann, extended this aesthetic appreciation beyond the realm of art and, in his concern to witness nature imitating art, he occasionally identified beautiful youths with ancient statues. Describing an Italian youth in Rome, in a letter to Robert Ross in 1900, Wilde wrote, 'He is so absurdly like the Apollo Belvedere that I feel always as if I was Winckelmann when I am with him.'[63]

Comment on contemporary sculpture features rarely in Wilde's writings and his classical interests encouraged him to admire the work of late-nineteenth-century academic sculptors more usually considered dry, lacking in inspiration and outmoded. Several among those he singled out for favourable mention were American. Of William Wetmore Story,[64] who was devoted to the antique and created statues of a heroic nature, Wilde wrote that he made 'marble musical in its harmony, and poetry in its perfection Parian'[65] Wilde was far more adulatory than Henry James, who wrote a biography of Story, which was carefully reserved in praise. Wilde described Story's son,[66] who followed his father in the profession, as 'the greatest sculptor'.[67] Beyond mere verbal praise, Wilde took an active part in launching the career of young American sculptor John Donoghue.[68] They met in America in 1882, when Donoghue showed Wilde a sculpture of a young girl that he had modelled, and that was inspired by the poem 'Requiescat'.[69] Wilde found the sculptor, not yet recognized, living in poor conditions, in spite of the fact that he had already created some very fine sculptural work, notably the Young Sophocles leading the chorus of victory after the Battle of Salamis,[70] much admired by Wilde, and which was eventually to become one of Donoghue's most famous works, exhibited in both Europe and America. Wilde publicized the sculptor in America and befriended him when he moved to Paris in 1883. The Young Sophocles is a perfect example of the nineteenth-century academic reworking of classical forms. Echoing the gracefulness of sculptural work of the late classical period, it is very much part of an established tradition of youthful male nudes, which found renewed popularity with the academics of the late century. Back in America, Donoghue carried out some heroic monumental sculptures, notably a figure of Science, executed in the grand style, for the Rotunda of the Library of Congress in Washington, DC.

While Wilde revealed himself as one steeped in classical dogma, he nonetheless, at the close of his life and of the century, reached beyond the stultifying confines of the academic in his admiration of Rodin. At this stage Wilde's sculptural interests appear to have shifted from the delicate and beautiful youths, the classical perfection of Winckelmann's theorizing, to the powerful and vigorous expression witnessed in the work of Rodin. That Rodin created sculptures of exquisite beauty scarcely needs reiteration here; however, it was the infamous portrait statue of Balzac that captured Wilde's imagination and that he described as 'an astonishing masterpiece'.[71] Wilde had earlier used precisely that term in connection with *La Comédie humaine*, which he described in 1886 as 'one of the masterpieces of the age'.[72] The monumental statue, forceful in its physical and spiritual presence, was exhibited at the Paris salon of 1898 to public uproar. Wilde was virtually unique in acclaiming the work[73] and was perhaps not just acknowledging, but even reaching out to, the somewhat mysterious expression of power in the statuesque figure, as his own body grew weaker and his strength, physical and spiritual, declined. Two years later, he was to tour the pavilion of Rodin's work at the Universal Exhibition in Paris in the company of the sculptor and to declare him the 'greatest poet in France'.[74] In 1900 to be acclaiming Rodin must be considered acceptably modern. Although at the time more progressive sculptural work was being created by painter/sculptors, such as Degas and Gauguin, their sculptures were little known publicly.

In keeping with other European and American cities in the nineteenth century, Dublin had a strong tradition of public commemorative sculpture. In Wilde's early years in the city, the variety of sculptural types and styles was marked, from eighteenth-century royal and particularly equestrian monuments, to soldier–hero commemorations of a monumental nature at the beginning of the nineteenth century and more significantly Irish statuesque memorials after the mid-century. It was in the 1850s and 1860s that the taste, largely French-inspired, for statues of men of letters emerged. Wilde would have been familiar with the portraits of Moore, Goldsmith and Burke, all in the College Green area at the entrance front of Trinity College. The authoritative and propagandist presence in College Green of the pompous and weighty equestrian statue of William III, erected in 1701, could not have escaped his notice as a student of the College. The presence of this monument was marked by continuous political activity throughout the nineteenth century, with the Orange Order employing it as a focal point of their processions in the city and the nationalists continually attempting to damage or destroy it. From this background, Wilde, in Washington in 1882, conveyed his dislike of aggressive equestrian monuments and suggested that more peaceful imagery should be encouraged.[75]

Unveilings of monumental statues were huge public events in Dublin, and occasionally prompted national holidays. Wilde was aged only nine when, on 8 August 1864, one of the most significant commemorations of the period was launched. The laying of the foundation stone for the O'Connell Monument in Sackville (now O'Connell) Street was a day of celebration, with processions through the streets and a great banquet in the evening. The parade was made up of a vast number of banner-carrying representatives of trades, confraternities, corporations and suchlike from all over the country. It passed along Merrion Square, where O'Connell had formerly resided, and it is reported that 'every window was filled with elegantly dressed ladies and gentlemen'[76] – and surely children also! A more politically controversial statue erected in Dublin during this period is that commemorating the Protestant nationalist revolutionary William Smith O'Brien,[77] who died in 1864. The unveiling of the monument on the south side of O'Connell Bridge, on 27 December 1870, was marked by processional marches through the streets and politically motivated speeches, all reported at length in the newspapers of the day. The press reported that some 20,000 people were present for the occasion.[78] Wilde was still a student at Portora in this year, but the event took place during the Christmas vacation and therefore (once again) there was an opportunity for the impact, the power of the public monument, to be registered on the young Irishman.

How much of this also registers in his work? Something of the positive ideology and the functional nature of monumental statuary is captured in Wilde's fairy tale 'The Happy Prince', in which he uses a public statue as a vehicle for exploring issues of compassion. Monuments are not only erected for propagandist purposes, but occasionally serve as promoters of peace and dialogue.[79] In their capacity to remind, their commemoration may be related to an individual who has had a concern for humanity as a *raison d'être* in life. However, Wilde's story also tells of the transformation of the public monument from a state of magnificent splendour to one of shabby decay. The statue, minus its gilding and precious stones, which the Prince himself offered up for the welfare of his subjects, is finally deemed ugly and is pulled down. Surely with more than a hint of self-mockery, Wilde puts the following words in the mouth of the Art Professor at the university: 'As he [the statue] is no longer beautiful he is no longer useful.'[80]

Like *The Picture of Dorian Gray*, the story of 'The Happy Prince' has loose connections with the Pygmalion legend, popular among *fin de siècle* artists, literary and visual. However, if in the Pygmalion story the statue of Galatea is brought to life, the lifelikeness in this case permits the art-work to self-destruct. This might be considered a remarkable premonition of twentieth-century avant-garde sculptural ideology, in which the traditionally permanent nature of sculpture is challenged by the new interest in transience and the ephemeral. It is certainly indicative of the changing perception of public monuments across time. Commemoration and/or style may become outmoded, until ultimately a monument finds peace simply as a curiosity and, even more significantly, as a landmark. However, long after monuments have ceased to fire the imagination, they continue to document a developing culture, revealing who or what it was important to commemorate at a given time. Joining the monumental statuary in the public spaces in Dublin, Oscar Wilde may have 'become noble in art forever'.[81] But it must also be observed that this commemoration will serve as an indication to future generations of changing attitudes in Ireland at the close of the twentieth century.

The Spirit of Play in *De Profundis*

FRANK MCGUINNESS

That wise woman, Cecily Cardew, says of her diary in *The Importance of Being Earnest*, 'it is simply a very young girl's record of her own thoughts and impressions, and consequently meant for publication. When it appears in volume form I hope you will order a copy.' She reveals here a seductive cunning that, allied to a fine commercial brain, augur well for her success in the game of love and chance that is marriage. She is addressing her future husband, Algernon, who is the imaginary subject of so many entries in this diary, and she is at once enticing and distancing, as she creates for him a character and a history of which he has no knowledge. This elaborate history centres upon their engagement which, he learns, was settled with suitable ritual on the previous St Valentine's Day. Presents have been given, 'neatly numbered and labelled, a ring . . . a pearl necklace . . . a little gold bangle with a turquoise and diamond heart'. Most significantly, she can produce a box where she has kept all his letters to her. He protests that he has never written any letters to her. Cecily replies, 'I remember it only too well. I grew tired of asking the postman every morning if he had a London letter for me. My health began to give way under the strain and anxiety. So I wrote your letters for you.' Here there is, obliquely, a hint of prophecy, as this episode anticipates the composition of *De Profundis, Epistula: In Carcere et Vinculis*, where Wilde wrote, 'Every single work of art is a fulfilment of a prophecy.'

De Profundis was written in 1897 to Lord Alfred Douglas, Bosie, a few months before Wilde's release from Reading Gaol near the end of his two-year sentence for 'acts of gross indecency with other male persons'. It could be regarded as an argument outlining Wilde's spiritual and sexual evolution, conveying the sincere feelings of the sinner who has converted into a penitent. It might equally be regarded as a love letter to Bosie, terrifying in its accusations and admissions, a fucking by verbal force, a demanding of rights. Its title and subtitle carry scriptural connotations, and Wilde is too skilled a playwright not to demand that his title be his guide. The cry of 'De Profundis' itself comes from Psalm 130:

Out of the depths have I cried unto thee, O Lord.
Lord, hear my voice: let thine ears be attentive to the voice of my supplications.

If thou, Lord, shouldest mark iniquities, O Lord, who shall stand?

But there is forgiveness with thee, that thou mayest be feared.

I wait for the Lord, my soul doth wait, and in his word do I hope.

My soul waiteth for the Lord more than they that watch for the morning: I say, more than they that watch for the morning.

Let Israel hope in the Lord: for with the Lord there is mercy and with him is plenteous redemption.

And he shall redeem Israel from all his iniquities.

Supplication, iniquities, forgiveness, waiting, hope, redemption − this is the Pilgrim's Progress of Wilde's text, if its controlling image is that of a man *in carcere et in vinculis*, if its justifying voice is that of the penitent at prayer. This is indeed Wilde's reductive desire at certain points in this letter, when he wishes 'humility' on himself and on Bosie. But Cecily Cardew's invaluable advice to authors must be heeded. Whatever is written can be published, and whatever is published is performed. *De Profundis* is not the meditation of a penitent at prayer. It is the act of a penitent as performer. It is a histrionic defiance of the histrionic judgement passed against Wilde at his trial, a theatrical explosion to break the silence of censorship that his prison sentence demanded; it is a play.

It is a strange play that limits itself to one spectator, but not so strange when it is realized that this play wished to create its spectator as much as its spectacle. Two characters propel the action, Oscar and Bosie, the writer and the written. Not since Shakespeare's purification of the role of actor through the part of Prospero in *The Tempest*, has any playwright made such correspondence between the initial participants in the act of making theatre. And Bosie is Ariel transformed into Caliban, he is Miranda and Ferdinand turned into Antonio and Sebastian, while Oscar is Prospero rewritten, having had his magic renounced for him. As in *The Tempest* a revenge must be taken, and revenge in *De Profundis* depends not on magic but on meaning, and the meaning is clear: Bosie destroyed Oscar's life because he destroyed Oscar's art. To recover that magic, that art, will require another act of destruction. This destruction will unleash itself through a tempestuous reply to Bosie's chaotic arrival and influence on the order of Oscar's life. The form this reply takes is soliloquy masked as dialogue, for it is written in a letter, and letters anticipate an acknowledgement. 'I have yet to know you. Perhaps we have yet to know each other', Oscar slyly concludes in *De Profundis*, after he has instilled his knowledge of all involved in this drama.

Drama it was, this relationship. The text repeatedly documents the ecstasies and exploitations, the cruelties and deprivations of their courtship and affair. That it had soon ceased to be sexual intensified the addictive dependence. That dependence is accounted for in the lists of financial recriminations, the presents given and taken, 'numbered and labelled', as Cecily foretold. Page after page records the screaming pitch of this melodrama, and acting as unifying motif through this 'terrible letter' are the many, many references to their previous letters. Loving letters of flirtation, abusive letters of rejection, pleading letters for forgiveness, concerned letters from Bosie's mother, all this writing leading finally to the scrawled note of sexual accusation from Bosie's father, the Marquess of Queensberry, which led to Wilde's downfall. Oscar observes how his wife Constance once joked that he received so many letters from Bosie's mother that they must be collaborating on a 'secret novel'. This epistolary novel ended up as no secret, and its tale once told brought ruin on the hero.

Oscar berates Bosie most viciously for the 'careless want of appreciation' that allowed him to leave Wilde's letters 'lying about for blackmailing companions to steal, for the servants to pilfer, for housemaids to sell'. But the whole motif of these letters is underlined by one great roar of desire. Oscar wants Bosie to write to him. The admonishing speech, the recriminating sermons, they are the tactics of an author deprived of his audience, so deprived it becomes necessary to invent its existence, and in that invention thereby invent himself. As the invention expands in the course of the letter to include all humanity in the suffering of the creator, so paradoxically does it contract until the audience is intensified into a single individual, created in the image of an unsuffering spectator. If all others are to share Oscar's suffering, then Bosie stares at it. Enduring his tragic fate, Oscar allows us empathic access to his prison cell. He tells us that the censorious regulations of the prison system allowed entry to his enemies, not his friends, but through taking advantage of his empathic access we have, like Oscar, defied his/our enemy and become friends. Yet one man defies the categories of enemy and friend. He is allowed such powerful defiance when he is created in the role of neither enemy nor friend, but in the role of lover. The lover maintains one mysterious power over Oscar. This is his silence. If Oscar asks us for our sympathetic eyes and ears to see and listen, then he is also ultimately asking Bosie to speak.

In *De Profundis* Oscar calls himself 'the lord of language'. Bosie is *Lord* Alfred Douglas, and the similarity of the titles is not accidental. Oscar may mock Bosie's vanity over his 'little title', but so too does Bosie's silence mock 'the lord of language'. It is a silence that threatened to strike Oscar dumb, and, fearing that threat, Oscar turns in his defence to the Saviour of 'those who are dumb under oppression and whose silence is heard only by God'; he turns to the figure of Christ. Identifying the precise figure of Christ is one of the key conflicts in the drama of *De Profundis*. If the voluble Oscar and the silent Bosie dominate the text, then midway through the action a crucial other presence is felt, and that is Wilde's creation of the character of Christ.

The first question to pose itself is obvious. Is this character a mirror image of Oscar himself? 'Feasting with panthers' is of course Wilde's own famous description of having 'entertained at dinner the evil things of life'. The pleasure of their company lay in their very danger, for 'the danger was half the excitement'. Into what danger does Wilde now tread? Is the tragic chorus from *The Ballad of Reading Gaol* a clue?

> Yet each man kills the thing he loves,
>   By each let this be heard,

Some do it with a bitter look,
   Some with a flattering word.
The coward does it with a kiss,
   The brave man with a sword!

The kiss of Judas and the betrayal of Bosie find easy parallel, but *The Ballad of Reading Gaol* is, as its echoes of *The Merchant of Venice* here hint, a meditation on justice and punishment. Any trace of a Messianic complex is kept to the periphery of the poem.

No such escape is possible in *De Profundis* with its concentration on suffering and the redemption that follows suffering. To map out our way through this terrain we must look for helpful clues, and the most helpful is the most ingenious statement made in *De Profundis*, when Wilde declares of the text, 'There is nothing in it of rhetoric.' The character of Christ is Wilde's supreme rhetorical creation here. This Christ is a supremely literary artefact. Oscar and Bosie bear within them the functions of their external histories to influence their dramatic development, but Christ is a creature of Wilde's pure imagination, as ahistorical as Salomé, as tantalizing as Willie Hughes. In 'The Soul of Man under Socialism' Wilde defends artists against over-identification between themselves and their subjects: 'To call an artist morbid because he deals with morbidity as his subject-matter is as silly as if one called Shakespeare mad because he wrote *King Lear.*' Oscar is tempting fate by calling Christ to his side, but he is too expert a dramatist and too good a critic to equate the two. So who is the Christ of *De Profundis*?

A creature of pure imagination, a literary artefact. What is remarkable about this character of Christ lies not in any similarity he shares with Oscar but in the precise dissimilarities which contrast him with Bosie. When we remember Douglas's dismissal of Wilde's Irishness in his life of Oscar Wilde, not the least of these dissimilarities is Wilde's erroneous claim that Christ is like an Irishman. He associates the bilingualism of the Irish peasant with that of the Galilean peasant of Christ's time. Speaking in specific terms of Bosie's family and of his own relations with it as 'the ruin of your race upon mine', Wilde extends his private grief into a national grief. Douglas, the English aristocrat, is pilloried as a fraud, his sensibility derided as sentimentality, his sophistication dismissed as cynicism, such sentimentality and cynicism being 'the perfect philosophy for a man who has no soul'.

The soulless Bosie is mocked as 'Philistine', lacking all talent, being utterly devoid of imagination, embodying the supreme vice of shallowness, and being pathetically vain of his 'little title'. His every cultural aspiration and political illusion stand maligned. They are the false and indulgent fantasies bestowed on Bosie by Narcissus, Bosie's self-love, and the great rival to Oscar's love. Wilde cleverly redraws the points of reference that constituted the relationship's original triangle, namely Oscar, Bosie and Narcissus. He substitutes for Narcissus the character of Christ, thereby replacing his own rival with Bosie's rival, Christ. Everything Christ is, Bosie is not. Everything Bosie wishes to be, 'a poet . . . a close union of personality with perfection', Christ already is. Under the guise of spirituality, this sexual taunting is savage. Christ may have been a 'young Galilean peasant', but he is more noble than the aristocratic Bosie because Christ's 'morality is all sympathy'. To Christ, imagination is simply a 'form of love'. Sympathy, imagination, love – Christ is assuming the status of a perfect partner. Made divine by that moral sympathy, illuminated by that imaginative love, Christ obtains the ultimate accolade: 'He is just like a work of art himself.' He is desire personified, his life eulogized as 'the most wonderful of poems', for out of his own imagination entirely 'did Jesus of Nazareth create himself'.

Throughout *De Profundis* Wilde repeatedly bows to Dante as the supreme literary authority, by means of references to *La Vita Nuova* and *The Divine Comedy*. And Christ has become Oscar's Beatrice, whose physical grace once glimpsed becomes the guide to great light through great love. Christ has, it appears, replaced Bosie, and it is Oscar's turn to do the rejecting. The play of *De Profundis* continues its plot. The discarded lover can now do the discarding with all the simple, powerful logic of a ballad or folk-tale. Justice, not jealousy, is the motive. There is about it all an air of inevitability. This is what must happen for the song to be sung, for the story to be told. There is in *De Profundis*, as there is in all of Wilde's major writings, the sense of a folk-tale. His parents, Sir William and Lady Wilde, were collectors of stories, and his first great fictions were fairy-tales. His stories for the stage have miraculous revelations at the core of their narratives. There is nothing more miraculous than the perfect plot of *The Importance of Being Earnest*. There Miss Prism, that failed novelist, declares, 'The good ended happily, and the bad unhappily. That is what Fiction means.' The folklorist knows differently, knows better. The stranger the story, the stronger the story, and, Wilde tells us in *De Profundis*, 'behind sorrow there is always a soul'.

Oscar may be in the process of selling his soul to Christ, but there is one who can stop this salvation, and save Oscar for himself. That one is Bosie, who can prove his power by replying to this letter. He provides Bosie with dangerous, irresistible information – Oscar may still be saved for damnation:

> As regards your letter to me in answer to this, it may be as long or as short as you choose. Address the envelope to 'The Governor, HM Prison, Reading.' Inside, in another, and an open envelope, place your letter to me: if your paper is very thin do not write on both sides, as it makes it hard for others to read. . . . What I must know from you is why you have never made any attempt to write to me, since the August of the year before last, more especially after, in the May of last year, eleven months ago now, you knew, and admitted to others that you knew, how you had made me suffer, and how I realised it. I waited month after month to hear from you. . . . There is no prison in any world into which Love cannot force an entrance. If you did not understand that, you did not understand anything about Love at all.

The need for the lover details its pain, its anxiety, the 'numbered and labelled' dates of correspondence and communications, and desire for contact, the longing for the real presence, albeit transubstantiated into pen and paper. The confrontation between writer and written collapses. A cry comes from the heart, and it is to hell with the soul:

> Let me know all about your article on me for the *Mercure de France*. I know something of it. You had better quote from it. It is set up in type. Also, let me know the exact terms of your Dedication of your poems. If it is in prose, quote the prose; if in verse, quote the verse. I have no doubt that there will be beauty in it. Write to me with full frankness about yourself: about your life: your friends: your occupations: your books. Tell me about your volume and its reception.

Write to me, tell me, let me know, as if in that writing, that telling, that knowledge, there is true redemption. The author is looking for a suitable conclusion, for any conclusion, and only his audience can provide it. In continuing the story, in answering this letter, Bosie may yet in writing, in telling his side of the story, create a work of art to stand beside the work of art that is *De Profundis*.

A work of art, Wilde defined in 'The Soul of Man under Socialism', is 'the unique result of a unique temperament'. *De Profundis* tells a great, terrible story. Its voices range from the most self-pitying to the most self-loathing tones. Its characters develop, regress, stand out in extraordinary light or lie in darkness, casting depraved shadows. Its heart can harden with the violence of its hatred and break with the longing for love reciprocated. It contradicts, celebrates and confounds itself. It is theatrical writing of the highest order. And its author knew its worth. He made one significant change to the text of *De Profundis*. At the letter's beginning he had written, 'an artist as I was'. This he altered to 'an artist as I am'.

Ellmann's Wilde

Derek Mahon

In September 1887, Oscar Wilde, three years married and the father of two sons, took on the editorship of *Woman's World*, a task he performed with decreasing enthusiasm for a year and a bit. He started with the best intentions, though, even if his primary motive was to provide for his family, itself a good intention. Going through back numbers he had decided the magazine was 'too feminine and not sufficiently womanly', and resolved to change matters. Its readership would consist henceforth not of air-heads but of 'women of intellect, culture and position', who would be treated as such. There would be articles on education, a serial story by an established writer, and fashion would be relegated to the back pages. New contributors included his mother on 'Irish Peasant Tales', his wife Constance on 'Muffs', and his brother Willie, improbably, on 'Soda Water'. But office routine, like home life, soon grew wearisome, answering letters being a particularly noxious chore: 'I have known men come to London full of bright prospects and seen them complete wrecks in a few months through a habit of answering letters.' Besides, his mind was really elsewhere, on his Socratic dialogues, 'The Decay of Lying' and 'The Critic as Artist', and on the novel he was gestating, *The Picture of Dorian Gray*.

But his feminist sympathies, like the universal elitism proposed in 'The Soul of Man under Socialism', were related to his main purpose, if purpose is the word. Like Rimbaud, he insisted that art should be absolutely modern; yet it is only now that the nature of his example is becoming clear. His involvement with the 'pre-Raff', his feminism and socialism (both of a more colourful variety than Shaw's), his sexual self-definition and 'elegant republicanism', his use of style as a weapon, have, as more than one critic has pointed out, a proleptic higher punkdom about them (Rimbaud too was a sort of punk) which will make him an apt *maître-à-penser* for our own Nineties. It is a measure of Wilde's complexity and originality that we should have had to wait a hundred years to understand, to be *allowed* to understand, exactly what he was about. Superficial biographers like Hesketh Pearson and H. Montgomery Hyde, deceived by his own carefully cultivated appearance of superficiality, have deceived generations into thinking of him as merely a consummate stylist and wit, the author of several amusing plays – plays with rather alarming subtexts, in fact. (Consider Algy's secret 'Bunburying' in *The Importance of Being Earnest*.)

Only in recent years have keener minds studied the enigmatic Wilde from the unexpected angles with which he was himself familiar, and discovered that the darling of the London drawing-rooms was not some sort of highbrow Noël Coward, but in reality a subversive, indeed a revolutionary figure; though why anyone should be surprised seems, at first glance, mysterious. He himself always claimed to be revolutionary, a Christian anarchist, but did so with such disarming urbanity that the liberation theology went unperceived, or only half believed. When he put theory into practice (his inversion of conventional eroticism a metaphor of political subversion), society responded in time-honoured fashion and locked him up. There were those who would have crucified him had crucifixion been on the statute book; and Wilde, in fact, felt himself to have been crucified. In the course of his transfer from Wandsworth to Reading, he had to wait for half an hour, handcuffed and in prison clothing, on the central platform at Clapham Junction, where a crowd formed to laugh and spit at him: 'For a year after that was done to me,' he wrote in *De Profundis*, 'I wept every day at the same hour and for the same space of time.' The Golgotha note is unmistakable and intentional.

The facts of his life have been related so often that the question arises, do we really need another biography? When the biographer is the late Richard Ellmann, however, we can be sure that we do; besides, Wilde still needs explaining. Ellmann died shortly before its publication after a long illness, and there is something heroic in the very existence of this book. If it does not measure up to his tremendous life of Joyce, perhaps the illness was to blame; or perhaps not that only. His *James Joyce* is a masterpiece of narrative organization on an epic scale; it flows hither and yon in river run fashion because there is no great point to be made, merely a tale to be told. With Wilde there is a tale to be told, certainly, but there is a point to be made too. Ellmann, unfortunately, though he gets close to it time and again, never quite brings himself to make it, though it might be argued that his chosen emphases make the point implicitly. The point is, as I have suggested, that Wilde was not an entertainer, even of a superior kind, or not that only; he not only posed as, he really *was*, the apostle of a new way of being. Ellmann does not follow up all the implications; but, if we can forget the Mayfair patina with which Pearson and his like have covered him from top to toe, the facts speak for themselves; and the key appears to have been his mother.

Lady Wilde, the patriotic 'Speranza', has been described as 'the silliest woman who ever lived', and her letters, as quoted by Ellmann, do tend to support this view; yet, like Yeats's father (and Wilde was his mother's son as Yeats was his father's), she said some memorable things. When someone asked her to receive a young woman who was 'respectable', she replied: 'You must never employ that description in this house. It is only tradespeople who are respectable; we are above respectability.' This sort of thing, which may or may not have been idiotic, certainly helped shape her son's mind. After her husband's death she moved to

London, remarking to the young Yeats, who must have been impressed: 'I want to live in some high place, like Highgate or Primrose Hill, because I was an eagle in my youth.' In the event she lived in Chelsea, at sea-level, and cheered on her rising son. When nemesis arrived, she insisted that he face the music; if he ran away, she warned, she would never speak to him again.

It has been suggested that she may have wished to see her son shine in the dock like Robert Emmet; but might not Oscar have had the same idea? His favourite novel was *Le Rouge et le noir*; his first play, *Vera*, was about Russian nihilism; when *Salomé* was refused a licence by the Lord Chamberlain, he announced his intention of becoming a French citizen, pointing out that he was 'not English but Irish, which is quite another thing'. (Beckett, much later, asked by a French journalist if he were not English, replied: 'Au contraire.') To a San Francisco audience Wilde had spoken in praise of the Fenians, his earliest heroes – of Smith O'Brien, John Mitchel and Michael Davitt. Hounded around London after his first trial, he went to his estranged brother's house in Chelsea saying, 'Willie, give me shelter or I shall die on the streets', and collapsed on the steps, in Willie's phrase, 'like a wounded stag'. It was Willie, also, who said that Oscar was determined 'to face the music like Christ'. Yeats, who collected letters of support at this time, was struck by this stag-and-Christ imagery, which he later took up in the *Autobiographies*. Ellmann has remarked elsewhere on this potent symbolism and its use in connection with Parnell.

James McNeill Whistler dubbed him *le bourgeois malgré lui* at a time when Oscar's home life seemed to be thriving; and Wilde resented this. Perhaps the most painful aspect of the whole story was the effect on Constance, a woman of some importance in her own right, with a far from ideal husband. Although 'advanced' in her views, she was slow to realize the true nature of her husband's sexual orientation. Ellmann speculates that he 'confessed to having caught syphilis at Oxford, perhaps telling her that he had suffered a recurrence of the disease after a long remission; celibacy was the only answer'. She was to behave throughout as generously as circumstances permitted. Meanwhile, Oscar spoke of a club called the 'Tired Hedonists' and explained, 'We are supposed to wear faded roses in our buttonholes when we meet, and to have a sort of cult for Domitian.' To the suggestion that the members must be bored with each other, he agreed: 'We are; that is one of the objects of the club.'

Thus, says Ellmann, Wilde 'smiled aestheticism away', developing 'a higher ethics' in which artistic freedom and full expression of personality were possible. Unfortunately they were not possible in Victorian London. They were possible in Paris, city of sin, where Wilde seduced Gide ('a French Protestant, the worst kind, except of course for the Irish Protestant'); but he had chosen London as his stage, perhaps with an unconscious premonition that a less tolerant society would the more readily gratify the penitential, even sacrificial, needs of his divided nature. He was nervous as he responded to the cries of 'Author!' on the opening night of *Lady Windermere's Fan* with a speech that delighted many and displeased some: 'Ladies and gentlemen, I have enjoyed this evening immensely. The actors have given us a charming rendition of a delightful play, and your appreciation has been most intelligent. I congratulate you on the great success of your performance, which persuades me that you think almost as highly of the play as I do myself.'

The famous paradoxes did not exist in isolation; they illustrate a difficult dialectic which Ellmann summarizes succinctly at each stage of its development. The underlying theme from start to finish was that life should imitate art, Christ being the perfect type of the artist in action (one of Wilde's favourite books was Thomas à Kempis's *Imitation of Christ*). In its most self-indulgent form, the theory demanded that life should aspire to the condition of a fairy-tale — an idea adopted by a not dissimilar figure, Scott Fitzgerald, another radical dandy who cracked up while trying to sustain an aesthetic fiction. Wilde's own fairy-tales, now we have the benefit of psychoanalysis, are especially revealing, or, to put the thing the right way round, it was natural that he should take an interest in the genre and put so much of himself into it, notably in 'The Happy Prince' and 'The Selfish Giant'. Children are puzzled and even repelled by the soppier features of these stories; but the Giant's garden (a childhood memory of Merrion Square?) never fails to enchant. Unfortunately it was not possible to go on living there, any more than it had been for Verlaine. The French poet, whose less brilliant career foreshadowed his own, was once brought by Wilde to a Paris salon. He had first asked the hostess if he could introduce 'a poet who has been in prison', and sat proudly listening while the ruined Verlaine read a new poem to those present. Wilde had been interested in prisons at least since his American tour.

Although he courted London society and apparently subscribed to its class distinctions, there was always something comically exaggerated about this. He liked to prescribe what 'a gentleman' should do, as in 'I never notice the view; a gentleman doesn't look out of the window'; and his comical exaggeration (by 'a gentleman' he meant, of course, 'a dandy like myself') disguised a very real impatience with the social structure. A certain kind of Anglo-Irishman (Synge is an obvious example) has always been intrigued by those who live on the edge of things, those beyond the pale; and Wilde was one of these. Although his liaison with the egregious Lord Alfred Douglas was the effective cause of his 'downfall' (in the light of his own dialectic, the word is open to question), it is clear from Ellmann's account of the trials that what really incensed his prosecutors was the insouciance with which he took other Alfreds, Taylor and Wood, male prostitutes both, to dine at the Café Royal and stay at the Albemarle Hotel. 'I am not going to be imprisoned in the suburbs for dining in the West End', declares Algy when, in the four-act version of *The Importance*, a solicitor calls with a summons for debt. The author seems to have known how the thing would turn out in reality.

Numerous legends have accumulated around Wilde's term of trial. 'That he accepted the idea of being a martyr may be true,' observes Ellmann, 'but must be reconciled with his obvious preference for not being one.' Hence, perhaps, his famous indecision when the police wanted him out of the country before he could be arrested. Then there is the yacht Frank Harris claimed to have moored in the Thames to take Wilde to safety. 'Much scepticism has been shown about this yacht', Ellmann notes; yet it seems to have existed. Yeats and Ada Leverson knew about it; and certainly, if it did not exist, it should have. Harris, widely regarded as a bad hat, emerges from Ellmann's account as 'a true friend', imaginative and active on Wilde's behalf, as also were Yeats and Shaw. Ada Leverson, 'the Sphinx' as Wilde called her, also behaved magnificently, lending him a nursery room in her house when he had nowhere else to go. 'Shall I remove the toys?' she asked, but he replied, 'Please leave them.' So he spent his last days of freedom among the dolls and rocking-horses of a strange house, where he received his wife, friends and advisers. It was Ada Leverson who said of homosexuals that she did not mind what they did so long as they did not do it in the street and frighten the horses; and she was among the first to greet him on his early-morning release from prison, which prompted Oscar to exclaim: 'My dear Sphinx, you can't possibly have *got* up; you must have *sat* up.'

The judge who passed sentence remarked, in his summing-up, that Wilde and Taylor must be 'dead to all sense of shame', and when he sent them down for two years, a cry of 'Shame!' was heard in the court. Lady Wilde had long ago disparaged shame while approving of sin as 'highly poetical', which may have been some consolation. The Golgotha note starts to be heard at this point, together with a new humility and egalitarianism, though there had been glimpses of this last as far back as his emotional meeting with Whitman. He now re-read Augustine, Pascal and Dante's *Inferno*, established friendships with fellow prisoners and warders both, and developed an interest in prison reform, about which he wrote to the press. Ellmann's chapter on Wilde's imprisonment is curiously reminiscent of Behan's *Borstal Boy*: the same harshness and tedium, the same gruff friendliness from unexpected quarters. *De Profundis*, written behind bars, suffers, in Ellmann's view, 'from the adulteration of simplicity by eloquence, by an arrogance lurking in its humility, and from its disjointed structure' – also, no doubt, because it was addressed to the abominable Bosie, as inadequate a source of inspiration as one could imagine. (Also because its author suffered from insomnia, chronic diarrhoea and constant humiliation, and was nearly out of his mind.) But *The Ballad of Reading Gaol*, written in Dieppe after his release, will surely live, for all its echoes of 'The Ancient Mariner' and 'A Shropshire Lad'. Ellmann compares it to the best of the 'Border Ballads':

> And all the woe that moved him so
>   That he gave that bitter cry,
> And the wild regrets, and the bloody sweats,
>   None knew so well as I;
> For he who lives more lives than one
>   More deaths than one must die.

'Wilde's final illness', says Ellmann, 'was almost certainly syphilitic in origin'; the French doctors diagnosed cerebral meningitis. Among his last remarks were, 'I am dying beyond my means; I will never outlive the century; the English people wouldn't stand for it' and; (with Parnell in mind) 'There is something vulgar in all success; the greatest men fail, or *seem to have failed*' (my italics). There is a sense in which, if we have the imagination to read him aright, Wilde's real success lies before him.

Ellmann appends a curious document: 'For an impression of how Wilde talked, especially on the lecture platform, the best guide is the American, Helen Potter, whose book *Impersonations* (New York 1891) offers a detailed account of his way of accenting and pausing.' There follows part of the text of a Wildean 'Lecture on Art', set out phonetically and illustrating not only speech-pattern but gesture, as in 'Right hand supine, palm up: to receive, give, support, rescue; things floating, good successful, etc.' The voice, notes Potter, is 'clear, easy and not forced . . . a general appearance of repose'. This is all very interesting, except that we already know instinctively how Wilde talked; it is evident from the cadences of his prose, and from our knowledge of Anglo-Irish speech. As to the texture of that speech, Lillie Langtry, to whom Oscar once professed a theatrical devotion (even sleeping one night, just one, on her doorstep), reported that he had 'one of the most alluring voices that I have ever listened to, round and soft, and full of variety and expression'.

Did the miners of Colorado think so too? Before drinking them under the table, Wilde spoke to them about the silversmith and amorist Benvenuto Cellini, and was reproved for not having brought him along. When he explained that Cellini was dead, they wanted to know who shot him; or so said Oscar. This visit to Colorado was one of the high points of his life. It was in a Denver saloon that he saw the sign 'Please don't shoot the pianist, he is doing his best', and considered the possibility that 'bad art merits the penalty of death'. The miners christened a new shaft 'The Oscar', in his honour, and Wilde later speculated that, 'in their simple artless fashion', they might have offered him shares in the mine, though 'in their artless untutored fashion they did not.' I have heard it said that the Hollywood Oscars are so called because they had their source in the Oscar shaft, which seems a *little* far-fetched; but Ellmann offers no opinion on the matter, so perhaps I am imagining things. In any case it would be inappropriate: though 'the kindest of men', Wilde was opposed to vulgarity in all things.

'His work', Ellmann concludes, 'survives as he claimed it would. We inherit his struggle to achieve supreme fictions in art, to associate art with social change, to save what is eccentric and singular from being sanitised and standardised, to replace a morality of severity with one of sympathy. He belongs to our world more than to Victoria's.' The full force of that last assertion is only now becoming evident.

Acting Wilde

Alan Stanford

In my experience of directing Wilde's plays or acting in them, there is no distinction in style between what I might present to an Irish audience or an English one. However, Irish audiences have never really understood Wilde. It is true that he is cursed by being claimed as an English playwright. And when the English claim him as such, some patriot inevitably stands up and declares, 'He's not English, he's Irish.' Unfortunately they do not grasp the full truth of it. Wilde was and indeed is Irish through and through. But he would also have thought of himself as Irish first and British second, despite a pronounced Celtic reluctance to admit to the political union of Great Britain and Ireland. Oddly enough, his Irish audience, as well as many of the English theatrical public, fail to grasp that Wilde wrote as an Irishman and what he wrote were savage satires on the war games of English society.

Why is it so hard to make the Irish audience see what Wilde is about? Because they are so damned middle class. It has been said that England has a class system, and boasts of it; America has a class system and denies it; and Ireland has a class system — but no one knows what it is. The Irish system is, of course, based on 'merit' — that is, always assuming that we interpret merit as the ability to earn and accumulate money and power. On this basis Ireland has two classes only: those in the middle and the underdogs. We have no aristocracy, and the aristocracy we did have, the Anglo-Irish, we have always refused to accept, considering them to be foreign and imposed rather than an integral part of the Irish identity. We have spent hundreds of years suppressing the notion that the Anglo-Irish were part of the Irish tradition. And the result is that we have now no national relationship with the idea of an upper, or self-regarding superior, class. Hence the Irish audience has no real notion of where Wilde is coming from.

Wilde's early environment formulated his way of thinking. His mother was a famous poetic patriot with a notoriously satiric tongue and a sublime contempt for all that was 'respectable'. We can be certain that at his mother's elbow, if not at her knee, Oscar learned the art of the barbed remark. His comment, 'You must meet my mother. We are founding a society for the suppression of virtue', tells us much of her influence on his young mind. She started a salon which gathered in the best intellects of the day, and Oscar was raised in the centre of this circle, at the dinner-table, the tea parties and conversaziones. And the people who came to call were not the aristocrats of English society but the Irish middle class: the doctors, lawyers, artists and academics, as well as the Castle Catholics and the minor members of the Anglo-Irish ascendancy. They were spectators of society, not just partaking of its pleasures, but observing it with a mind and temperament similar to that of Speranza.

The Irish audience is, in general, ignorant of this background or its implications for Wilde's work. When we Irish look at a character like Lady Bracknell, for instance, we mistake her for a model of a British aristocrat. But she is not an aristocrat. She is a middle-class woman, intelligent and manipulative, married into the ranks of the aristocracy and cynical enough to have learned the rules of society and how to manipulate them. She had no need to 'rise from the ranks of the aristocracy'; she was already born in 'the purple of commerce' with all its guile and wit. She is a classic Wilde character, not because she is funny, but because she is dangerous. She understands power and the way it is deployed. She is possibly Wilde's greatest creation in his war on the authority of a pompous upper class. She is almost anarchic in her exposure of pomposity in rank.

That misreading of Lady Bracknell illustrates just where the Irish have Wilde wrong. We tend to think of him as merely witty. We have confused Oscar Wilde the wit with Oscar Wilde the artist. True, Wilde's epigrams are striking — but they are by no means the essence of his genius. Anyone can think up a Wildean epigram. You simply take any shibboleth of the moment and invert it; it is quite mechanical really, like 'work is the curse of the drinking classes'. What makes Wilde a genius is the degree of jaundice in his eye when he looks at society at large. Wilde understands power. Power that has to do with manipulating systems and people rather than overthrowing them. Look at *An Ideal Husband*, a shocking play about political corruption. In Robert Chiltern you have a politician who, in younger days, sold a government secret for money. He has no guilt. He fears nothing but the shame of exposure, and when he manages to blackmail the blackmailer, and thus put her out of action, he feels completely vindicated. One might consider him a quite wonderful example of the hardened British upper classes, the kind that kept the empire together. Or you might consider him purely the creation of an Irish imagination. Ireland is (and was), after all, not a guilt society but a shame society. It does not matter here what you do as long as you do not get found out. Oscar the Irishman understood the importance of the dirty secret as the wellspring of power.

And as this play illustrates, Wilde also understands, cynically, that in the modern world the root of all power is, to put it baldly, money. And money is something you can always get if you have the capacity to manipulate the rules. In *Lady Windermere's Fan*, the Duchess of Berwick, for all her snobbery or, as they like to call it, breeding, is delighted to welcome the moneyed Mr Hooper as a suitor for her daughter. Keeping the aristocracy in the style to which it is accustomed depends on such expedient arrangements. And speaking of 'breeding', the list that Lady Bracknell shares with 'the dear Duchess of Bolton' smacks more of the livestock breeder than anything else.

Because it deployed that kind of political critique of the empire at its pitch, Patrick Mason's landmark production of *The Importance of Being Earnest* at the Gate Theatre in Dublin was, in concept, brilliant. The England of the 1890s was evoked by the Britain of the 1980s, one ruled by the imperatives of the free-market economy. It was all done in modern dress. Lady Bracknell was rendered as the then Prime Minister, Margaret Thatcher; Gwendolen and Cecily were cast in the manner of the new Princesses Diana and Fergie, Sloane Rangers in their element. The satire also pointed in the other historical direction. When I was cast as Dr Chasuble, I went back to Wilde's formative years at Oxford which, more than a generation before his attendance there, had been in the throes of what was known as the Oxford Movement, the development within the Anglican Church of a move towards Rome. As a result of its influence, the men trained at Oxford for doctorates in Divinity were prepared as theologians, and then thrust into local parish work — with predictably disastrous results. Nowadays, Chasuble is usually played as a doddering old fart. But I wanted to play him as one of the period's Young Fogeys who were trained in the kind of Anglo-Catholic casuistry which made the Oxford Movement famous — all that nonsense about 'the heretical views of the Anabaptists' and the position on matrimony of the Primitive Church. Chasuble should have stayed in Oxford as a theologian and converted, in due course, like Newman, to Catholicism. Instead, he is inflicted on a country parish. It was a joy to discover Chasuble as not an absent-minded old relic, but rather an all too present danger to the society of his parish; a mission in which he is backed by the monstrous Miss Prism, another mistress of the twisted logic that made the British empire what it was — yesterday.

As a satire on a dying empire, Mason's production was simply the best production of *The Importance of Being Earnest* I have ever been in — and I have acted in quite a few. But Mason went too far. At the very last line, when Jack says — 'On the contrary, Aunt Augusta, I've now realised for the first time in my life the vital Importance of Being . . .' — he is interrupted by a taped voice that says loudly: 'Oscar Wilde, you have been found guilty of . . .' and so forth, continuing with Mr Justice Wills's judgement which ended Wilde's last trial. Suddenly, what had been exquisitely beautiful had become ugly. It was all wrong. The whole point of the play is that it is to be kept on the surface, and on the surface everything should have remained. As Wilde said, 'All art is at once surface and symbol. Those who go beneath the surface do so at their peril.' In this Wilde play, you should not go beneath the superficial banter or seek to engage the heart. Follow Wilde's principle that 'The first duty in life is to be as artificial as possible.' In Mason's production, even the roses were artificial. To emphasize the price of that exquisitely artificial way of life, Mason put back the Grimsby episode, in which Algernon is threatened with imprisonment for debt. That works because, while stressing the cruelty of the system — its insatiable need for cash, the ugly sanctions on which it drew — the production kept them at a distance by an equally cruel artifice of evasion and denial. Cold cruelty is essential to Wilde's comedy. Bringing in all this sincerity and realism into the last line makes the artifice no longer cruelly funny — just cruel.

If we start being sincere about Wilde, we are all in trouble: directors as well as actors. Unfortunately, in Ireland, we have a tradition of being 'sincere' about Wilde. We have not come to the understanding that only an Irishman could have written these plays about English society and the English aristocracy. Only an Irishman, a Dubliner from the days when Dublin still felt that it was the second city of the empire, could view England with such a cynical eye; as an Irishman, of the Anglo-Irish class, Wilde could recall 700 years of being an outsider who was also the insider; he was, if you wish, the enemy from within.

And, while Wilde could play at being a member of English society, an aristocrat *manqué*, as a boy he had seen a different world, the primitive peasant culture of rural Ireland. When his father brought him to the West of Ireland — to Galway and Mayo — in the late 1870s, Wilde would have encountered a society which was within a generation of the Great Hunger. There would still have been much evidence of the devastation — not only in the landscape of deserted villages, but also in the songs and stories collected by his father. As he grew older, studied the classics at school and university and later travelled to Greece, Wilde would have found a comparable culture, one in which songs and stories were transmitted mouth to ear: for the West of Ireland still preserved an oral culture, a culture essentially still pagan and peasant, to which Christianity gave only a veneer.

I recall myself, over twenty-five years ago and still fresh from England, working in a theatre season in the old Town Hall in Killarney, County Kerry. Outside the entrance to the Hall was a pile of stones under a tree, which seemed to me something of a public nuisance. It collected beer bottles and fast-food wrappers; and after dances people peed on it or puked in it. I could not understand why the whole thing was not tidied away. Then one Sunday morning, as we were arriving for rehearsal, we fell over people, a big crowd of them, all dressed in Sunday finery, black suits and dresses, kneeling their way around this pile of stones, reciting Aves to the click of their beads. When I inquired about the purpose of this assembly, I was informed that this was a Holy Well and this the Sunday on which prayers were said there. 'But', I said, 'people pee into that well.' 'Not this Sunday they don't' was the reply. The sight of those people in such obvious fervour for a long-forgotten saint seemed to me to owe more to pagan devotion than to Christian piety.

I recalled that incident years later when making a recording of Oscar Wilde's poetry. I sensed something of the pagan in his soul so influenced by the world from which he came. It surfaces in 'Santa Decca':

The Gods are dead: no longer do we bring
   To grey-eyed Pallas crowns of olive-leaves!

Demeter's child no more hath tithe of sheaves,
And in the noon the careless shepherds sing,
For Pan is dead, and all the wantoning
  By secret glade and devious haunt is o'er:
  Young Hylas seeks the water-springs no more;
Great Pan is dead, and Mary's son is King.

And yet — perchance in this sea-trancèd isle,
  Chewing the bitter fruit of memory,
  Some God lies hidden in the asphodel.
Ah Love! if such there be, then it were well
  For us to fly his anger: nay, but see,
  The leaves are stirring: let us watch awhile.

Wilde was influenced by the native tradition of his own 'sea-trancèd isle' — that of writing for the ear. The importance of Wilde is the importance of the word and the word is sound. On the page Wilde can look tedious — complicated to the eye. He himself was a talker who found writing a tiresome duty. His magic is in the power of the spoken word, words which are themselves events, which change reality: the words of the primitive tradition of charms and spells, which rely on cadence and repetition. The rhythm of a piece like *The Ballad of Reading Gaol* is bardic. It is a ballad in the style of the Irish *sean-nós* — the old style — a lament with a relentless refrain, an insistent rhythm. For Wilde the written word was only a means by which the oral word could preserve itself, to be returned again to delight the ear. My experience of performing Herod in *Salomé* is one of luxuriating in the fabric of sound, a golden necklace of spoken words.

Wilde was himself, above all, a *seanchaí*, a teller of tales. He enjoyed the lecture circuit; he dominated the dinner-tables and enlivened the lounges of London; he talked himself into society and talked himself, eventually, out of it. And now, by the performance of his texts, he talks still.

It has always struck me as curious — and it struck me again during the rehearsals of Mason's *Importance* — that when actors rehearse an Oscar Wilde play something unusual happens to them. Usually actors (and as an actor I am free to say this) are monsters of egotism. The director's work is initially bent on reforming what the actor perceived as an extension of his or her own personality into something resembling a characterization. But with Wilde it is different. From the start of those rehearsals, there was an anxiety about what Wilde would have wanted, how he would have this spoken or that played, as if he were in the back row listening. The sense of his presence in his own plays is overwhelming. Indeed when I had to cast an actor in the role of Dorian Gray some years ago, the sense of Wilde's attendance at the auditions was palpable. You can hear his voice in every line. Perhaps because he was a performer or perhaps because his personality was so compelling, for many actors it is as if Wilde were there to consult.

There is, of course, the opposite danger: that of excessive identification. Take the case of Herbert Beerbohm Tree, who had made such a success of Lord Illingworth in *A Woman of No Importance*. The part had a strange effect on Tree. He came in time to identify with it, and to the end of his life, it is said, retained a distinct resemblance to the character of the original. 'Ah,' Wilde cracked, 'every day Herbert becomes *de plus en plus Oscarisé*; it is a wonderful case of Nature imitating Art.'

And that is what happens with Wilde. You either love him or detest him. Either you fall under his spell — as Dorian Gray falls under that of Lord Henry Wotton — or, like Salomé, you resist the honeyed phrases of the serpent Herod and find him slightly ridiculous clothed in his robe of purple prose. Long after he is dead, though, his words still exercise a kind of dictatorship over the spirit and, for those willing to listen, they will draw them into his presence and the anarchy of his wit.

Women of No Importance: Misogyny in the Work of Oscar Wilde

Victoria White

Oscar Wilde did not come out, like a drowning soul from the belly of a whale, and climb aboard the raft of homosexuality. He does not do well as a hero in the great gay defining myth. Nor did he follow his coming out with cosy chats about the oppression of women. Those of us who care about gay rights and women's liberation must look elsewhere for help.

Wilde was euphemistic about his sexual orientation, dressing it up as Greek ideal love when the other man concerned was of his own class or higher, and barely recognizing the fact that he had sex with young lower-class boys. Both of these facts have implications for his relationship with women: it was not just that he did not want to sleep with them, he did not want an adult relationship at all. And women of the Victorian age, with their bothersome wombs, escaped physical adulthood with difficulty.

The curious nature of Wilde's homosexuality is an essential key to understanding the fear and hatred of women which runs through his work like a dark thread, plaited with the brighter thread of near-feminist sentiments. (It seems impossible to write about Wilde without him mocking you, from the grave, for having a moral code as adamantine as Miss Prism's.) There is a sentence in *De Profundis* which astonishes: 'What the paradox was to me in the sphere of thought, perversity became to me in the sphere of passion.'[1] Wilde describes his sex life as the physical equivalent of the paradoxes for which he is famous, and which still startle, although they rattle through his comedies: 'All women become like their mothers. That is their tragedy. No man does. That's his.'[2]

What Wilde does in the paradoxes is very simple and rarely alters: he takes a wise saw and inverts it, so that it mocks the norms of the society in which he lived. What he is saying, then, about his sex life, is fairly serious. He is saying he did it because it was fun, because it was exactly the opposite of what was expected of him, and because he despised and scorned that expectation. He is saying that he was reacting against a system, rather than creating a new one.

That system against which he reacted had the relationship between men and women at its very core, and, to a lesser extent, still does. In Wilde's work, women embody the most conservative norms of society. Mighty dowagers heft their way through the plays and prose of Wilde, like lumbering elephants. They are not so much people as institutions; indeed, the Duchess of Berwick is described in *Lady Windermere's Fan* as a 'public building'.

However, Wilde's life and his art exploit the cracks in these 'public buildings'; he has no ambition to build new ones. Wilde never scorned the values of his parents, as a true anarchist would have done, and he continued to hold his mother in high esteem despite the fact that she definitely shared many attributes of his dowagers. In fact, Ellmann notes that he based a speech attributed to Lady Agatha in *The Picture of Dorian Gray* on his mother's ramblings, and then removed it out of filial piety: 'Sir Humpty Dumpty − you know − Afghan frontier. Russian intrigues: very successful man − wife killed by an elephant − quite inconsolable − wants to marry a beautiful American widow − everybody does nowadays − hates Mr Gladstone − but very much interested in beetles: ask him what he thinks of Schouvaloff.'[3] In *Oscar Wilde: A Long and Lovely Suicide*, a psychoanalytical study of Wilde, Melissa Knox makes much of Lady Wilde's aspirations for her son, and argues that he did his best to live them out.[4] These aspirations were not for his happiness, but that he play a hero's role in society. When her son won the Newdigate Prize for Poetry at Oxford, she crowed, in a letter addressed 'to the Olympic Victor': 'You have got *honour* and *recognition* − and this at only 22 is a grand thing.'[5]

Wilde did not despise her desperate need for public validation and excelled himself in exaggeration when he wrote of her death to Bosie in the letter later published as *De Profundis*: 'She and my father had bequeathed me a name they had made noble and honoured not merely in Literature, Art, Archaeology and Science, but in the public history of my own country in its evolution as a nation.'[6] He clung to his mother's snob values all his life, delighted in Lord Alfred Douglas's title, as Ellmann notes, and happy to 'feast with panthers', or have sex with endless rentboys, to feed his 'perversity', as if they did not count as people. The feminist notes in Wilde's life can best be explained as throwbacks to his mother's ideals, the misogynistic notes being part of the rebellion against her domination which he carried on all his life, the endless perverting of values which he could not escape.

When he took over the editorship of the *Lady's World: A Magazine of Fashion and Society* in 1887, he argued that 'We should take a wider range, as well as a high standpoint, and deal not merely with what women wear, but with what they think, and what they feel.' He immediately changed the name of the magazine to *Woman's World*, which was, he said, 'applicable to a magazine that aims at being the organ of women of intellect, culture, and position'.[7] Constance Wilde had come under Lady Wilde's influence while she was still in Dublin, and later became an advocate of Rational Dress. In that most absurd play, *The Importance of Being Earnest*, Cecily has a line which stands out from the rest for its normality, and is probably a direct quote from Constance: 'That leads to Rational Dress, Miss Prism. And I suppose that when a woman is dressed rationally, she is treated rationally. She certainly deserves to be.'[8]

Thus, while Wilde's conscious self may have been in favour of women's advancement, it is clear that he also feared it; his women are either lily-like virgins, whores or honorary men, who invert all the convention of their roles, as when Gwendolen drawls that home is 'the best place for a husband'. The dowagers in Wilde's plays are likewise hermaphroditic creatures who combine in their impressive bulk the union between man and woman which is the fulcrum of that bourgeois society around which Wilde's life turned. In the hilarious denouement of *The Importance of Being Earnest*, as the cast desperately work through the Army Lists to find Jack's father's Christian name, in the hope he may be an Ernest, the effete Jack beseeches Lady Bracknell: 'Aunt Augusta, I beg you to bring your masculine mind to bear on this subject.'[9] Dowagers such as Aunt Augusta are the subject of ridicule partly because they have passed beyond child-bearing to become, not people, but the sum total of their title, occupation and position in society. They are like huge, empty husks.

There seems to be just one kind of woman who has no place in Wilde's cosmology, and that is a mature, sexually active, reproductive woman. Mrs Erlynne, Lady Windermere's mother, and Mrs Arbuthnot, Gerald's mother in *A Woman of No Importance*, are both women condemned by their reproductive sexuality; the physical fact of a baby makes it difficult for a woman to keep any 'depravity' secret, as Mrs Arbuthnot's former lover, Lord Illingworth, can do. While these 'fallen' women are redeemed, in different ways, by Wilde, using the language of Christian redemption, their escape does not come easily. The moralistic language of these redemptions, the language of his mother, pulls against Wilde's own clever, amoral banter. Perhaps Wilde needed to summon all the power of received wisdom to redeem these women in his own mind.

In his own life, Wilde could not tolerate his wife when she moved from virgin status to sexually expressive womanhood. His friend Frank Harris related that he told him:

> When I married, my wife was a beautiful girl, white and slim as a lily, with dancing eyes and gay rippling laughter like music. In a year or so the flowerlike grace had all vanished; she became heavy, shapeless, deformed. She dragged herself about the house in uncouth misery with drawn blotched face and hideous body, sick at heart because of our love. It was dreadful. I tried to be kind to her; forced myself to touch and kiss her; but she was sick always, and − oh! I cannot recall it, it is all loathsome. . . . I used to wash my mouth and open the window to cleanse my lips in the pure air.[10]

It is impossible to ascertain why Wilde feared reproductive women, but it is equally impossible not to try to guess. He described himself to Leon Daudet as 'just like a tiny, tiny child',[11] and his infantilism is obvious throughout his work. While he waged the great Freudian war for his mother, he did not win it. He remained her child, and could not take on the mantle of her potential lover, and the lover of other women. Just as a child fears his mother's reproductive body, in case he may be again engulfed by it perhaps, so Wilde feared the reproductive bodies of young women.

If his system and aesthetics are an act of 'perversity', they are most of all a reaction against the female reproductive body. The reproductive body is nature at work. 'The Portrait of Mr W. H.', which tells a fictionalized story of the beautiful young man to whom many of Shakespeare's sonnets are dedicated, contains the most obvious expression of Wilde's condemnation of the woman's body: 'I could not understand', writes the narrator,

> how it was that Shakespeare set so high a value on his young friend marrying. He himself had married young and the result had been unhappiness, and it was not likely that he would have asked Willie Hughes to commit the same error. The boy-player of Rosalind had nothing to gain from marriage, or from the passions of real life. The early sonnets with their strange entreaties to have children seemed to be a jarring note.[12]

Rescue is imminent, however, for it is not real children we are talking of, reasons the narrator, but rather literary works. The supremely creative act of giving birth to a child is here challenged, as it is in Genesis, by comparison with male acts of creation. Disembodied acts of creation, indeed, occur throughout Wilde's work. The actual portrait of Mr W. H., a forgery which gives the fiction life, is succeeded by the picture of Dorian Gray, which consigns the original to the status of unchanging art. Jack in *The Importance of Being Earnest* is cradled in a big, battered handbag – the nearest thing to a womb of which Wilde could have approved – while poor Miss Prism's three-volume romantic novel is wheeled away in a perambulator.

In *Sexual Personae*, Camille Paglia brilliantly describes Lord Henry's moulding of Dorian Gray as 'an act of homosexual generation', a 'hermaphroditic cloning of sexual personae'.[13] She focuses on the candle-lit dinner at which the older man imparted himself to the beautiful boy in a quasi-sexual act: 'To project one's soul into some gracious form, and let it tarry there for a moment; to hear one's own intellectual views echoed back to one with all the added music of passion and youth,' breathes Lord Henry, 'to convey one's temperament into another as though it were a subtle fluid or a strange perfume; there was a real joy in that. . . .'[14] So the narrator of 'The Portrait of Mr W. H.' explains that when Shakespeare speaks to Willie Hughes of 'the marriage of true minds', he is really quoting the prophetess Diotima, who said that 'friends are married by a far nearer tie than those who beget mortal children, for fairer and more immortal are the children who are their common offspring'.[15] Predictably, Plato's *Symposium* is duly trotted out to validate the theory:

> It is only when we realise the influence of neo-Platonism on the Renaissance that we can understand the true meaning of the amatory phrases and words with which the friends were wont, at this time, to address each other. There was a kind of mystic transference of the expressions from the physical world to a

sphere that was spiritual, that was removed from gross bodily appetite, and in which the soul was Lord.[16]

This Platonic reasoning only holds up in the absence of active homosexuality. There is nothing 'pure' or 'incorporeal' about these friendships if it is admitted that men desire other men as sexual beings. Wilde did admit that men desire men, but he was able to live a sort of half-truth; his love for Bosie was apparently not sexual in the usual sense, but it was certainly obsessive. Paglia says that his great break with his Greek aesthetic theory was to be physically close to him.

Then, on the side, there was a procession of beautiful, lower-class boys, with whom Wilde had an impressively active sex life. What did they think, I wonder, of Wilde's famous self-validation from the dock: 'The "Love that dare not speak its name" in this century is such a great affection of an elder for a younger man as there was between David and Jonathan, such as Plato made the very basis of his philosophy, and such as you find in the sonnets of Michelangelo and Shakespeare. It is that deep, spiritual affection that is as pure as it is perfect.'[17]

Within this system, women are dross because they inspire only physical desire, which is ironic, because by this stage they inspired very little desire in Wilde at all, but he seems not to have been able to pass up on the opportunity of venting his misogyny. 'The Portrait of Mr W. H.', written when he was two or three years into his life as a homosexual, but before he met Bosie, is a horribly misogynistic work. In his eulogy of Willie Hughes, the little Shakespearean boy-actor, the (unnamed) narrator explains that a boy playing, say, Rosalind, adds a welcome layer of artifice to the production. It never occurs to him to suggest that women might play men to produce the same effect. As the narrator continues, it is clear that he is determined to scatter women from the Shakespearean stage; the wit and romance of so many of Shakespeare's heroines was perhaps occasioned by the fact that young men played them and imbued the parts with 'passionate purity, quick mobile fancy, and healthy freedom from sentimentality', he says.[18]

But when the narrator begins to speak of the 'Dark Lady of the Sonnets', his reasoning descends to that of the paranoid misogynist. The dark lady is 'black-haired, and married, and of evil repute',[19] and her great crime is to make Willie Hughes fall in love with her. Shakespeare tries to come between them by fascinating the dark lady himself. He becomes temporarily infatuated with her, although he knows her to be 'evil and unworthy', but for her (and here it is hard to believe that Wilde is not sending himself up, though there is no indication that he is) 'the genius of a man is as nothing compared to a boy's beauty'.[20]

The relationship of this work, and any work, to its writer's life is problematic, of course; the fact that the whole Willie Hughes story is a forgery masterfully throws a delicate gossamer of doubt over the whole narrative. But the authorial voice makes itself heard when the narrator speaks of reading and re-reading Shakespeare's sonnets, to the point where it seems to him that 'I was deciphering the story of a life that had once been mine, unrolling the record of a romance that, without my knowing it, had coloured the very texture of my nature, had dyed it with strange and subtle dyes.'[21]

Wilde did not need the voice of a narrator to denigrate women, either. When working on *Salomé* in Paris, he replied to a friend, who had said that women were beautiful: 'How can you say that? Women aren't beautiful at all. They are something else, I allow: magnificent, when dressed with taste and covered with jewels, but beautiful, no. Beauty reflects the soul.'[22]

A sexual woman is immediately a threat. Her sexuality is automatically evil. Salomé's mother Herodias is portrayed as a nymphomaniac, but Salomé has beauty as long as she is virginal. However, the prophet Jokanaan rouses her sexuality and she proceeds to enact the myth of the great castrating bitch, with her mother's encouragement. Not only does she cut off his head, a handy penis-substitute in dream theory, she fetishizes it, by turning it into an object of sexual desire.

There is evidence that this fear and suspicion of sexually active women did not confine itself to Wilde's writing. In Paris, before he married, he was vigorously counselling his friend Robert Sherard not to marry, and declared to Louis Latourette: 'All the great men of France were cuckolds. Haven't you observed this? All! In every period. By their wives or by their mistresses.' The fact that those with mistresses were themselves adulterers seems to have passed him by. Wilde's work, in fact, thrives on such double standards.

At this stage, Wilde did not know that he would treat his own wife appallingly, although he was always strangely prescient about his life, probably because it is the same story retold again and again, driven by the motor of immovable obsessions. Constance comes across as gentle, tender and astonishingly innocent. With two young children and only middle-class means, there was no possibility of her playing with her sexual identity in a way which would have made her interesting to Wilde. In his plays, only very evil or very rich women could escape their own children; Mrs Erlynne, the forty-year-old *femme fatale* in *Lady Windermere's Fan*, is the former, while her daughter is the latter – Lady Windermere remains of the virgin type of innocent Wilde women. Having children and looking after them was decidedly bourgeois in Victorian days, anyway, and Wilde, an inveterate snob, must have felt that his wife was letting down the side.

On the other hand, detaching sexual identity from bodily functions was smart, and the currency of the kind of drawing-rooms which Wilde frequented. Oscar Wilde hardly invented 'camp', but his life and work is its most clear articulation, and this is perhaps his most lasting legacy; Susan Sontag dedicates her 'Notes on Camp' to him.[23] 'Camping it up' is the taking on of an exaggerated female identity. The Freudian semiotician Jacques Lacan saw the essence of femininity as a mask created so that the man is not threatened, and thus does not seek vengeance. Female identity is so much more complex than that; but, nevertheless, Lacan's notion is a useful one in looking at 'camp'. We have already seen Wilde refusing at the fence of the Oedipal struggle; his taking on of the exaggerated female personality which is 'camp' could be seen as another symptom of that refusal. 'Camping it up' can also be seen as a way of denying women their role and their power by appropriating it for male uses.

It was also great fun, however, because it was upper class and slightly shocking, and because the roles which Victorian society offered a man once he had cleared the Oedipal fence would have been enough to send him hopping back over it again. Wilde turned his neuroses into an aesthetic system which in turn influenced his behaviour, and both became simultaneously true for him. Paglia is impressed with the cruelty of Wilde's pure aestheticism, because it produced the best of his art. But she is forgetting the nature of perversity and paradox; they work only by relation to their opposite. Wilde's nature contained the model against which his perversities and paradoxes were worked out. If it had not, he would have been truly radical, and either ridiculous or magnificent, but certainly not funny.

Paglia seems to lament Wilde's turning to mother nature in *De Profundis*, and explains this by saying it was written 'in tears and at the midnight hour, not in Apollonian sunlight'.[24] Perhaps he simply no longer needed to be perverse about nature because his perversity was already catered for by his being behind bars. Prison offered him another role, another system of detachment, and he no longer needed to fight off the mantle of husband and father, and the bed of a sexual woman. He was now outside nature in a new way. He writes:

We have forgotten that Water can cleanse, and Fire purify, and that the Earth is mother to us all. As a consequence our Art is of the Moon and plays with shadows, while Greek art is of the Sun and deals directly with things. I feel sure that in elemental forces there is purification, and I want to go back to them and live in their presence.[25]

Wilde suffered much in prison, but he was free of the demand that he be an adult, and perhaps it was that demand, ultimately, which forced him to be perverse. After his plays, Wilde's fairy-tales are his best work; his least perverse voice is the voice he uses to speak to children. The fears which fairy-tales explore are fears which seem to have been real for him: fears of castration, annihilation and humiliation.

Let us remember that Wilde did not stop sleeping with women just to sleep with men; he slept, almost always, with men much younger than himself. Most of the time, they were boys. Although the stigma attached to homosexuality has, to a great extent, faded, the stigma attached to paedophilia has not. No, Wilde did not sleep with children, but he did sleep with boys in their teens. He is one of the great writers for children who had an unhealthy obsession with youth, a club he shares with Lewis Carroll and J. M. Barrie.

Wilde's great search was the search for the innocent and beautiful. What led him to see sexually mature nature as fallen is a difficult question; was it the death of his beloved little nine-year-old sister, who with her golden hair and pale face would seem to be the prototype of his obsession, as Melissa Knox has argued? Was it the spectre of his mother, from which he never escaped? It is impossible to know, but the effects of this terrible immaturity are plain enough, and meant that that obviously mature body, the pregnant woman, was physically repugnant to him. One notes an obsessive repetitiveness in Wilde's beautiful prose: his words for beauty are always variations of 'white', 'golden-haired' and 'flower-like'. It is obvious that Constance was on a losing wicket when she could no longer, as Wilde said, be called 'white' or 'slim as a lily'. Similarly, Wilde's words for beautiful are all synonyms for 'innocent'. As for the dark lady of the sonnets, her black hair denounces her immediately.

So that to explain Wilde by calling him 'homosexual', and to explain his fear of women by referring to his homosexuality, is a ridiculous simplification. What attracted him to Bosie (derived from 'boysy') was his childlike quality: 'My sweet rose, my delicate flower, my lily of lilies,' he wrote to Douglas, 'it is perhaps in prison that I am going to test the power of love.'[26] Sadly, the end of the affair was so inevitable that, like most events in his life, he foretold it over and over. When the little dwarf dies of a broken heart in 'The Birthday of the Infanta', the little Princess, about as physically perfect as a female could be in Wilde's world, is peeved: 'Her dainty rose-leaf lips curled in pretty disdain. "For the future let those who come to play with me have no hearts," she cried, and she ran out into the garden.[27]

The Secret Fall of Constance Wilde
(An Excerpt from a New Play)

THOMAS KILROY

A dark stage. The attendant figures, mute, emerge out of the darkness: white, faceless masks, bowler hats, tight Victorian jackets, chequered pants, white gloves, a cross between Victorian toffs and street-theatre performers, stagehands and puppeteers, dressers, waiters, and Figures of Fate.

Out of the darkness four of the attendant figures roll a great white disc, a performance space like a circus ring, into place downstage under a brilliant spot. (Note: the disc effect throughout may be accomplished through the use of lighting.)

At the same time the voice of Constance from the darkness crying: 'No! No! No!'

Then two other attendant figures lead Oscar and Constance into the spot, on to the disc, rather like hospital attendants with frail patients. All six attendant figures then melt back into darkness, leaving Oscar and Constance on their own.

Oscar and Constance perform on the disc, circling one another. They are both at the end of their lives, he in frock coat and hat, she in a cape, both unsteady and worn, both leaning heavily on walking sticks.

At first the exchange between them is rapid.

CONSTANCE:	– no – no – no – no –
OSCAR:	I must see them! They're my children, too, Constance.
CONSTANCE:	I've never denied that – that's *not* what this is about!
OSCAR:	(*Deliberate shift: nervous, uncertain*) Let's see – Cyril's birthday is June the fifth, isn't it? A twelve-year-old already! And Vyvie will be what? My God, is it eleven? In November?
CONSTANCE:	Stop it, Oscar! Stop it!
OSCAR:	What? What?
CONSTANCE:	Playacting!
OSCAR:	– not playacting!
CONSTANCE:	You never face the situation as it really is. Never! Nothing exists for you unless it can be turned into a phrase. For once, would you say it as it actually is, Oscar!

OSCAR: *(Low)* I must see them. Before I die. That's all. Why are you doing this to me? Why? Why?

CONSTANCE: Protection —

OSCAR: Protection! My two little boys are protected from me, is it? Because I'm a pervert? Is that it? A gaol-bird? Two years' hard labour in the clink for gross indecency with male persons known and unknown.

CONSTANCE: Don't, Oscar.

OSCAR: Don't, Oscar! I can't touch my little boys because I'm a poof, a Marjorie, a Mary Ann. A prick lover. All you see is the invert. Barren. Yes! They cannot breed. So! Let them be without children. That's it, isn't it?

CONSTANCE: Funny. A few years ago I wouldn't have known what you're talking about. And a few months ago I would have been sickened by such offensive language. How I've changed simply by living with you!

OSCAR: *(Yell)* Say it as it really is, Oscar! That's what you want, isn't it? Say it as it really is, Oscar! Constance the realist!

CONSTANCE: Don't bully, Oscar. It makes you seem tiresome. Besides you know it doesn't work with me. Actually, what I really want now is to face myself, to face, finally, what it was that made me end up like this. Here. With you. I want to face my own role in this whole sorry spectacle.

OSCAR: What on earth are you talking about?

CONSTANCE: Evil.

OSCAR: Evil? Evil! You know, Constance, you positively drip with goodness. You drench everyone around you with your virtue. Drip, drip, drip, wet, wet, wet. Just like your sanctimonious relatives. Aunt Mary and Cousin Lizzie. Lizzie Busybody. Leaky, that's what you are, Constance. You leak, drowning in that wet, deadly morality of yours.

CONSTANCE: *(Surprised)* Why I'm not at all like that. You know perfectly well that I find that sort of thing — comic —

OSCAR: *(Pause)* I am sorry. That was utterly inexcusable of me. Sorry. I've had that word evil thrown in my face by every Tom, Dick and Harry and now coming from you of all people!

CONSTANCE: You know you're the most self-obsessed, self-indulgent, self-self-self person that I have ever — I wasn't talking about you, for Heavensakes! I was taking about myself!

OSCAR: I don't understand —

CONSTANCE: Evil! In me! Which I've never been able to confess.

OSCAR: You're not evil, Constance —

CONSTANCE: No, Oscar, not that, not any more. Never again will I be invented as the good woman. Never! Constance who never screamed aloud at what was being done to her, the good woman who ran with her children, away from the horror, the filth, the good wife who kept him in money throughout even while he betrayed her. No. I want myself restored to me now. As I really am! Even if it is to be at the very end.

OSCAR: But you always acted out of − goodness.

CONSTANCE: Most times I acted out of rage! Rage! Deep, silent rage! Oh, it was so easy to appear meek, so easy. It was like dressing to go outdoors, one felt − safe. But it was always different when one was alone in the house.

Do you know, sometimes I broke things. But you wouldn't have noticed, Oscar, would you?

OSCAR: You mustn't punish yourself like this, Constance, mustn't!

CONSTANCE: Why did you like having the good woman as your wife, Oscar? Have you ever asked yourself that? Have you? Did it make your wretched debauchery more easy? Hm? Did it somehow − protect you?

OSCAR: We had − happiness −

CONSTANCE: I think we were imprisoned by happiness.

OSCAR: What on earth do you mean?

CONSTANCE: Do you remember in the early days? How we wouldn't leave the house for days on end? Our House Beautiful! People would ask: Where on earth have you two been for the past few days? And we would smile at one another across the room. I thought no one is as tender, as loving, as exquisite, as mysterious as this man and he is mine! He is my prisoner in this white palace. Then one day, I remember the moment exactly, I saw your face actually change −

OSCAR: Please, Constance −

CONSTANCE: Dripping with goodness, did you say? Wet, indeed! How you turned away from me with that stylish disgust of yours! I blamed myself, of course, lying there in the darkness. Women always do. Thinking in the night. What is wrong with me? Why is he unable to look me in the face in the act of love? Why does he make me turn my back on him, on all fours, like an animal when all I want to do is look into his eyes?

OSCAR: It was not like that!

CONSTANCE: And when I conceived with Cyril I will never, never

	forget that look of revulsion on your face, the disgust at what my body had become. When I tried to touch you, you sprang away from me as if from something rancid.
OSCAR:	*(Cry)* Oh, God of Creation, what you have given us to live with! *(Shift)* What is − mysterious is that none of this makes any difference to my love for you. Or the children. *(Discovery)* There is so much truth in failure and destruction.
CONSTANCE:	At least you've sometimes expressed the truth to me, Oscar. Even when you surrounded me with lies.
OSCAR:	*(Heavy irony)* The problem with *my* marriage is that my wife understands me − *(Rush)* You went back on our agreement. You sat across from me in that filthy prison cage and you promised! Yes, Oscar, you said. Everything will be the same as before. You and I. Cyril and Vyvyan.
CONSTANCE:	I've learned that nothing is ever the same as before, nothing −
OSCAR:	And where did you learn that, may I ask?
CONSTANCE:	From your friend Alfred Douglas.
OSCAR:	*(Shocked pause)* Bosie! What's he got to do with this?
CONSTANCE:	Can you really ask that? After all that has happened?
OSCAR:	I have nothing more to do with him! Nothing!
CONSTANCE:	Oh, really?
OSCAR:	You don't believe me?
CONSTANCE:	No, I don't believe you because on this one subject you are capable of endless lying. And you wonder why I must protect the children! This is ridiculous!
OSCAR:	Protect. The children. *(Working it out)* From Bosie! Bosie? Did he do something?
CONSTANCE:	I see! You believe he's corrupt, too, don't you?
OSCAR:	Bosie! What did he do? Did he do something to the children? Did something happen? Answer me, woman! By God, I will kill him! My own sons − What did he do?
CONSTANCE:	Nothing.
OSCAR:	But he tried to?
CONSTANCE:	I wouldn't allow it.
OSCAR:	It? You wouldn't allow 'it'? What is this 'it'? Maybe it's just something in your mind, Constance, hm? Thinking up something monstrous about someone else −
CONSTANCE:	Why did I marry you, Oscar? Why? Why?
OSCAR:	*(Long pause. Brokenly)* Because. We loved.
CONSTANCE:	People keep asking me: What was it like, Constance, really like, to be married to him? Of course, they're

thinking of you-know-what. It's as if they are undressing me with their eyes. Why, I answer them in my best wifely voice, it was theatre, m'dears, theatre! Theatre all the way! You know what Oscar is like! Every day a different performance. With frequent costume changes, of course. They are also wondering although they never ask: *When did she know?* All those young men and boys about the place. All those late dinners in Kettner's and the Café Royal. When you consorted with sodomites and — what's that curious term? Rentboys! You didn't become someone else. You were the same person I had married. What is more, you were the same person I had wanted to marry. What does that say, Oscar? About us? About me?

OSCAR: Why *did* you marry me, Constance?

CONSTANCE: I fear that I may be about to find out. *(She suddenly doubles up in pain)*

OSCAR: Constance! Are you in pain?

CONSTANCE: *(Breaking)* I fell —

OSCAR: I know that, dear. You were alone —

CONSTANCE: Alone. In the house. I fell. Or flew. Down flights. Our House Beautiful, oh, Oscar! Number One Tite Street in the Borough of Chelsea. The most desirable, the most sought after entrée in London!

OSCAR: Are you in constant pain?

CONSTANCE: There are times when I cannot walk.

OSCAR: And will they operate again?

CONSTANCE: They say there's little point. The injury — the paralysis is progressive. What a word. Progressive. You used to use that word of me, Oscar. Remember? My wife is progressive! She campaigns for Peace, the dockers, Rational Dress and Lady Sandhurst. A modern woman, my wife. Remarkably broad-minded, I must say. Progressive. Paralysis. Do you really care about my pain?

OSCAR: Of course I care. Terribly.

CONSTANCE: I've decided something about you. I said this to someone the other day. He's absolutely deficient, I said, in certain areas of feeling. And absurdly intense in others. A sort of imbalance that is extremely dangerous. If you have anything to do with him, that is. That's what I said.

OSCAR: *(Pause)* Constance. What actually happened to you? On that staircase?

CONSTANCE: Don't wish to speak about it —

OSCAR: But something happened?

CONSTANCE:	— fall —
OSCAR:	But something else?
CONSTANCE:	— on the landing —
OSCAR:	What was it, Constance?
CONSTANCE:	*(Whisper. In tears)* Unspeakable. Evil. Crouching there on the landing. Squat. Evil.
OSCAR:	What did you see, Constance?
CONSTANCE:	I cannot tell you!
OSCAR:	Please —
CONSTANCE:	No! It cannot be told. It can only be — discovered. Revealed.
OSCAR:	Please confide in me, Constance! Please! Don't you see? If you did it would — save me. Talk to me, Constance! Otherwise I'm finished. Back on the streets. Alone.
CONSTANCE:	But firstly, firstly, it has to be — acted out. Then I will be able to face it. They're waiting for us, Oscar.
OSCAR:	*(Frantic)* No — no. Tell me, Constance. Please!
CONSTANCE:	They're waiting for us, Oscar. Back there. In the darkness.
OSCAR:	*(Surrender)* Yes.
CONSTANCE:	Waiting to put us through our paces. One more time. To perform. This time to face it as it really was!
OSCAR:	See how we've both ended up on sticks, Constance. How demeaning! Used to admire a decent cane. In the old days. But never as a mere aid to walking.
CONSTANCE:	There has always been your story, Oscar, but this time there has to be mine as well! You and I. Our — marriage. Our — children.
OSCAR:	*(Sadly: towards walking stick)* When something becomes useful it ceases to be beautiful. Don't you think?
CONSTANCE:	*(Shift to anxiety)* What's the matter?
OSCAR:	*(Desperate rush)* As a family we rather frequented the Continent, did we not? Look how we've ended up! You with the children under the Italian sun and I alone on the streets of Paris. *(Breaks)* Cyril is the one I worry about most. He is such a perfectionist that he may do something terrible with his life! *(Pulls himself into the debonair mode, with difficulty and without complete success)* Each country exports its scandals. When in doubt take the boat. Otherwise life would be extremely tedious for the rest of the world.
CONSTANCE:	*(Now deeply concerned for him)* What is it, Oscar? When you go on like this I know there is something —
OSCAR:	*(Disturbed)* Simply cannot go through all this again,

	from the beginning, Constance. Cannot. Cannot.
CONSTANCE:	It is the only way in which I can go back.
OSCAR:	— cannot — cannot —
CONSTANCE:	— for me, so that I may face myself.
OSCAR:	For you —
CONSTANCE:	For my secret journey, Oscar.
OSCAR:	For you, Constance. E finita la commedia!

Loud clapping from the darkness around them. Lights up and for the first time we see the full stage.

The clapping we have heard has come from the six attendant figures who stand waiting, equipped with clappers. All about on stands are full-sized puppets waiting to be used: two child puppets for the Wilde children, nightgowns/sailor suits. Puppets of: several Victorian gentlemen in frock-coats, top hats; a judge and barristers; a gaoler and policemen.

A set of stairs which may become an elaborate staircase with banisters, a court-room dock, a railway carriage.

The disc is rolled back upstage by attendants, where it leans against the back wall, a gigantic moon or wafer.

The attendants lead Oscar and Constance to either side of the stage, downstage and, there, facing the audience, they communicate with one another across a distance, without looking at one another. As they speak, they are transformed by the attendants into their youthful selves. When the canes are taken from them they straighten up at once, alert. Wig and costume changes complete the transformation.

Bás Wilde Mar a Tharla
(The Real Death of Wilde)

GABRIEL ROSENSTOCK

An choróineach ag dul in éag,
Barraí príosúin an tsaoil ag leá,
Cuntanós séimh an Aingil . . .
Siúlann saoránaigh Pháras thar bráid
Ina n-imprisin.
I gCarcair Reading eisítear uimhir eile fós.
Nach éachtach iad figiúirí an duine!
Líonmhaire iad ná deora uile na Séine.

(The carnation withers,
And the prison bars of life dissolve,
The soft countenance of an Angel . . .
Citizens of Paris pass
Like figures in a painting.
In Reading Gaol another number is given out.
Mighty the figures created by man
More plentiful than all the tears of the River Seine.)

TRANSLATION: NOEL GRIFFIN

Oscar Wilde Dedication: Westminster Abbey, 14 February 1995

SEAMUS HEANEY

'Poetry is human existence come to life.' 'Poetry surprises by a fine excess.' 'The road of excess leads to the palace of wisdom.' 'Wisdom is a butterfly and not a gloomy bird of prey.'

In Poets' Corner, the way of quotation is an obvious way and the quotations you have just heard — from Hugh MacDiarmid, John Keats, William Blake and W. B. Yeats respectively — all have to do in one way or another with Oscar Wilde, with the vocation that he followed so exactingly in his life and in his work, with the liberation that his name represents and the exhilaration that it promotes. But they also remind us that, within the universe of the quotable, Oscar himself has become a kind of first cause, an original source from whom witticisms proceed as freely and abundantly as creation proceeds from the hand of the creator. Indeed, there are times when it can seem that the Holy Quip of St Oscar has replaced the Holy Writ of the other prophets and evangelists and that the Book of Life itself could be rendered down into a new compendium of Phrases and Philosophies for the Use of the Young.

Oscar has entered the language as decisively as he once entered America — with nothing to declare except his genius. In the meantime, he has given the language a new adjective in the word 'Wildean', a new myth in *The Picture of Dorian Gray* and, in the dialogue of *The Importance of Being Earnest*, a new linguistic element that bears about the same relation to our actual speech as ozone bears to stale air. On and off the stage, his one-liners had the perfect pitch and promise of a struck tuning-fork, but they issued from an imagination in which far deeper harmonies were latent and constantly in search of more resonant forms of expression. For Wilde was not only a brilliant entertainer but a dedicated poet, one who in the end fulfils our most solemn expectation that the poet should be (in the words of Nadezhda Mandelstam) both 'a vehicle of world harmony' and 'a source of truth'.

The great reward of Oscar's verbal brilliance, in other words, is that it completely earns its intellectual and imaginative keep. His aesthetic came to encompass not only the perfection of blue china but the desolation of blues singing. The cry of hurt is every bit as audible in *The Ballad of Reading Gaol* as it is in the song of St James's Infirmary, although the provenance of Wilde's chain-gang poem is Irish rather than American and looks back to all the convict ballads, gaol journals and political poetry of Irish nationalist literature in the nineteenth century – a literature to which Wilde's mother famously contributed under the pseudonym of Speranza.

But if it looks back to Irish patriots in the dock for felony in Dublin and an Irish playwright in the dock for homosexuality in London, the ballad also looks forward to English soldier–poets in the trenches of Flanders. Wilde prefigured the War Poets in being a voice from a world of a penal system where the suffering and humiliation on the ground were matched only by the complacency and arrogance at the highest levels; so it is entirely appropriate and deeply gratifying that he is commemorated here side by side with Wilfred Owen, Isaac Rosenberg and all those other sad captains of doomed youth.

Wilde liked to compare his ballad to the cry of Marsyas, the centaur whom the establishment god Apollo flayed after Marsyas had challenged his pre-eminence as a musician; and Wilde's comparison was valid in as much as he too had challenged the music of what happened in Victorian society, especially what happened in the area of sexual behaviour, where the register mounted all the way from an undersong of evasion, denial and cover-up to the discords of prejudice, righteousness and vindictiveness. In a reckless tactic that prefigured the non-violent politics of the century ahead, he provoked the violence of the system and suffered it in order to expose it. And his challenge, like that of Marsyas, was offered as a style of playing, as an artistic performance. Whether he was going down a mine in a bucket or undergoing cross-examination in a court, Oscar's conduct was both a display and a discipline, an extreme summoning of all his intellectual principles and self-dramatizing instincts. 'Style, not sincerity' was more than a quip. It was a masquerade which his society recognized as a taunt, a flaunt, a front, something oppositional, resistant and liberationist. Declan Kiberd, for example, has pointed out how Wilde's lifelong performance as a stage Englishman was a commentary on the hollowness of the stereotype of the stage Irishman as well, and an unmasking, as we have learned to say – ultimately from Oscar himself – an unmasking of the distinction between English and Irish in the first place. And between heterosexual and homosexual. Which is to say that all our current awareness about the way gender roles and sexual orientation are constructs rather than destinies, all our lost trust in the essential stability of a category such as 'human nature', all our nascent tolerance of diversity, all these things were foreshadowed in Oscar Wilde's life and writings.

And then, of course, in yet another foreshadowing of the consequences of intellectual dissidence and artistic integrity in the twentieth century, Oscar was sent to the Gulag; with the result that *The Ballad of Reading Gaol* is the one example I can think of of a modern classic in English which first appeared as samizdat literature – published, as it was, in a limited edition which was in effect a clandestine edition, and not under the author's own name but under the prisoner code number which was Oscar's number at Reading, Convict C.3.3.

The ballad is Wilde's poem of solidarity with the outcasts, his attempt to produce, in Franz Kafka's great phrase, a book that would be an axe to break the frozen sea in each of us, and I have concentrated on it in this place at this moment because it repeats in the medium of verse the achievement which Wilde very properly claimed for himself in the realm of drama. 'I took the drama,' he said in *De Profundis*, 'the most objective form known to art, and made it as personal a mode of expression as the lyric or the sonnet.' In *The Ballad of Reading Gaol* he did something similar with the melodramatic recitation, transforming it from an interlude in the music hall to an episode in the history of conscience.

And yet the literary fact of the matter is that the axe which is keenest, the one which is still most capable of shattering the surfaces of convention, is not the high lament of the ballad but rather the hard-edged, unpathetic prose that Wilde created in dialogues like 'The Decay of Lying' and in dramas like *The Importance of Being Earnest*. His heady paradoxes, his over-the-topness at knocking the bottom out of things, the rightness of his wrongfooting, all that high-wire word-play, all that freedom to affront and to exult in his own uniqueness — that was Wilde's true path to solidarity. The lighter his touch, the more devastating his effect. When he walked on air, he was on solid ground. Which is why a window, 'that little patch of blue/that prisoners call the sky', is such an appropriate memorial. A window that lets us see through, makes us look up, and lets the light in. A window that is the sky's threshold, not just a practical means of illumination in the simplest literal sense, but a poetic image of illumination at its most spiritual as well. The kind of illumination represented by the good decision of the Dean and Chapter of Westminster Abbey to honour the name of Oscar Wilde in this historic corner of his adopted homeland. And the kind of illumination which T. S. Eliot experienced in the church at Little Gidding, where he discovered that, after all the lesions of the past, reconciliation was possible and that the use of memory was 'for liberation'. And it is such a reconciliation that we are here to celebrate, one which Oscar Wilde's descendants must rejoice in particularly, but one which all his admirers, in this generation and in generations to come, will be able to share in from now on in this place where his name is inscribed on high and he is honoured, as he of all people would want to be, in style. 'See,' Eliot wrote in that redemptive poem,

See, now they vanish,
The faces and places, with the self which, as it could, loved them,
To become renewed, transfigured, in another pattern.

Notes

Oscar Wilde: The Artist as Irishman
DECLAN KIBERD

1. Henry Craik, letter to John Forster, Forster MS 48.E.25, British Library.
2. W. B. Yeats, *Autobiographies* (London: Macmillan, 1955), 138.
3. Ibid., 138.
4. Ibid., 137.
5. Richard Ellmann, *Oscar Wilde* (New York: Alfred A. Knopf, 1988), 14.
6. *Complete Works of Oscar Wilde* (Glasgow: HarperCollins, 1994), 369.
7. Ibid., 770.
8. Ibid., 371.
9. Quoted in H. Montgomery Hyde, *Oscar Wilde* (London: Eyre Methuen, 1976), 31.
10. *The Letters of Oscar Wilde*, ed. Rupert Hart-Davis (London: Rupert Hart-Davis, 1963), 54.
11. Quoted in Hyde, *Oscar Wilde*, 232.
12. 'Je suis Irlandais de race, et les Anglais m'ont condamné à parler le langage de Shakespeare.' *Letters*, 304.
13. Quoted in Hyde, *Oscar Wilde*, 85.
14. Quoted in Richard Ellmann, *James Joyce* (Oxford: Oxford University Press, 1959), 226.
15. Richard Ellmann, *Eminent Domain: Yeats among Wilde, Joyce, Pound, Eliot and Auden* (Oxford: Oxford University Press, 1967), 12–13.
16. *Letters*, 469.
17. See Hyde, *Oscar Wilde*, 38 ff.
18. *Complete Works*, 1142.
19. Oscar Wilde, *The Artist as Critic*, ed. Richard Ellmann (London: W. H. Allen, 1970), 136.
20. On this, see Lionel Trilling, *Sincerity and Authenticity* (Oxford: Oxford University Press, 1972), 118–22.
21. *Complete Works*, 395, 396.
22. Ibid., 397.
23. James Laver, *The Concise History of Costume and Fashions* (New York: Random House, 1969), 182.
24. *Complete Works*, 415.
25. On Wilde's critique of determinism, see Christopher Nassaar, *Into the Demon Universe* (New Haven, Conn.: Yale University Press, 1974), 135–7.
26. Quoted in Rodney Shewan, *Oscar Wilde: Art and Egotism* (London: Macmillan, 1977), 193.
27. *Complete Works*, 366.
28. Ibid., 378.
29. See L. P. Curtis Jnr, *Anglo-Saxons and Celts: A Study of Anti-Irish Prejudice in Victorian England* (Bridgeport, Conn.: Conference on British Studies, 1968).
30. *Letters*, 143.
31. Otto Rank, *The Double: A Psychoanalytic Study* (New York: Alfred A. Knopf, 1971).
32. *Complete Works*, 364.
33. Erich Stern, review of Rank's *The Double*, *Die Literatur*, XXIX, 1926–7, 555.
34. Rank, *The Double*, 48 ff.
35. *Complete Works*, 388.
36. Quoted in Harry Tucker, 'Introduction', Rank, *The Double*, xvi.
37. G. W. F. Hegel, *The Phenomenology of Mind* (London: Routledge & Kegan Paul, 1966), 229–40.
38. Ashis Nandy, *The Intimate Enemy: Loss and Recovery of Self Under Colonialism* (Bombay: Oxford University Press, 1983), 7–8.

39. Ibid., 79–113.
40. Ibid., 11.
41. *Complete Works*, 1152.
42. Quoted in R. K. R. Thornton, *The Decadent Dilemma* (London: Edward Arnold, 1983), 68.
43. Quoted in H. Kingsmill-Moore, *Reminiscences and Reflections* (London: Batsford, 1930), 45.
44. Nandy, *Intimate Enemy*, 32–5.
45. Percival W. H. Almy, 'New Views of Mr O. W.', *Theatre*, London, 1894, 124.
46. *Complete Works*, 370.
47. Ibid., 369.
48. Quoted in Ellmann, *Oscar Wilde*, 20.
49. Quoted in Hyde, *Oscar Wilde*, 71.
50. *Letters*, 80.
51. Ellmann, *Oscar Wilde*, 186.
52. Quoted in Tom Nairn, *The Enchanted Glass: Britain and its Monarchy* (London: Hutchinson, 1988), 328.
53. Quoted in ibid., 332.
54. Ibid., 340.
55. *Letters*, 339.
56. *Complete Works*, 1147.
57. Ibid., 1131.
58. Ibid., 1153.
59. Jorge Luis Borges, *Labyrinths* (Harmondsworth: Penguin Books, 1970), 216.
60. George Russell, *Letters from AE*, ed. Alan Denson (London: Abelard-Schuman, 1961), 20.
61. Wilde, *The Artist as Critic*, 130.
62. Quoted in Ellmann, *Oscar Wilde*, 186.
63. *Complete Works*, 1140.

The Story-Teller at Fault:
Oscar Wilde and Irish Orality
DEIRDRE TOOMEY

1. W. B. Yeats, *Autobiographies* (London: Macmillan, 1955), 130–9. A shorter version of this essay was published in C. George Sandulescu (ed.), *Rediscovering Oscar Wilde* (Gerrards Cross: Colin Smythe, 1994), 405–20.
2. See *Uncollected Prose by W. B. Yeats I*, ed. John P. Frayne (London: Macmillan; New York: Columbia University Press, 1970), 354.
3. Yeats, *Autobiographies*, 135.
4. Ibid., 286.
5. W. B. Yeats, *Prefaces and Introductions: Uncollected Prefaces and Introductions by Yeats to Works by Other Authors and to Anthologies Edited by Yeats*, ed. William H. O'Donnell (London: Macmillan, 1988), 147–50. The version given in this introduction differs slightly from that of the *Autobiographies*.
6. Ibid., 149.
7. Yeats, *Autobiographies*, 135.
8. See Percival W. H. Almy, 'New Views of Mr Oscar Wilde', *Theatre*, March 1894, and André Gide, *Oscar Wilde* (London: William Kimber, 1951), 29.
9. Gide, *Oscar Wilde*, 29.
10. In *Les Songes merveilleux du Dormeur éveillé / Le Chant du Cygne / contes parlés d'Oscar Wilde* (Paris: Mercure de France, 1942). Ian Small firmly refers to this collection as 'apocrypha', but this assumes a chirographic–typographic mind-set (*Oscar Wilde Revalued: An Essay on New Materials and Methods of Research* [Greensboro, NC: ELT Press, 1993], 206). Gabrielle Enthoven, the theatre historian and collector, recalled in a letter to Cecil Oldman (enclosed in her *Echoes* [nd, privately printed], BL) that she would write down a version of an oral tale as soon as Wilde had left her house 'in order to remember'; others who have recorded Wilde's tales, such as Yeats, had a strongly developed recall for oral material.
11. Vincent O'Sullivan, *Aspects of Wilde* (London: Constable, 1936), 34, 75; Laurence Housman, *Echo de Paris: A Study from Life* (London, 1923), 34; Yeats, *Autobiographies*, 138. Ian Small has questioned the assumption that Wilde abandoned writing after *The Ballad of Reading Gaol*, pointing to Wilde's careful proof corrections to the Smithers editions of *The Importance of Being Earnest* and *An Ideal Husband* (unpublished paper). However, Wilde's weary assertion, in December 1898, that he was 'going to make an effort and try to write a poem in prose' for a journal of La Jeunesse's indicates aversion to writing, as does the apology to Ross in April 1900, 'I simply cannot write. . . . It is a mode of paralysis – a *cacoethes tacendi* [itch to be silent] – the one form that malady takes me' (*The Letters of Oscar Wilde*, ed. Rupert Hart-Davis [London: Rupert Hart-Davis, 1963], 766, 820).
12. O'Leary serialized part of the tale in the

Gaelic Journal, 1894–97. He had heard it in West Cork before the Famine.

13. W. B. Maxwell, *Time Gathered: Autobiography* (London: Hutchinson, 1937), 97.

14. See *Letters*, 809.

15. In Frank Harris, *Unpath'd Waters* (London: John Lane, 1913), 3–27. 'The King of the Jews' (49–57) also owes something to Wilde's oral tale, 'Simon of Cyrene'.

16. First published in *The Smart Set* in October 1902, and collected in *Spiritual Adventures* (London: Constable, 1905), 55–82.

17. In *Harper's Bazaar*, March 1933 first collected in *Work Suspended and Other Stories* (London: Chapman & Hall, 1949), 101–12.

18. For an excellent survey of orality theory, see Walter J. Ong, *Orality and Literacy: The Technologising of the Word* (London and New York: Routledge, 1991). See also Eric Havelock, *The Muse Learns to Write* (New Haven, Conn.: Yale University Press, 1986).

19. *Le Chant du Cygne*, 124–7.

20. Ernest Horry La Jeunesse (1847–1917), French littérateur. O'Sullivan, *Aspects of Wilde*, 41, 37.

21. Ernest La Jeunesse, *Recollections of Oscar Wilde*, ed. Percival Pollard (Boston and London: J. W. Luce, 1906), 71, 83.

22. Ong, *Orality and Literacy*, 32–3, 72.

23. *Complete Works of Oscar Wilde* (Glasgow: HarperCollins, 1994), 29.

24. Ong, *Orality and Literacy*, 67–8.

25. '[D]esire has her dwelling near the muses.' See Eric Havelock, *Preface to Plato* (Oxford: Basil Blackwell, 1963), 154–5.

26. *Complete Works*, 1115.

27. Jean Paul Raymond and Charles Ricketts, *Oscar Wilde: Recollections* (London: Nonesuch, 1932), 13.

28. 'The rounded sentence began its career in the . . . days of oral communication, when indoctrination depended on word of mouth and retention of doctrine depended on the memory' (Eric Havelock, *The Liberal Temper in Greek Politics* [New Haven: Yale University Press, 1957], 126). Wilde was doubly sensitive to orality in that not only did he come from an oral culture, but in studying classics for more than seven years he would have been aware of the interplay of orality and literacy at the time of Plato.

29. See Havelock, *Preface to Plato*, passim.

30. La Jeunesse, *Recollections of Oscar Wilde*, 70–1.

31. *Le Chant du Cygne*, 98.

32. See *De Profundis*, *Letters*, 476–7.

33. *Le Chant du Cygne*, 287. This tale and a subsequent tale were undoubtedly given in French (as below) by Wilde:

    Et Lazare marcha. Tous s'en furent alors en criant au miracle.

    Mais Lazare, ressuscité, demeurait triste.

    Au lieu de tomber aux pieds de Jésus, il restait a l'écart, avec un aspect de reproche.

    Et Jésus s'approchant demanda tendrement:

    —Toi qui reviens de chez les morts, ne me diras-tu rien, Lazare?

    Et Lazare lui dit:

    —Pourquoi m'as-tu menti, pourquoi mens-tu encore en leur parlant du ciel, de la gloire de Dieu? Il n'y a rien Rabbi, rien par delà la mort, et celui qui est mort est bien mort, je le sais, moi qui m'en reviens de là-bas.

    Et Jésus un doigt sur la bouche avec un regard implorant vers Lazare, lui répondit:

    —Je le sais. Ne le leur dis pas.

34. Yeats, *Autobiographies*, 137.

35. Kernahan used what he had heard as the basis of a novel, *The Man of No Sorrows* (London: Cassell, 1911). This work also uses the *topos* of 'The Doer of Good'. The genesis of Wilde's tale can be dated since it responds directly to a controversy of January 1895. Ferdinand Brunetière published, in the *Revue des Deux Mondes*, which he edited, an article, 'Après une visite au Vatican'. He attacked the cult of science and denounced the failure of science either to understand human nature or to develop a new morality. Zola's *Paris* (Paris, 1898) outlines the themes of the debate.

36. This passage closely resembles one in *De Profundis*: 'the sufferings of those whose name is Legion and whose dwelling is among the tombs, oppressed

nationalities, factory children, thieves, people in prison, outcasts, those who are dumb under oppression and whose silence is heard only of God' (*Letters*, 477). However, it seems likely that the oral version came first.

37. See 'The Soul of Man under Socialism'; '"Know thyself"' was written over the portal of the antique world. Over the portal of the new world, "Be thyself" shall be written. And the message of Christ to man was simply "Be thyself." That is the secret of Christ' (*Complete Works*, 1179).

38. *Le Chant du Cygne*, 170–2. This is clearly Wilde's French rather than that of a native speaker; certain usages are literary and obsolete, viz. 'illusionnées':

Un jour, un terrassier arabe au service d'un entrepreneur de fouilles qui ne recherchait que des monnaies anciennes, heurta de son pic per hasard, au flanc de la montagne du Calvaire, la pierre d'un tombeau. Et s'étant fait aider par ses camarades pour soulever la lourde dalle, il découvrit au creux de étroit sépulchre creusé dans un roc un mort encore, enveloppé dans son linceul intact.

L'entrepreneur de fouilles fit transporter cette macabre découverte dans un musée où les savants à lunettes se penchant sur elle avec soin démaillotèrent le défunt de ses bandelettes et découvrirent avec stupéfaction un corps momifié, portant évidentes, encore ourlées d'un sang desséché, noirâtre et craquelant, des plaies aux poignets, aux pieds et au flanc. C'était bien là, sans nul doute, le corps même de celui-là qui avait été crucifié sous Ponce-Pilate.

Ainsi des générations avaient été illusionnées comme le furent les saintes femmes et les premiers disciples, illusionnés également ceux-là qui avaient cru pouvoir établir avec certitude l'emplacement du sépulcre appartenant à Joseph d'Arimathie et construire sur cet emplacement un sanctuaire où les genoux des fidèles étaient venus user les pierres.

Les journaux s'emparèrent de l'événement, le Pape fut chassé du Vatican dont on fit une sorte de temple de la Vérité Scientifique où l'on exposa sous verre à la curiosité publique le cadavre par qui le mensonge séculaire avait été assassiné. Et de ce fait, foi chrétienne, basée sur le dogme de la Résurrection subit une éclipse passagère.

Mais, le dimanche de Pâques suivant, un triste dimanche sans cloches, au premier pâle rayon de soleil qui vint le toucher assez tard dans la matinée, le corps inerte reprit la vie, brisa les vitres de son cercueil transparent et, devant les visiteurs et les gardiens prosternés, traversant d'un essor glorieux la Voûte Vaticane, disparut à leurs yeux. Une nouvelle religion dut naître et se répandre, ayant d'autres apôtres, d'autres martyrs aussi. De-ci, de-là, le Christ apparut à autres pèlerins pour se justifier aux hommes et fonder un culte de beauté sur des bases nouvelles. Il prêcha que, si l'on suivait sa doctrine, il n'y aurait plus ni riches, ni pauvres, ni luttes de classes, ni guerres, mais seulement, dans la grande unité des races divisées, des hommes s'aimant les uns les autres devant l'ephémère et constant miracle de la vie. Il affirma qu'il était revenu pour abolir les souffrances de ceux-là qui sont légion et dont la demeure est parmi les tombes, tous les opprimés, les enfants des usines, les voleurs, les vagabonds des grands chemins, les gens en prison, les proscrits, bref de tous ceux qui sont muets sous le glaive de l'oppresseur, et dont le silence est entendu par Dieu seul. Il dit à chacun: 'Sois toi-même. Ta perfection est en toi. Mais sans doute était-il venu trop tard dans un monde trop vieux'.

A cette revélation suprême par une bouche de lumière, des savants donnérent des explications rationellement scientifiques. Jésus renonça pour toujours à reparaître aux yeux des hommes, et tout retomba dans l'apathie des jours sans croyance et sans joie.

39. For which see Marjorie Reeves and Warwick Gould, *Joachim of Fiore and the Myth of the Eternal Evangel in the Nineteenth Century* (Oxford: Clarendon Press, 1987), 180–4.

40. See Warwick Gould, Philip L. Marcus and Michael Sidnell (eds.), *The Secret Rose, Stories by W. B. Yeats: A Variorum Edition* (London: Macmillan, 1992), 125–73.

41. Gide, *Oscar Wilde*, 18–19.

42. See Raymond and Ricketts, *Oscar Wilde: Recollections*, 18.

43. Ibid., 17.

44. Hester Travers Smith (ed.), *Psychic Messages from Oscar Wilde* (London: T. Werner Laurie, 1924).

45. Ricketts to T. S. Moore, December 1923 (BL Add MS 61719). Ricketts got little satisfaction on this matter from Hester Dowden .

46. Even if Wilde had not seen the centaurs while at Olympia, he would certainly have known E. Curtius, F. Adler et al., *Die Ausgrabungen zu Olympia*, 5 vols (Berlin, 1875–81). Plate XXIV of vol. 3 shows Deidameia and the Centaur Eurytion from the west pediment.

47. Yeats, *Autobiographies*, 96–7. The speech was given to the Law Students' Debating Society on 24 October 1901. It is also quoted in *Ulysses*, chapter 7 ('Aeolus'). In the recording studio, Joyce chose to read the speech of J. F. Taylor from *Ulysses*.

48. Report of the Intermediate Education (Ireland) Commission (1899).

49. W. B. Yeats, 'Academic Class and the Agrarian Revolution', first published in the [Dublin] *Daily Express*, 11 March 1899, 3: see *Uncollected Prose II*, ed. John P. Frayne and Colton Johnson (London: Macmillan, 1975), 149–52.

50. Evidence of 22 February reported in the [Dublin] *Daily Express*, 23 February 1899, 2.

51. The Atkinson controversy festered for weeks in the *Daily Express* and other nationalist papers and letters, and articles by those attacking Atkinson's position were collected in a series of Gaelic League pamphlets. The Gaels had their revenge on Atkinson when in 1902 Whitley Stokes reviewed his *Glossary* to the first volume of *Ancient Laws of Ireland*. Stokes expanded the review into *A Criticism of Dr Atkinson's Glossary* (London, 1903), listing forty-three pages of errors, including 'linguistic monstrosities which . . . some knowledge of Old and Middle-Irish would have enabled him to avoid or correct' (5). Douglas Hyde's revenge was in his bilingual satire *An Pleusgadh na Bulgoide* (*The Bursting of the Bubble*) (Dublin: Gill and Son, 1903) in which Dochtúir Mac h-Aitcinn [Atkinson] initially mistakes modern Irish for Japanese and is attacked by a posse of enraged and enchanted Trinity dons, including Mac Eathfaidh [Mahaffy] – 'Villain, don't you understand Irish. And we always saying that there was no other Irish scholar in Ireland but yourself . . . you leprechaun of the beard. Oh, was it not greatly this college was deceived in you.' See Lady Gregory (trans.), *Poets and Dreamers* (Gerrards Cross: Colin Smythe, 1974), 1987.

52. Wilde was a nationalist. He always insisted on his Irish status, admired O'Connell and Parnell and was very proud when his son Cyril announced that he was a Home Ruler. Vincent O'Sullivan confused Wilde's anti-Boer position and his admiration for Queen Victoria with a Unionist or Conservative stance (O'Sullivan, *Aspects of Wilde*, 25–6). Shaw was also anti-Boer – and none could doubt his radicalism.

53. W. B. Yeats, 'What is "Popular Poetry?"', in *Essays and Introductions* (London: Macmillan, 1961), 6.

54. 'Some Words about Unpublished Literature', *Gael*, 7 January 1888. See Douglas Hyde, *Language, Lore and Lyrics*, ed. Brendan Ó Conaire (Dublin: Irish Academic Press, 1986).

55. 'ag seinm cheoil do phócaí falamh'.

56. Guillot de Saix (ed.), *Contes et Propos d'Oscar Wilde* (Paris: Arthème Fayard, 1949), 9.

57. Lady Wilde ('Speranza'), *Ancient Legends, Mystic Charms, and Superstitions of Ireland* (Boston: Ticknor, 1887; London: Ward & Downey, 1888), I, 31–5.

58. Yeats, *Autobiographies*, 191.

59. See Seán O'Suilleabháin, *The Types of the Irish Folk Tale* (Helsinki: F. F. Communications No. 188, 1963), type 2421b. It has been collected all over Ireland and is usually told in a simple version: a man is asked to tell a tale in exchange for hospitality; he has no tale to tell, is turned out of the house, has a series of magical adventures and returns to tell his tale. Yeats uses part of the expanded version of this tale in 'Swedenborg, Mediums and the Desolate Places'; see *Explorations*, selected by Mrs W. B. Yeats (London: Macmillan, 1962), 57–8.

60. 'All the old writers ... wrote to be spoken or to be sung, and in a later age to be read aloud to hearers ... who gave nothing up of life to listen, but sat, the day's work over, friend by friend, lover by lover' (*Samhain*, 1906; in *Explorations*, 221). See also 'Speaking to the Psaltery' and 'The Return of Ulysses' (*Essays and Introductions*, 14, 199).

Hunting Out the Fairies:
E. F. Benson, Oscar Wilde and the
Burning of Bridget Cleary
ANGELA BOURKE

1. An early version of this paper was presented at the Synge Summer School in County Wicklow in June 1994. I thank those who attended for their comments and for valuable discussions which followed.

2. Richard Ellmann, *Oscar Wilde* (New York: Alfred A. Knopf, 1988), xvi.

3. Brian Masters, *The Life of E. F. Benson* (London: Pimlico, 1991), 111.

4. E. F. Benson, 'The Recent "Witch-Burning" at Clonmel', *Nineteenth Century*, no. 220, June 1895, 1053–8.

5. For a discussion of the newspaper coverage of Bridget Cleary's death, see Angela Bourke, 'Reading a Woman's Death: Colonial Text and Oral Tradition in Nineteenth-Century Ireland', *Feminist Studies*, 21 (3), 1995, 553–86.

6. Andrew Lang, author of the *Red, Green, Yellow*, and several other *Fairy Books*, was one of the prominent people who entered the debate about the death of Bridget Cleary and how it should be understood: first in a general essay inspired by 'the late melancholy events in a peasant family of Tipperary', on the subject of 'Changelings', in the *Illustrated London News*, 25 May 1895, and later, after the prisoners had been sentenced, in a letter to *The Times*, 19 July.

7. Anon., 'The "Witch-Burning" at Clonmel', *Folk-Lore: Transactions of the Folk-Lore Society*, vi (4), December 1895, 373–84. The writer concludes: 'It would only seem necessary to add a protest, in the interest of the due administration of the law, against the article by Mr E. F. Benson in the *Nineteenth Century* for June last. Some of Mr Benson's interpretations of the evidence before the magistrates are disputable; but whether they are right or wrong is not the point. The article in question was published before the trial. It was an attempt to influence public opinion upon a case that was still *sub judice*. And, however unlikely to reach the jurymen who would have to try the guilt of the prisoners, it ought not to have been published at that time.'

8. See Bourke, 'Reading a Woman's Death'.

9. Hubert Butler, *Escape from the Anthill*, with a foreword by Maurice Craig (Mullingar: Lilliput, 1985), 63–74, 'The Eggman and the Fairies' (1960). See also Richard P. Jenkins, 'Witches and Fairies: Supernatural Aggression and Deviance among the Irish Peasantry', *Ulster Folklife*, 23, 1977, 33–56, republished in Peter Narváez (ed.), *The Good People: New Fairylore Essays* (New York: Garland, 1991); and Thomas McGrath, 'Fairy Faith and Changelings: The Burning of Bridget Cleary in 1895', *Studies*, Summer 1982, 178–84. Carlo Gébler's 1994 novel, *The Cure* (London: Hamish Hamilton), acknowledges a debt to Butler. His account of Bridget Cleary's life and death is partly based on contemporary reports, partly invented.

10. Peter Narváez, 'Newfoundland Berry Pickers "In the Fairies": Maintaining Spatial, Temporal, and Moral Boundaries through Legendry' in his (ed.) *The Good People: New Fairylore Essays* (New York and London: Garland, 1991), 336, 360.

11. Hyde notes that the officers of the court deliberately delayed issuing the warrant for Wilde's arrest until after the boat train for France should have left. H. Montgomery Hyde, *The Trials of Oscar Wilde* (New York: Dover Publications, 1973), 151–2.

12. Gary Schmidgall, *The Stranger Wilde: Interpreting Oscar* (London: Abacus, 1994).

13. For a sense of the idiom and range of fairy legend, see the collection, Seán Ó hEochaidh, Máire Ní Néill and Séamas Ó Catháin (eds.), *Síscéalta Ó Thír*

Chonaill/Fairy Legends from Donegal (Dublin: Comhairle Bhéaloideas Éireann, 1977).

14. Similar traditions are found in Scotland and in parts of Canada. See, for instance, Narváez, 'Newfoundland Berry Pickers'.

15. Geoffrey Palmer and Noel Lloyd, *E. F. Benson as He Was* (Luton: Lennard, 1988), 50; Ellmann, *Oscar Wilde*, 416.

16. Masters, *E. F. Benson*, 108.

17. Ibid., 111; cf. Ellmann, *Oscar Wilde*, 421. Palmer and Lloyd suggest, however, that Wilde and Benson were introduced in Cambridge by Robert Ross in 1888–89: 'Fred [Benson] was charmed by Wilde; they often met and talked about their writing projects' (1988), 32.

18. E. F. Benson, *As We Were* (London: Longmans, 1930).

19. Masters, *E. F. Benson*, 114.

20. Ibid., 272.

21. Benson, *As We Were*, 235; quoted in Masters, *E. F. Benson*, 246.

22. Masters, *E. F. Benson*, 245.

23. Frank Kinahan, *Yeats, Folklore and Occultism* (Boston: Unwin Hyman, 1988), chapter 2, 'The Philosophy of Irish Fairylore'.

24. Lady Wilde ('Speranza'), *Ancient Legends, Mystic Charms, and Superstitions of Ireland* (Boston: Ticknor & Co., 1887; London: Ward & Downey, 1888).

25. Quoted in Kinahan, *Yeats, Folklore and Occultism*, 45.

26. W. B. Yeats, *Letters to the New Island* (Cambridge, Mass.: Harvard University Press, 1934), 78; quoted in Davis Coakley, *Oscar Wilde: The Importance of Being Irish* (Dublin: Town House, 1994), 101.

27. 'Some Literary Notes', by the Editor, *Woman's World*, II (16), February 1889, 221. Reprinted in Richard Ellmann (ed.), *The Artist as Critic: Critical Writings of Oscar Wilde* (London: W. H. Allen, 1970), 130–5.

28. 'Some Literary Notes', 222.

29. Coakley, *Oscar Wilde*, 94–104.

30. Angela Bourke, 'Fairies and Anorexia: Nuala Ní Dhomhnaill's "Amazing Grass"', *Proceedings of the Harvard Celtic Colloquium*, XIII, 1993, 25–38, and 'Reading a Woman's Death'. See also Séamas Mac Philib, 'The Changeling (ML 5058): Irish Versions of a Migratory Legend in their International Context', *Béaloideas*, 59, 1991, and the essays by Patricia Lysaght, Diarmuid Ó Giolláin, Joyce Underwood Munro and Peter Narváez in Narváez (ed.), *Good People*.

31. Lady Wilde, *Ancient Legends*, 210.

32. Ibid., 89–90.

33. Coakley, *Oscar Wilde*, 99, refers to D. A. Upchurch, *Wilde's Use of Irish Celtic Elements in 'The Picture of Dorian Gray'* (American University Studies, Series IV, English Language and Literature, vol. 140).

34. Compare Mrs Sheridan, who told Lady Gregory, 'I know that I used to be away among them myself, but how they brought me I don't know, but when I'd come back, I'd be cross with the husband and with all.' Lady Gregory, *Selected Writings*, ed. Lucy McDiarmid and Maureen Waters (London: Penguin Books, 1995), 71.

35. Tony Butler, "The Burning of Bridget Cleary: The 100th Anniversary', *The Nationalist* (Clonmel), 25 March 1995, 21.

36. See, for instance, Joyce Underwood Munro, 'The Invisible Made Visible: The Fairy Changeling as a Folk Articulation of Failure to Thrive in Infants and Children', in Narváez, (ed.) *Good People*, 251–83; Susan Schoon Eberly, 'Fairies and the Folklore of Disability: Changelings, Hybrids, and the Solitary Fairy', ibid., 227–50.

37. I am grateful to Karen Lewicki for pointing this out in my Harvard Celtic 180 class in 1993.

38. Cf. Brad Evans, letter to the *New Yorker*, 6 June 1994, 9, on the subject of American petroleum interests in Ecuador, and accounts of indigenous peoples' culture there: 'the language of "savagery," "barbarism," and the "progress of civilization" which dominated America's western expansion in the nineteenth century can apply all too easily to today's corporate colonialism in South America. . . . we now prefer the terms "remote" and "isolated" to "savage" and "barbarian," but the effect is about the same.'

39. Hubert Butler, 'The Eggman and the Fairies'. The reference to the eggman is

in *The Irish Times*, 8 April 1895.

40. 'The Recent "Witch-Burning" at Clonmel', 1054.
41. See 'Reading a Woman's Death'.
42. 'The Recent "Witch-Burning" at Clonmel', 1058.
43. Masters, *E. F. Benson*, 242.

Impressions of an Irish Sphinx
OWEN DUDLEY EDWARDS

1. *Complete Works of Oscar Wilde* (Glasgow: HarperCollins, 1994), 874–5.
2. Vincent O'Sullivan, *Aspects of Wilde* (London: Constable, 1936), 231.
3. *Complete Works*, 884.
4. Declan Kiberd, *Inventing Ireland: The Literature of the Modern Nation* (London: Jonathan Cape, 1995), 380–94.
5. Richard Pine, *The Thief of Reason: Oscar Wilde and Modern Ireland* (Dublin: Gill & Macmillan, 1995).
6. 'Speranza' [Lady Wilde], *Poems* (Dublin: James Duffy, 1864), 5–7.
7. *Complete Works*, 218–19.
8. 'Speranza' [Lady Wilde], 'The Famine Year', *Poems*, 7.
9. Julian Symons, *The Detling Secret* (Harmondsworth: Penguin Books, 1984), 31.
10. Micheál macLíammóir, *The Importance of Being Oscar* (Dublin: Dolmen Press, 1963), 2–3.
11. O'Sullivan, *Aspects of Wilde*, 63. Isola seems to be the obvious family death.
12. Oscar Wilde, *The Artist as Critic*, ed. Richard Ellmann (London: W. H. Allen, 1970), 150.
13. American University Studies, Series IV, English Language and Literature, vol. 140, 70.
14. *Complete Works*, 748–9.
15. *The Letters of Oscar Wilde*, ed. Rupert Hart-Davis (London: Rupert Hart-Davis, 1963), 365.
16. *Complete Works*, 198–9.
17. *The Picture of Dorian Gray, Complete Works*, 27.
18. Daniel Corkery, *The Hidden Ireland: A Study of Gaelic Munster in the Eighteenth Century* (Dublin: M. H. Gill & Son, 1967), 13 and note.
19. *Letters*, 483.
20. *Complete Works*, 1189.
21. *The Artist as Critic*, 118.
22. *Complete Works*, 762.

Venus in Blue Jeans: Oscar Wilde, Jesse James, Crime and Fame
FINTAN O'TOOLE

1. H. Montgomery Hyde, ed., *The Trials of Oscar Wilde* (Sydney: Butterworth, 1948), 123.
2. William A. Settle Jr, *Jesse James Was His Name* (Lincoln, Nebr.: University of Nebraska Press, 1977), 127.
3. Ibid..
4. *The Letters of Oscar Wilde*, ed. Rupert Hart-Davis (London: Rupert Hart-Davis, 1963), 115.
5. See Dee Brown, *Wondrous Times on the Frontier* (London: Arrow Books, 1994), 166.
6. Frederic Jameson, *Postmodernism or the Cultural Logic of Late Capitalism* (London: Verso, 1991), 11.
7. Hyde, *Trials of Oscar Wilde*, 124.
8. Walter Benjamin, *One-Way Street* (London: New Left Books, 1979), 48–9.
9. Robert M. Utley, *Billy the Kid: A Short and Violent Life* (London: I. B. Tauris, 1990), 4.
10. 'The American Invasion', *Court and Society Review*, 23 March 1887. Reprinted in John Wyse Jackson (ed.), *Aristotle at Afternoon Tea: The Rare Oscar Wilde* (London: Fourth Estate, 1991), 36–9.
11. *Letters*, 163.
12. Tom Wolfe, 'Introduction', in René Koning, *A la Mode: On the Social Psychology of Fashion* (New York: Seabury Press, 1973), 22–3.
13. Susan Sontag, 'Notes on "Camp"', *Against Interpretation and Other Essays* (New York: Doubleday, 1990), 289.
14. Hyde, *Trials of Oscar Wilde*, 127.
15. Quoted in Richard Ned Lebow, *White Britain and Black Ireland: The Influence of Stereotypes on Colonial Policy* (Philadelphia: Institute for the Study of Human Issues, 1976), 46.
16. Quoted in Liz Curtis, *Nothing but the Same Old Story: The Roots of Anti-Irish Racism* (London: Information on Ireland, 1984), 58.
17. Quoted in Noel O'Donoghue, *Proud and Upright Men* (Tuam: privately published 1986), 8–9.
18. See Eric Mottram, *Blood on the Nash Ambassador: Investigations in American*

Culture (London: Hutchinson Radius, 1983), 27–8.

19. Utley, *Billy the Kid*, 61.

20. Mottram, *Blood on the Nash Ambassador*, 28.

21. Richard Ellmann, *Oscar Wilde* (New York: Alfred A. Knopf, 1988), 152.

22. Reproduced in Gary Schmidgall, *The Stranger Wilde: Interpreting Oscar* (London: Abacus, 1994), 339.

23. Ellmann, *Oscar Wilde*, 184.

24. Reproduced in Schmidgall, *The Stranger Wilde*, 204.

25. Dale T. Knobel, *Paddy and the Republic: Ethnicity and Nationality in Antebellum America* (Middletown, Conn.: Wesleyan University Press, 1986), 93.

26. Quoted in R. F. Foster, *Paddy and Mr Punch* (London: Allen Lane, 1993), 184.

27. *Letters*, 724.

The Wilde Irishman:
Oscar as Aesthete and Anarchist
JERUSHA MCCORMACK

1. Theodore Wratislaw, *Oscar Wilde: A Memoir* (London: The Eighteen Nineties Society, 1979), 13.

2. Joy Melville, *Mother of Oscar: The Life of Jane Francesca Wilde* (London: John Murray, 1994), 40.

3. Ibid., 108.

4. Ibid., 61.

5. *The Letters of Oscar Wilde*, ed. Rupert Hart-Davis (London: Rupert Hart-Davis, 1963), 148.

6. Melville, *Mother of Oscar*, 45.

7. 'The Decay of Lying', in *Complete Works of Oscar Wilde* (Glasgow: HarperCollins, 1994), 1084.

8. John Quail, *The Slow Burning Fuse* (London: Paladin, 1978), 12.

9. Richard Ellmann, *Oscar Wilde* (New York: Alfred A. Knopf, 1988), 153.

10. Robert Kee, *The Laurel and the Ivy* (London: Hamish Hamilton, 1993), 278.

11. Melville, *Mother of Oscar*, 159.

12. H. Montgomery Hyde, *Oscar Wilde* (London: Eyre Methuen, 1976), 71.

13. Ibid., quoting the *Philadelphia Press*, 9 May 1882.

14. 'The Truth of Masks', in *Complete Works*, 1173.

15. *Complete Works*, 1083.

16. Fénéon was a promoter of avant-garde artists such as the Impressionists and Post-Impressionists, and was a formidable dandy in his own right; cf. Joan Ungersma Halperin, *Félix Fénéon: Aesthete and Anarchist in Fin-de-Siècle Paris* (New Haven, Conn.: Yale University Press, 1988), 249.

17. Ellmann, *Oscar Wilde*, 281.

18. Deirdre Toomey, 'The Story-Teller at Fault: Oscar Wilde and Irish Orality', above, 27.

19. Matthew Arnold, *Culture and Anarchy*, ed. J. Dover Wilson (Cambridge: Cambridge University Press, 1966), 71–97.

20. *Complete Works*, 1182.

21. Ibid., 1176.

22. Quail, *Slow Burning Fuse*, 313.

23. No sustained critical response is recorded by Karl Beckson (ed.), *Oscar Wilde: The Critical Heritage* (London: Routledge & Kegan Paul, 1970).

24. Yeats comments (in 1923) on the popularity of the essay in the Young China party; cf. *Critical Heritage*, ed. Beckson, 396. Montgomery Hyde gives the report of Robert Ross in 1908 that copies of the essay, translated into Chinese and Russian, were on sale in the bazaars of Nijni Novgorod; cf. Hyde, *Oscar Wilde*, 381. 'The Soul of Man under Socialism' is commonly read 'straight' by political theorists, such as George Woodcock in *Anarchism* (Harmondsworth: Penguin Books, 1962), 423–6.

25. 'On the Study of Celtic Literature', *The Complete Prose Works of Matthew Arnold*, vol. III: *Lectures and Essays in Criticism*, ed. R. H. Super (Ann Arbor: The University of Michigan Press, 1962), 347.

26. Cf. the analysis offered by Michael S. Helfand and Philip E. Smith II in 'Anarchy and Culture: The Evolutionary Turn of Cultural Criticism in the Work of Oscar Wilde', *Texas Studies in Literature and Language*, 20 (2), Summer 1978, 119–215.

27. *Fortnightly Review*, 55 (n.s. 49), 1 February 1891, 272.

28. Matthew Arnold, 'Renan's "La Réforme intellectuelle"', in *Prose Works*, VII, 45. Although Arnold thought that the recognition of the Celtic strain in English

character would create a real cultural improvement, he was not sanguine about the political liberation and recognition of Ireland; cf. his comment that Ireland should be 'a nation poetically only, not politically', 'From Easter to August', *Nineteenth Century*, 22 September 1887, 321.

29. Allen, 'The Celt in English Art', *Fortnightly Review*, 273.

30. 'The Incompatibles', in *Prose Works*, IX, 267.

31. 'Soul of Man', in *Complete Works*, 1194.

32. *Letters*, 483.

33. Vyvyan Holland, *Son of Oscar Wilde* (Oxford: Oxford University Press, 1988), 54, who gives the first line inaccurately; its correct version is 'Tá mé i mo chladh, is ná dúisaigh mé', as given by Richard Pine, *Oscar Wilde* (Dublin: Gill & Macmillan, 1983), 54.

34. *Letters*, 289.

35. 'I am French in sympathy, Irish by race, but the English have condemned me to speak the language of Shakespeare.' *Letters*, 304. At the time, Wilde was composing *Salomé* in French.

36. Paradox may be defined as a statement that is seemingly contradictory or opposed to common sense but may in fact be shown (by rational analysis) to be true. Thus some paradoxes, such as those of Zeno or Heraclitus, may even be taken as the starting point of philosophical discussion. As opposed to this sort of paradox, identified with Greek philosophers, there is the Irish Bull, which assumes the form of logic while violating it, such as the famous question by Boyle Roche: 'Why should we do anything for Posterity; what has Posterity done for us?' Similarly, when Miss Prism is informed by Jack that his brother Ernest is dead, she exclaims: 'What a lesson for him! I trust he will profit by it.' In the context of Irish writing, it might be seen as one of the many forms of colonial disruption of the imposed imperial language, such as the verbal sabotage enacted by Mrs Malaprop in Sheridan's *The Rivals*. See also Maria Edgeworth's *An Essay on Irish Bulls* (1802).

37. Quoted in Regenia Gagnier, *Idylls of the Marketplace: Oscar Wilde and the Victorian Public* (Aldershot: Scolar, 1986), 76.

38. 'The Painter of Modern Life: IX. The Dandy', *Baudelaire: Selected Writings on Art and Artists* (Harmondsworth: Penguin Books, 1972), 419.

39. *Dandyism*, 23. Quoted in Gagnier, *Idylls*, 221, 74.

40. 'The Dandy', *Baudelaire: Selected Writings*, 421.

41. 'The Decay of Lying', in *Complete Works*, 1086.

42. 'The Incompatibles', *Prose Works*, IX, 272, 282.

43. *Complete Works*, 552.

44. Ibid., 553.

45. Ibid., 579.

46. Ibid.

47. Parnell belonged to the Anglo-Irish landowning class, one to which Sir William Wilde was linked by virtue of his Mayo estate. Like Wilde, he was a Protestant, although idolized by his populist Catholic following. Fatally, Parnell's aristocratic background came into conflict with bourgeois values as represented by the courts and the press. For ten years preceding the crisis which led to his downfall, Parnell and Captain and Mrs O'Shea had preserved a 'civilized' *ménage à trois* in the manner of the aristocracy (in which a blind eye was systemically turned on every aspect of the love triangle). But once made public, through the divorce suit taken by the Captain on Christmas Eve 1889, their private arrangements were placed under public (and thus middle-class) judgement. Rather than, at that moment, taking decisive action to limit public damage, Parnell chose to stay at the side of Mrs O'Shea, in every respect the 'ideal husband'. In this private role, Parnell left himself exposed to the public storm which ensued (and which is credited not only with Parnell's fall from political power but with his actual death).

48. *Complete Works*, 553.

49. *Letters*, 492.

50. *Critical Heritage*, ed. Beckson, 28.

51. 'Wilde and Nietzsche', from 'Nietzsche's Philosophy in the Light of Recent History', *Last Essays*; reprinted in *Oscar Wilde: A Collection of Critical Essays*, ed. Richard Ellmann (Englewood Cliffs, NJ: Prentice-Hall, 1969), 169.

52. *Complete Works*, 1244.

53. *Complete Works*, 17.
54. *Critical Heritage*, ed. Beckson, 177.
55. *Complete Works*, 17.

The Journey to Reading Gaol: Sacrifice and Scapegoats in Irish Literature
BERNARD O'DONOGHUE

1. Richard Kearney, 'Myth and Terror', *The Crane Bag Book of Irish Studies (1977–81)*, ed. Mark Patrick Hederman and Richard Kearney (Dublin: Blackwater Press, 1982), 273–86.
2. Ibid., 280.
3. Ibid., 275.
4. Ibid., 281.
5. See Owen Dudley Edwards, 'Introduction: The Stories of Oscar Wilde', *Complete Works of Oscar Wilde* (Glasgow: HarperCollins, 1994), 14.
6. For a comparison of the shaming methods of Gandhi and Wilde, see Jerusha McCormack, 'Oscar Wilde: The Once and Future Dandy', in C. Georges Sandulescu (ed.), *Rediscovering Oscar Wilde* (Gerrards Cross: Colin Smythe, 1994), 269–74.
7. *The Collected Poems of W. B. Yeats* (London: Macmillan, 1958), 179.
8. *A Concordance to the Poems of W. B. Yeats*, ed. S. M. Parrish and J. A. Painter (Ithaca: Cornell University Press, 1963).
9. Maud Ellmann, *The Hunger Artists: Starving, Writing and Imprisonment* (Cambridge, Mass.: Harvard University Press, 1993).
10. *The Collected Plays of W. B. Yeats* (London: Macmillan, 1952), 114.
11. Ibid., 109.
12. Ibid., 108.
13. *A Commentary on the Collected Plays of W. B. Yeats*, ed. A. N. Jeffares and A. S. Knowland (London: Macmillan, 1975), 43–7.
14. *Complete Works*, 377.
15. Leviticus 16: 20–2.
16. Maud Ellmann, *The Hunger Artists*, 67.
17. *Complete Works*, 213.
18. Ibid., 422.
19. Ibid., 448.
20. P. H. Pearse, *Plays, Stories, Poems* (Dublin: Talbot Press, 1924), 285.

Against Nature? Science and Oscar Wilde
JOHN WILSON FOSTER

1. W. B. Yeats, *Essays and Introductions* (London: Macmillan, 1961), 187.
2. *The Letters of W. B. Yeats*, ed. Allan Wade (London: Rupert Hart-Davis, 1954), 335.
3. W. B. Yeats, 'Four Years: 1887–1891', *Autobiographies* (London: Macmillan, 1955), 115.
4. Yeats, *Essays and Introductions*, 444.
5. 'Modern Poetry: A Broadcast', in ibid., 491.
6. See my articles 'Natural History, Science and Irish Culture', *Irish Review*, 9, 1990, 61–9, and 'Natural Science and Irish Culture,' *Eire-Ireland*, 26(2), 1991, 92–103.
7. Richard Ellmann, *Eminent Domain: Yeats among Wilde, Joyce, Pound, Eliot and Auden* (Oxford: Oxford University Press, 1967), 9–27. I am using the edition of *The Picture of Dorian Gray* to be found in *Complete Works of Oscar Wilde* (Glasgow: HarperCollins, 1994), 17–159. Basil Hallward's phrase is really Arnold's phrase 'the Greek spirit' from the latter's essay 'Hebraism and Hellenism', in *Culture and Anarchy* (1869). Wilde's interest in Greek culture derived as much from his Trinity College Dublin tutor, the celebrated Irish wit and Hellenist John Pentland Mahaffy, as from the writings of Arnold: see W. B. Stanford, *Ireland and the Classical Tradition* (Dublin: Allen Figgis, 1976), 235–43.
8. See, for example, 'The Critic as Artist', in *Complete Works*, 1121–2, 1138–9. Future references to 'The Critic as Artist' will be to this edition. The distinction between the contemplative man and the man of action is implicit in Yeats's 'Easter 1916'. In 'Yeats and the Easter Rising', reproduced in *Colonial Consequences: Essays in Irish Literature and Culture* (Dublin: Lilliput Press, 1991), I offered several sources of Yeats's famous phrase 'terrible beauty' without remembering Wilde's use of it in chapter 8 of *Dorian Gray*.
9. Wilde wrote to Grant Allen in early 1891 praising his essay in the *Fortnightly Review* for its 'scientific demonstration'

of the Celtic spirit of art that Arnold had merely 'divined'. See *The Letters of Oscar Wilde*, ed. Rupert Hart-Davis (London: Rupert Hart-Davis, 1963), 286–7. (Allen wrote several books on evolution.)

10. Laziness, imaginativeness and an attraction to the unrealistic are attributes of Wilde's Celt: see *Letters*, 429, 666, 751.

11. For the reference to 'the great Celtic school', see *Letters*, 339. Although not an Irish nationalist, I have myself engaged in the exclusion of Shaw and Wilde, choosing in *Fictions of the Irish Literary Revival* (Syracuse: Syracuse University Press, 1987), like most Irish critics, to see the Irish Literary Revival starting in Dublin with Standish James O'Grady, Yeats and Douglas Hyde.

12. I am quoting from the edition of 'The Decay of Lying' in *Complete Works*, 1071.

13. Camille Paglia, *Sexual Personae: Art and Decadence from Nefertiti to Emily Dickinson* (London: Yale University Press, 1990), 523.

14. Without explanation, Hart-Davis believes Wilde may have been urging upon William Sharp (who was assembling an anthology of sonnets) the merits of Poe's sonnet 'Silence', even though the letter quite clearly says 'Edgar Allan Poe's sonnet to Science'. *Letters*, 182.

15. Richard Ellmann, *Oscar Wilde* (New York: Alfred A. Knopf, 1988), 31, 87, 166. The white carnation was dyed green, according to Ellmann, in homage to Huysmans' Des Esseintes, who preferred natural flowers that resembled artificial flowers to artificial flowers that resembled natural ones. Ellmann, 'The Uses of Decadence', in *a long the riverrun: Selected Essays* (New York: Knopf, 1989), 3–4.

16. *Letters*, 169. According to Hart-Davis, Hopps read this amusing letter aloud to the FMR meeting in Wilde's absence.

17. *Letters*, 172–3.

18. Paglia, *Sexual Personae*, 512.

19. 'the art that is frankly decorative is the art to live with. . . . The marvels of design stir the imagination.' 'The Critic as Artist', in *Complete Works*, 1148.

20. *Oscar Wilde's Oxford Notebooks: A Portrait of Mind in the Making*, ed.

Philip E. Smith II and Michael S. Helfand (New York: Oxford University Press, 1989), 144.

21. William Kingdon Clifford, *Lectures and Essays*, ed. Leslie Stephen and Sir Frederick Pollock (London: Macmillan, 1901), I, 162–6.

22. Clifford, 'On the Scientific Basis of Morals', in ibid., II, 88–9. 'The word "design"', writes Clifford, 'might then be kept for the special case of adaptation by an intelligence'.

23. Tess Cosslett (ed.), *Science and Religion in the Nineteenth Century* (Cambridge: Cambridge University Press, 1984), 173.

24. The young Wilde was reading J. A. Symonds's *Shelley* (1878) at this time, and possibly John Tyndall's 'Belfast Address', which discusses Goethe in such terms: see *Oscar Wilde's Oxford Notebooks*, 206.

25. *Letters*, 236–7.

26. See, for example, ibid., 287, 489.

27. We can quickly gauge the importance of the scientific element of Anglo-Irish culture (which since the Irish Literary Revival has been consigned to the status of a 'hidden Ireland') from Gordon L. Herries Davies's essay, 'Irish Thought in Science', in Richard Kearney (ed.), *The Irish Mind* (Dublin: Wolfhound Press, 1985). More pertinently focused is T. G. Wilson's *Victorian Doctor; Being the Life of Sir William Wilde* (New York: L. B. Fischer, 1946), which recreates not only the varied pursuits of its subject (ophthalmologist, archaeologist, ethnologist, statistician and naturalist) but also the commendable standard of Irish science during the Victorian period; see especially chapters 2, 8 and 14.

28. J. K. Huysmans, *Against Nature*, trans. Robert Baldick (London: Penguin Books, 1959), 36. Christopher Lloyd has suggested that *Against Nature* might better be entitled *Against Culture*, on the grounds that it is not nature itself that is rejected but a certain conception of nature: 'facile notions of the picturesque'. *J. K. Huysmans and the Fin de Siècle Novel* (Edinburgh: Edinburgh University Press, 1990), 95.

29. Clifford defines science as 'the getting of knowledge from experience on the

assumption of the uniformity of nature, and the use of such knowledge to guide the actions of men'. 'On the Scientific Basis of Morals', in *Lectures and Essays*, II, 78. Much earlier, Bacon wrote that a correct scientific method 'leads with constant path through the woodlands of experience to the open country of Axioms'. *Novum Organum* (Oxford: Oxford University Press, 1855), 60. The cynicism of a Wilde character such as Lord Henry derives from his assumption of the uniformity (and therefore predictability and typicality) of human nature: the piquant humour is, of course, original.

30. *Complete Works*, 53, 54.

31. Ibid.

32. And, we might add, its destructive capability. Alan Campbell is the literal experimental scientist in *Dorian Gray*, blackmailed into getting rid of Basil Hallward's body through 'a certain scientific experiment' (124). (According to Ellmann, 'a friendly surgeon informed [Wilde] how this could be done by chemical means'. *Oscar Wilde*, 314.) But Campbell had already courted notoriety 'in connection with certain curious experiments' (122) and is unhealthily absorbed in biological research; it is implied that he traffics like Frankenstein in the secrets of the charnel-house and frequents the world of Burke and Hare. (Science and crime conspired to initiate *Dorian Gray*, for it was at a dinner-party in the presence of Arthur Conan Doyle that Wilde offered to write a novel in the spirit of friendly rivalry to Doyle's Sherlock Holmes mystery, *The Sign of Four*. Ellmann, *Oscar Wilde*, 313–14.) In his secretiveness, Campbell recalls Des Esseintes the experimenter; in the amorality of his experimentation, he recalls Lord Henry Wotton.

33. *Complete Works*, 53. For all the more important differences, it is diverting to compare Wilde's Lord Henry Wotton with history's Sir Henry Wotton (1568–1639). Sir Henry, like Wilde, was an Oxford man; he was interested in science (like Wilde's father he studied the human eye) as well as literature, and, like his much greater friend John Donne, lived before that dissociation of

sensibility we call the Two Cultures. He sent Bacon an account of experiments he witnessed at Kepler's house in Linz, and he procured foreign plants while he was James I's ambassador in Venice. He was an epigrammatist of note, and one of his paradoxes was to the effect that a diplomat should always speak the truth, for he shall never be believed. Another aphorism landed him in hot water with King James: 'an ambassador is an honest man, sent to lie abroad for the good of his country.' Sir Henry has been described as 'an amiable dilettante or literary amateur, with a growing inclination to idleness in his later years'. He became provost of Eton but, despite his interest in education (or, as he termed it, 'moral architecture'), 'he found the boys more interesting than their work'. See Izaak Walton's 'Life of Sir Henry Wotton', *Dictionary of National Biography*, and Keith Thomas, *Man and the Natural World* (Harmondsworth: Penguin Books, 1984).

34. *Oscar Wilde's Oxford Notebooks*, 135, 162, 234. In his Commonplace Book, Wilde wrote: 'In the modern attempt to rest morals on a scientific basis . . . a return to the old Hellenic ideal [to live by nature] can be seen.' Ibid., 135, 191.

35. Ibid., 135.

36. *Complete Works*, 1139. It is ironic, therefore, that Wilde spent his last years in eloquent beggary, and in Reading Gaol requested the works of Dickens.

37. Ibid., 46, 106.

38. Ibid., 1119. Wilde might implicitly be taking issue with Arnold's influential and more ponderous view that 'for the creation of a master-work of literature two powers must concur, the power of the man and the power of the moment'. Matthew Arnold, 'The Function of Criticism at the Present Time', in *Essays in Criticism* (London: Macmillan, 1898), 5.

39. Quoted by Ellmann, *Eminent Domain*, 16.

40. *Complete Works*, 1154.

41. *Oscar Wilde's Oxford Notebooks*, 121.

42. Ibid., 110.

43. *Complete Works*, 28, 156.

44. I discuss the idea of self-realization in Moore, Joyce and other Irish writers in *Fictions of the Irish Literary Revival*.

45. *Letters*, 448.
46. Ibid., 467. Later in *De Profundis*, however (488), Wilde calls self-realization inadequate, with the wise acceptance of the enigma of man's soul being the ultimate virtue.
47. *Letters*, 479, 491.
48. *Oscar Wilde's Oxford Notebooks*, 121. A second analogy, which derived from Herbert Spencer but was attributed by Wilde to Plato, was that between the individual and the social organism (ibid., 109).
49. Clifford, *Lectures and Essays*, I, 87. Smith and Helfand seem to have overlooked this lecture as a source for the ideas on p. 121 of their edition of the *Oxford Notebooks*.
50. *Oscar Wilde's Oxford Notebooks*, 121. Smith and Helfand do not supply a source for this remark; if there is one, it is probably Clifford, who wrote on both uniformity and the cognitive–organic analogy.
51. It is therefore ironic (despite its brevity of tenure) that among Dorian's later enthusiasms is evolutionary theory: 'for a season he inclined to the materialistic doctrines of the *Darwinismus* movement in Germany'. *Complete Works*, 101.
52. Ibid., 39, 40, 64, 38.
53. Ibid., 53. Arnold connected English Philistinism to the strain of vulgarity and insensitivity in the Anglo-Saxon breed signified by 'such hideous names' as Higginbottom, Stiggins, Bugg and Wragg. 'The Function of Criticism at the Present Time', in *Essays in Criticism*, 20–5.
54. *Complete Works*, 108.
55. Clifford develops the analogies between disease and wrongdoing, and health and moral sense (both in the individual and in society), in 'On the Scientific Basis of Morals', in *Lectures and Essays*, II, 74–95. For a discussion of Huysmans and sickness, see Lloyd, *Huysmans*, 83–96.
56. *Oscar Wilde's Oxford Notebooks*, 125, 159, 159, 155. Hunter was also an anatomist; he embalmed Martin Van Butchell's wife, and her husband kept her in a glass case in his drawing-room. See Samuel Foare Simmons and John Hunter, *William Hunter 1718–1783*, ed. C. H. Brock (Glasgow: University of Glasgow Press,

1983), 32. In a figurative sense, Dorian Gray is embalmed, and only at the end of the novel resumes his natural *moral* age. In the light of Lord Henry's musings on self-experimentation, and Wilde's interest in William Hunter, the career of John, William's younger brother, is not without interest. It was said by several memoirists and biographers that John (pioneer of scientific surgery, anatomist, botanist, zoologist) had inoculated himself with syphilis in order to study the disease and that his death had syphilitic origins. In his biography, George Qvist is at pains to challenge the claim: *John Hunter 1728–1793* (London: William Heinemann, 1981), 42–53. That Ellmann and others have claimed that Wilde's death had the same origin adds to the oddity of the Hunterian connection.
57. *Letters*, 448, 433, 440, 451.
58. The career of this concept in the nineteenth and early twentieth centuries is traced in a collection of essays, J. Edward Chamberlin and Sander L. Gilman (eds.), *Degeneration: The Dark Side of Progress* (New York: Columbia University Press, 1985). The essay by Chamberlin, 'Images of Degeneration', is particularly relevant to my own.
59. *Letters*, 401–2; Max Nordau, *Degeneration* (London: William Heinemann, 1913), 318–19.
60. *Complete Works*, 1137, 1138.
61. Unlike Yeats, Wilde was receptive to the idea that imagination is part of the method of successful science, something that Tyndall was fond of arguing: see, for example, 'Scientific Use of the Imagination', in *Fragments of Science* (London: Longmans, Green, 1907), II, 101–34.
62. *Oscar Wilde's Oxford Notebooks*, 120, 133–4. Clifford summarizes Spencer during his lecture, 'The Philosophy of the Pure Sciences', *Lectures and Essays*, I, 301–409.
63. Scientists like Clifford could not, however, encourage belief to go beyond inherited experience: see, for example, Clifford's review of a book bearing the Yeatsian title *The Unseen Universe*, *Lectures and Essays*, I, 268–300.
64. See, for example, Declan Kiberd's introduction to his selection of Wilde for *The*

Field Day Anthology of Irish Writing, General Editor, Seamus Deane (Derry: Field Day Publications, 1991), II, 372–6.

65. *Letters*, 47.

The Quare on the Square: A Statue of Oscar Wilde for Dublin
PAULA MURPHY

This essay would not have been possible without the generous assistance of the artists who were involved in the competition for the Oscar Wilde commemoration. I am grateful to them for their time, their information and their insights.

1. Oscar Wilde, letter to the editor of the *St James's Gazette*, 26 June 1890. *The Letters of Oscar Wilde*, ed. Rupert Hart-Davis (London: Rupert Hart-Davis, 1963), 259.

2. Richard Ellmann, *Oscar Wilde* (New York: Alfred A. Knopf, 1988), 93–4.

3. The Wilde commission is the first of a series of public sculptural works, commemorating Irish writers, sponsored by Guinness Ireland. Guinness contracted to pay £25,000 for the sculpture.

4. Danny Osborne was born in Bournemouth in 1949 and studied at the Bournemouth & Poole College of Art. He has lived in Cork since 1969, where he produces small porcelain sculptural work. However, he is also an explorer, and landscape paintings have been the creative result of his extensive journeys. The Wilde statue was his first commission for a monumental public sculpture.

5. The Dublin monument is the first public sculptural commemoration of Wilde. Epstein's sculpture in the Père Lachaise Cemetery in Paris, while public, is nonetheless a tomb monument. An appeal to erect a statue in London was launched in May 1995, with the intention that the work would be completed in 1997 to mark the centenary of Wilde's release from gaol. Wilde has also joined the literary heroes in Poets' Corner in Westminster Abbey. However, this commemoration, unveiled on 14 February 1995, takes the form of an inscription placed in a modern stained-glass window. The window, erected in June 1994,

was designed expressly to house such commemorative inscriptions.

6. Long before the advent of ephemeral sculpture, Wilde, in a letter concerning the Chatterton Monument, pointed out that 'a memorial should be permanent'. *Letters*, 189.

7. 'The human figure concealed under a frock coat and trousers is not a fit subject for sculpture,' said English sculptor John Gibson. Quoted in Lady Eastlake (ed.), *Life of John Gibson, R.A., Sculptor* (London, 1870), 90–1.

8. Sir Joshua Reynolds, *Discourses on Art* (New Haven, Conn.: Yale University Press, 1981), 187. Reynolds's lectures were published in his lifetime. The lecture on sculpture, 'Discourse X', was delivered at the Royal Academy on 11 December 1780, and published shortly after. Reynolds continued his attack on the reproduction of contemporary dress in sculpture in the following manner: 'Working in stone is a very serious business; and it seems to be scarce worth while to employ such durable materials in conveying to posterity a fashion of which the longest existence scarce exceeds a year.'

9. 'The Decorative Arts', in *Complete Works of Oscar Wilde* (Glasgow: HarperCollins, 1994), 930.

10. *Letters*, 460.

11. *Birmingham Daily Post*, 11 October 1888. The unveiling of the monument was performed by Lady Hodgson, the Lady Mayoress, and Wilde was the second speaker at the ceremony. His praise for the monument, the work of English sculptor Lord Ronald Gower, and his comments on the ideal, the poetic and the imaginary nature of the work were noted in several of the Birmingham newspapers. I am grateful to Dr Philip Ward-Jackson of the Courtauld Institute for drawing Wilde's participation in this event to my attention.

12. Alfred Gilbert, 1854–1934.

13. Gilbert to the Shaftesbury Memorial Committee, quoted in Isabelle McAllister, *Alfred Gilbert* (London: A & C Black, 1929), 104.

14. In the original proposal, the boulder on which Wilde reclines was intended to be executed in Connemara marble. In the

final work white quartz was substituted. While the substitution was carried out for financial reasons, obviously there is an inherent aesthetic dimension as well. I believe that the white boulder serves more satisfactorily to project the image of Wilde, whereas the fussiness of the green marble might have overpowered the statue. In conversation with the sculptor, 22 October 1995, I learned that when the boulder was put in place in Merrion Square 'the quare on the square' became known instead as 'the fag on the crag'.

15. Wilde, 'The Decorative Arts', *Complete Works*, 930.

16. *Letters*, 41–2.

17. Charles Francis Fuller, 1830–75. Fuller died in Florence the year after the monument was erected.

18. *Illustrated London News*, 14 November 1874. The article describes a marble bust painted in encaustic, the face – a deep brown; the embroidered vest – black gold, with a gold and white drape (a burnous); the turban – crimson and gold, with precious stones and jewels attached; the whole situated under a polychrome stone canopy with bronze columns.

19. Porcelain also rejects mosses and lichens and, not insignificant in this particular work, is easily cleaned of graffiti. The porcelain is a half-inch thick with a concrete core.

20. The tomb of the Duke of Clarence, 1892–1928, is in the Albert Memorial Chapel, Windsor Castle. Gilbert employed a rich variety of materials in the execution of this work. The recumbent lifesize effigy of Prince Albert is worked in aluminium and bronze, with the head and hands picked out in white marble. Surrounding the sarcophagus are twelve doll-like polychromed figures of saints, the design for which included ivory faces and hands, as can be seen particularly in the figure of St George.

21. Osborne identifies the torso as an uncomplicated expression of both freedom and the ideal. Conversation with the sculptor, 6 October 1995.

22. Many artists, particularly painters, have worked on this theme – Dürer, Rubens, Annibale Carracci and Delacroix, to mention just four.

23. Bernini's statue of Louis XIV for Versailles and Falconet's statue of Peter the Great at Leningrad are well-known sculptures where this symbolism has been employed.

24. *Letters*, 481.

25. Wilde in letter to the editor of the *St James's Gazette*, 26 June 1890. *Letters*, 259.

26. 'A mirror will give back to one one's own sorrow. But Art is not a mirror, but a crystal. It creates its own shapes and forms.' Ibid., 415.

27. Art 'is not meant to instruct, or to influence action in any way. It is superbly sterile, and the note of its pleasure is sterility. If the contemplation of a work of art is followed by activity of any kind, the work is either of a very second-rate order, or the spectator has failed to realise the complete artistic impression.' Ibid., 292.

28. The selection panel comprised Dorothy Walker, art critic, chairperson; Janet Mularney, sculptor; Seamus Heaney, poet; Declan McGonagle, director, Irish Museum of Modern Art; Brian Reid, Guinness Ireland; Ronald Tallon, architect.

29. Melanie le Brocquy began working on the commission but ultimately withdrew for two reasons. She does not normally work from maquettes and is unhappy with the transfer of an image from small-scale sketch model to full-scale finished work. It was also her opinion that it would be difficult to complete the work in the allocated time. Several of the selected artists agreed with her on both these issues. Ultimately le Brocquy was proved right with regard to the time-scale, since the completed sculpture was intended to be unveiled on 16 October 1995. Le Brocquy's commemoration, had she pursued it, would have taken the form of an over-life-size bronze bust of Wilde. The supporting plinth was to be decorated with three plaques encircled with art nouveau ornamentation and depicting different aspects of Wilde's life: *De Profundis*, represented by a man seated on a stool with his head in his hands; the family portrayed in an image of Constance holding her son Cyril; the creative *oeuvre* of

Wilde depicted by its varied symbols. Although she withdrew from the competition, Melanie le Brocquy continued to work on the bust of Wilde.

30. Guinness Ireland undertook to pay £1,000 for each of the maquettes.

31. Harper Pennington, 1854–1920.

32. Don Cronin was born in 1969, in Cork, and studied at the Crawford College of Art and Design. This is the first time that he has been involved in a competition for a public monument.

33. Conversation with the sculptor, 15 June 1995.

34. *Letters*, 429.

35. Wilde, 'The Decay of Lying', in *Complete Works*, 1089.

36. Brian King was born in Dublin in 1942. He studied at the National College of Art and Design in the 1960s and is currently Head of the Sculpture Department there. He is a modernist sculptor and has executed several public sculptural works.

37. Conversation with the sculptor, 13 June 1995. This is of particular interest because King is not normally associated with figurative imagery, and is known for his minimalist style.

38. The style of the completed maquette is of interest in the context of a conversation the author had with the sculptor in the early stages of the work (15 May 1995), in the course of which he pointed out that he might end up 'producing a work that looks most RHA'.

39. A night alarm; a weaponed crowd;
One blow, and with the rest I ran,
I warmed my hands, and said aloud:
I never knew the man.

40. Cathy Carman was born in Portlaoise, County Laois, in 1952. She studied at the National College of Art and Design in the early 1970s and later at the Chiswick Art School in London. Carman has executed many public sculptures. Her work, in which she reveals a concern for sculptural materials, shows a very particular interest in the dark and mysterious side of life.

41. Carman was aware of Wilde's essay on masks, but she did not read it. Conversation with the artist, 30 May 1995.

42. Louise Walsh was born in 1963 in Cork. She studied at the Crawford College of Art and Design and at the University of Ulster. She has executed many public works and has a particular interest in gender issues.

43. Conversation with the artist, 19 July 1995.

44. Benedict Byrne was born in Dublin in 1956.

45. Wilde, '"Sermons in Stones" at Bloomsbury', *Pall Mall Gazette*, 15 October 1887.

46. William Wilde loaned a modern bronze version of the *Dying Gladiator* to the Dublin Exhibition in 1872.

47. Bertel Thorvaldsen, 1770–1844.

48. Johann Joachim Winckelmann, 1717–68.

49. John Hogan, 1800–58.

50. *Dublin Builder*, 1 July 1865, reveals the involvement of William Wilde in the O'Connell Monument commissioned for Ennis.

51. William Wilde published a *Proposal Relative to the Nelson Testimonial* in 1839, in which he suggested that one of the many fallen Egyptian obelisks should be brought to London to serve as a public testimonial to Lord Nelson.

52. See John Turpin, *John Hogan, Irish Neoclassical Sculptor in Rome, 1800–1858* (Dublin: Irish Academic Press, 1982).

53. Christopher Hewetson, c. 1736–98.

54. Ellmann, *Oscar Wilde*, 257–8.

55. Francis Haskell and Nicholas Penny, *Taste and the Antique* (New Haven, Conn.: Yale University Press, 1981), 271–2.

56. Gisela Richter, *The Sculpture and Sculptors of the Greeks* (New Haven, Conn.: Yale University Press, 1929). The attribution to Praxiteles has subsequently been much disputed through the twentieth century and it has not been possible to ascertain whether the Hermes and Dionysus is an original work or a later copy. J. J. Pollitt, *The Art of Ancient Greece: Sources and Documents* (Cambridge: Cambridge University Press, 1965).

57. J. J. Winckelmann, *Writings on Art*, ed. David Irwin (London: Phaidon Press, 1972), 132.

58. *Catalogue of the National Gallery of Ireland* (HMSO, 1868), 111.

59. Wilde, 'The Decay of Lying', in *Complete Works*, 1083.

60. J. W. Goethe, *Italian Journey (1786–1788)* (Harmondsworth: Penguin Books,

61. Wilde, 'The Decay of Lying', in *Complete Works*, 1083.

62. Wilde, 'The English Renaissance of Art', in *Aristotle at Afternoon Tea*, ed. John Wyse Jackson (London: Fourth Estate, 1991), 14. 'The English Renaissance of Art' was the first lecture given by Wilde on his American tour in 1882. Within a month he simplified and shortened the text, changing the title to 'The Decorative Arts'.

63. *Letters*, 825. The Apollo Belvedere was most particularly associated with Winckelmann and it was the statue about which he wrote so passionately.

64. William Wetmore Story, 1819–95.

65. *Letters*, 131.

66. Thomas Waldo Story, 1855–1915.

67. Wilde in a letter to Waldo Story 22 January 1884. *Letters*, 155.

68. John Donoghue, 1853–1903.

69. Ellmann, *Oscar Wilde*, 197.

70. A bronze variant of the Young Sophocles is in the collection of the National Gallery of Ireland.

71. *Letters*, 738.

72. *Pall Mall Gazette*, 13 September 1886.

73. Ruth Butler, *Rodin: The Shape of Genius* (New Haven, Conn.: Yale University Press, 1993), 317.

74. *Letters*, 831.

75. Ellmann, *Oscar Wilde*, 180.

76. *Freeman's Journal*, 9 August 1864.

77. The statue was originally more prominently and more successfully positioned in the city. However, it was moved in 1929 because of traffic congestion and is now unsatisfactorily located on O'Connell Street, behind the O'Connell Monument, at the junction with Abbey Street.

78. Paula Murphy, 'The Politics of the Street Monument', *Irish Arts Review Yearbook*, vol. 10, 1994, 202–8.

79. An example of this in Wilde's day is revealed in the unveiling of the Grattan statue in College Green in 1876. In his speech from the platform, A. M. Sullivan indicated his wish that the youth of Ireland 'might learn lessons of concord, of good-will, of public virtue, of toleration and of patriotism', from the presence of Grattan in their midst. See *The Origins, Progress and Completion of the Grattan Statue*, compiled by the Hon.

John P. Vereker, 1881. Ms 1703, Trinity College Dublin.

80. Wilde, 'The Happy Prince', in *Complete Works*, 276.

81. Ellmann, *Oscar Wilde*, 193. Wilde on the gracefulness of a Colorado mineshaft worker: 'at any moment he might have been transformed into marble or bronze and become noble in art forever'. While Wilde was musing on the possibility of such sculptural representation in the early 1880s, the Belgian sculptor Constantin Meunier was actually executing realist imagery. However, if Wilde's focus was aesthetic, Meunier's concern was socialist. Wilde would perhaps not have seen Meunier's work until the Exposition Universelle in Paris in 1900.

Women of No Importance: Misogyny in the Work of Oscar Wilde

VICTORIA WHITE

1. *The Letters of Oscar Wilde*, ed. Rupert Hart-Davis (London: Rupert Hart-Davis, 1963), 466.

2. *Complete Works of Oscar Wilde* (Glasgow: HarperCollins, 1994), 371.

3. Richard Ellmann, *Oscar Wilde* (New York: Alfred A. Knopf, 1988), 125.

4. Melissa Knox, *Oscar Wilde: A Long and Lovely Suicide* (New Haven, Conn.: Yale University Press, 1994).

5. Joy Melville, *Mother of Oscar: The Life of Jane Francesca Wilde* (London: John Murray, 1994), 139.

6. *Letters*, 458.

7. Ibid., 203.

8. *Complete Works*, 377.

9. Ibid., 417.

10. Quoted in Ellmann, *Oscar Wilde*, 266.

11. Ibid., 347.

12. *Complete Works*, 40.

13. Camille Paglia, *Sexual Personae: Art and Decadence from Nefertiti to Emily Dickinson* (London: Yale University Press, 1990), 518.

14. *Complete Works*, 40.

15. Ibid, 325.

16. Ibid.

17. *The Trials of Oscar Wilde*, ed. H. Montgomery Hyde (Sydney: Butterworth, 1948), 236.

18. *Complete Works*, 330.

19. Ibid, 334.
20. Ibid., 340.
21. Ibid., 343.
22. Ellmann, *Oscar Wilde*, 342.
23. Susan Sontag, 'Notes on "Camp"' in *Against Interpretation and Other Essays* (New York: Doubleday, 1990), 273–92.
24. Paglia, *Sexual Personae*, 569.
25. *Letters*, 509.
26. Ibid., 397.
27. *Complete Works*, 235.

Selected Bibliography

Almy, Percival W. H. 'New Views of Mr Oscar Wilde'. *Theatre*, March 1894.

Beckson, Karl, ed. *Oscar Wilde: The Critical Heritage*. London: Routledge & Kegan Paul, 1970.

Benson, E. F. *As We Were*. London: Longmans, 1930.

——, 'The Recent "Witch-Burning" at Clonmel'. *Nineteenth Century, A Monthly Review*, no. 220, June 1895.

Coakley, Davis. *Oscar Wilde: The Importance of Being Irish*. Dublin: Town House, 1994.

de Saix, Guillot, ed. *Les Songes merveilleux du Dormeur éveillé / Le Chant du Cygne / contes parlés d'Oscar Wilde*. Paris: Mercure de France, 1942.

——, ed. *Contes et Propos d' Oscar Wilde*. Paris: Artheme Fayard, 1949.

Ellmann, Richard, ed. *Eminent Domain: Yeats Among Wilde, Joyce, Pound, Eliot and Auden*. London: Oxford University Press, 1967.

——, *Oscar Wilde*. New York: Alfred A. Knopf, 1988.

——, 'The Uses of Decadence'. *a long the riverrun: Selected Essays*. New York: Alfred A. Knopf, 1989.

——, ed. *Oscar Wilde: A Collection of Critical Essays*. Englewood Cliffs: Prentice-Hall, 1969.

Foster, John Wilson. *Fictions of the Irish Literary Revival*. Syracuse: Syracuse University Press, 1987.

Gagnier, Regenia. *Idylls of the Marketplace: Oscar Wilde and the Victorian Public*. Aldershot: Scolar, 1986.

Gide, André. *Oscar Wilde*. London: William Kimber, 1951.

Helfand, Michael S., and Philip E. Smith II. 'Anarchy and Culture: The Evolutionary Turn of Cultural Criticism in the Work of Oscar Wilde'. *Texas Studies in Literature and Language*, 20 (2), Summer 1978.

Holland, Vyvyan. *Son of Oscar Wilde*. Oxford: Oxford University Press, 1988.

Housman, Laurence. *Echo de Paris: A Study from Life*. London, 1923.

Hyde, H. Montgomery. *Oscar Wilde*. London: Eyre Methuen, 1976.

——, ed. *The Trials of Oscar Wilde*. Sydney: Butterworth, 1948.

Kernahan, Coulson. *The Man of No Sorrows*. London: Cassell and Company, 1911.

Kiberd, Declan. *Inventing Ireland: The Literature of the Modern Nation*. London: Jonathan Cape, 1995.

——, 'The London Exiles: Wilde and Shaw'. *The Field Day Anthology of Irish Writing II*. General Editor Seamus Deane. Derry: Field Day Publications, 1991.

Kinahan, Frank. *Yeats, Folklore and Occultism*. Boston: Unwin Hyman, 1988.

Kingsmill-Moore, H. *Reminiscences and Reflections*. London: Batsford, 1930.

Knox, Melissa. *Oscar Wilde: A Long and Lovely Suicide*. New Haven, Conn.: Yale University Press, 1994.

La Jeunesse, Ernest. *Recollections of Oscar Wilde*. Edited by Percival Pollard. Boston & London: J. W. Luce & Co., 1906.

macLíammóir, Micheál. *The Importance of Being Oscar*. Dublin: Dolmen Press, 1963.

Masters, Brian. *The Life of E. F. Benson*. London: Pimlico, 1991.

Maxwell, W. B. *Time Gathered: Autobiography*. London: Hutchinson, 1937.

Melville, Joy. *Mother of Oscar: The Life of Jane Francesca Wilde*. London: John Murray, 1994.

Nassaar, Christopher. *Into the Demon Universe*. New Haven, Conn.: Yale University Press, 1974.

Nordau, Max. *Degeneration*. London: Heinemann, 1913.

O'Sullivan, Vincent. *Aspects of Wilde*. London: Constable, 1936.

Paglia, Camille. *Sexual Personae: Art and Decadence from Nefertiti to Emily Dickinson*. London: Yale University Press, 1990.

Palmer, Geoffrey, and Noel Lloyd. *E. F. Benson As He Was*. Luton: Lennard, 1988.

Pine, Richard. *The Thief of Reason: Oscar Wilde and Modern Ireland*. Dublin: Gill & Macmillan, 1995.

Raymond, Jean Paul, and Charles Ricketts. *Oscar Wilde: Recollections*. London: Nonesuch, 1932.

Sandulescu, C. George, ed. *Rediscovering Oscar Wilde*. Publications of the Princess Grace Library: 8. Gerrards Cross: Colin Smythe, 1994.

Shewan, Rodney. *Oscar Wilde: Art and Egotism*. London: Macmillan, 1977.

Small, Ian. *Oscar Wilde Revalued: An Essay on New Materials and Methods of Research*. Greensboro, N.C.: ELT Press, 1993.

Schmidgall, Gary. *The Stranger Wilde: Interpreting Oscar*. London: Abacus, 1994.

Smith, Hester Travers, ed. *Psychic Messages from Oscar Wilde*. London: T. Werner Laurie, 1924.

Sontag, Susan. 'Notes on "Camp"'. *Against Interpretation and Other Essays*. New York: Doubleday, 1990.

Symons, Julian. *The Detling Secret*. Harmondsworth: Penguin Books, 1984.

Thornton, R. K. R. *The Decadent Dilemma*. London: Edward Arnold, 1983.

Trilling, Lionel. *Sincerity and Authenticity*. Oxford: Oxford University Press, 1972.

Tyndall, John. 'Scientific Use of the Imagination'. *Fragments of Science*. London: Longmans, Green, 1907.

Upchurch, D. A. *Wilde's Use of Irish Celtic Elements in 'The Picture of Dorian Gray'*. American University Studies, Series IV, English Language and Literature, 140.

Wade, Allan, ed. *The Letters of W. B. Yeats*. London: Rupert Hart-Davis, 1954.

Wilde, Lady [Jane Francesca Wilde as 'Speranza']. *Ancient Legends, Mystic Charms, and Superstitions of Ireland*. Boston: Ticknor & Co., 1887; London: Ward and Downey, 1888.

———, *Poems*. Dublin: James Duffy, 1864.

Wilde, Oscar. *Aristotle at Afternoon Tea: The Rare Oscar Wilde*. Edited by John Wyse Jackson. London : Fourth Estate, 1991.

———, The Artist as Critic: Critical Writings of Oscar Wilde. Edited by Richard Ellmann. London: W. H. Allen, 1970.

———, *Complete Works of Oscar Wilde*. Glasgow: HarperCollins, 1994.

———, *The Letters of Oscar Wilde*. Edited by Rupert Hart-Davis. London: Rupert Hart-Davis, 1963.

——, *Oscar Wilde's Oxford Notebooks: A Portrait of Mind in the Making*. Edited by Michael S. Helfland and Philip E. Smith II. New York: Oxford University Press, 1989.

——, '"Sermons in Stones" at Bloomsbury'. *Pall Mall Gazette*, 15 October 1887.

Wilson, T. G. *Victorian Doctor; Being the Life of Sir William Wilde*. New York: L. B. Fischer, 1946.

Woodcock, George. *Anarchism*. Harmondsworth: Penguin Books, 1962.

Wratislaw, Theodore. *Oscar Wilde: A Memoir*. London: The Eighteen Nineties Society, 1979.

Yeats, W. B. *Autobiographies*. London: Macmillan, 1955.

——, *The Collected Plays of W. B. Yeats*. London: Macmillan, 1952.

——, *The Collected Poems of W. B. Yeats*. London: Macmillan, 1956.

——, *Essays and Introductions*. London: Macmillan, 1961.

——, *Letters to the New Island*. Cambridge, Mass.: Harvard University Press, 1934.

——, *Prefaces and Introductions: Uncollected Prefaces and Introductions by Yeats to Works by other Authors and to Anthologies edited by Yeats*. Edited by William H. O'Donnell. London: Macmillan, 1988.

——, *The Secret Rose, Stories by W. B. Yeats: A Variorum Edition*. Edited by Warwick Gould, Philip L. Marcus and Michael Sidnell. London: Macmillan, 1992.

——, *Uncollected Prose by W. B. Yeats I*. Edited by John P. Frayne. New York: Columbia University Press, 1970.

——, *Uncollected Prose by W. B. Yeats II*. Edited by John P. Frayne and Colton Johnson. London: MacMillan, 1975.

Index